TABLE OF CONTENTS

Editor's Note

Sometimes viewed as a challenging building site, the narrow lot actually presents very unique living possibilities: waterfront vacation home; zero-lot-line city home; suburban tract home; and more. In this book you'll find a wide range of your favorite styles to meet the challenge of building on a narrow lot. From classic Cape Cods to eclectic Bungalows, you'll find modern floor plans and many of the amenities often associated with larger homes. All of this testifies to the fact that the home for your narrow lot can be a totally successful building and living experience!

About The Designers

The Blue Ribbon Designer Series™ is a collection of books featuring the home plans of a diverse group of outstanding home designers and architects known as the Blue Ribbon Network of Designers. This group of companies is dedicated to creating and marketing the finest possible plans for home construction on a regional and national basis. Each of the companies exhibits superior work and integrity in all phases of the stock-plan business including modern, trendsetting floor planning, a professionally executed blueprint package and a strong sense of service and commitment to the consumer.

Design Basics, Inc.

For nearly a decade, Design Basics, a nationally recognized home design service located in Omaha, has been developing plans for custom home builders. Since 1987, the firm has consistently appeared in *Builder* magazine, the official magazine of the National Association of Home Builders, as the top-selling designer. The company's plans also regularly appear in numerous other shelter magazines such as *Better Homes and Gardens*, *House Beautiful* and *Home Planner*.

Design Traditions

Design Traditions was established by Stephen S. Fuller with the tenets of innovation, quality, originality and uncompromising architectural techniques in traditional and European homes. Especially popular throughout the Southeast, Design Traditions' plans are known for their extensive detail and thoughtful design. They are widely published in such shelter magazines as *Southern Living* magazine and *Better Homes and Gardens*.

Alan Mascord Design Associates, Inc.

Founded in 1983 as a local supplier to the building community, Mascord Design Associates of Portland, Oregon, began to successfully publish plans nationally in 1985. With plans now drawn exclusively on computer, Mascord Design Associates quickly received a reputation for homes that are easy to build yet meet the rigorous demands of the buyers' market, winning local and national awards. The company's trademark is creating floor plans that work well and exhibit excellent traffic patterns. Their motto is: "Drawn to build, designed to sell."

Larry W. Garnett & Associates, Inc.

Starting as a designer of homes for Houston-area residents, Garnett & Associates has been marketing designs nationally for the past ten years. A well-respected design firm, the company's plans are regularly featured in *House Beautiful*, *Country Living*, *Home* and *Professional Builder*. Numerous accolades, including several from the Texas Institute of Building Design and the American Institute of Building Design, have been awarded to the company for excellence in architecture.

Home Planners, Inc.

Headquartered in Tucson, Arizona, with additional offices in Detroit, Home Planners is one of the longest-running and most successful home design firms in the United States. With over 2,500 designs in its portfolio, the company provides a wide range of styles, sizes and types of homes for the residential builder. All of Home Planners' designs are created with the care and professional expertise that fifty years of experience in the home-planning business affords. Their homes are designed to be built, lived in and enjoyed for years to come.

Donald A. Gardner, Architect, Inc.

The South Carolina firm of Donald A. Gardner was established in response to a growing demand for residential designs that reflect constantly changing lifestyles. The company's specialty is providing homes with refined, custom-style details and unique features such as passive-solar designs and open floor plans. Computer-aided design and drafting technology resulting in trouble-free construction documents places the firm at the leading edge of the home plan industry.

Home Design Services, Inc.

For the past fifteen years, Home Design Services of Longwood, Florida, has been formulating plans for the sun-country lifestyle. At the forefront of design innovation and imagination, the company has developed award-winning designs that are consistently praised for their highly detailed, free-flowing floor plans, imaginative and exciting interior architecture and elevations which have gained international appeal.

Houses Under 30' Wide

Today's narrow-lot home—what does it offer the modern home builder? Aside from the opportunity to build on some of the most delightful sites (such as those found within historical city neighborhoods, and those that carry the name "beachfront" or "lakefront"), the modern narrow-lot house presents many of the large-lot amenities we've all come to appreciate. Vaulted ceilings, master suites and courtyards are just a few of the features that add to the livability of this type of home.

For the new family looking for the perfect starter home or the established family looking to add a guest cottage or mother-in-law quarters, our first section of houses under 30' wide offers several prime candidates to meet both needs and wants. Just imagine a two-car garage, three bedrooms—including a luxurious master suite—and ample storage space in a plan just under 1,500 square feet! Page 6 presents such a plan and would easily serve the new family. Its street-facing garage—with an abundance of storage space—provides easy access as well as a noise buffer for the major living areas; single-room widths lend themselves to quiet as well as privacy.

Also noteworthy, page 12 introduces a collection of "zero-lot-line" homes—ideal for those that have purchased property within city limits. These houses boast a number of applications: bought in conjunction with one another, they become excellent condominiums or multi-family living units. Bought singly, they serve as divine center-city, in-fill homes. In any case, their amenities will cause guests to do a double-take: walk-in closets, sumptuous master baths with whirlpool tubs and second-floor utility areas all characterize the modern urban dweller's abode.

For the more country-minded, pages 8 and 9 feature two cottage designs that make delightful additions to a village community. Each one extends livability through the use of porches and sunlit baths. If used as a guest house or mother-in-law quarters, the house on page 9 offers complete independence through its full kitchen, space for a washer/dryer unit and generous attic storage.

For those with subdivision property, pages 10 and 11 carry two very attractive "tract" homes. Both further enhance their thoughtful floor plans by offering two different exterior elevations—again, proof-positive that the narrow-lot home can make for a most gratifying building and living experience.

Design AA9174

First Floor: 640 square feet
Second Floor: 780 square feet
Total: 1,420 square feet
Width 24'-6"
Depth 51'

● Just a short trek around the two-car garage, the entry to this fine family home introduces the living room with its corner fireplace. A dining room brings up the rear of the plan and gains outdoor access through a French door. The kitchen boasts a pantry and direct passage to the utility area. Upstairs, the best in sleeping arrangements is offered through three private bedrooms. Bedroom 3 includes a generous walk-in closet while sharing a full hall bath with Bedroom 2. The master bedroom has a ten-foot tray ceiling. Lending a sense of the dramatic, French doors open to a balcony overlook to the living room below. Two walk-in closets grace this room. Plant shelves through-out the house add a special touch.

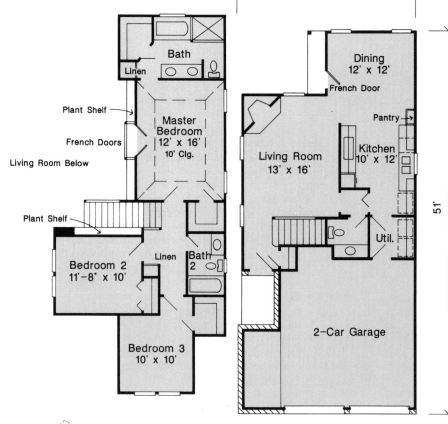

Design by
Larry W.
Garnett &
Associates, Inc.

Bath

Bedroom 2
14'-4" x 11'-8"

Master Bedroom
15'-8" x 13'

Linen
Plant Ledge

Bath 2

Bedroom 3
11'-4" x 10'

28'

French Door

Dining
12' x 11'

Kitchen
15' x 10'

Pantry

Stor.

1/2
Bath

Util.

Foyer

Living Room
15'-8" x 20'

Garage

Fireplace

Sitting Area

42'-4"

Design by
Larry W.
Garnett &
Associates, Inc.

Design AA8956

First Floor: 845 square feet
Second Floor: 845 square
Total: 1,690 square feet
Width 28'
Depth 42'-4"

● An angled staircase lends diversity to this three-bedroom plan. The large living room, with a front-facing sitting area, affords amenities such as a fireplace and lots of wall space for various furniture arrangements. The roomy kitchen features a corner sink and bar that services the dining room. Here you'll find a French door opening to the rear yard. A storage closet accommodates odds and ends. With a powder room and a utility area accessing the garage, the first floor meets the family's needs well. The second floor offers two family bedrooms that share a full bath, and a master bedroom that boasts a fine angled bath. With a double-bowl vanity, compartmented toilet and corner spa tub, this bath easily competes with today's finest.

Design AA9150

First Floor: 588 square feet
Second Floor: 397 square feet
Total: 985 square feet
Width 19'
Depth 40'-2"

Design by
Larry W.
Garnett &
Associates, Inc.

● This quaint little Victorian cottage serves perfectly as a starter or second home; or maybe you have it in mind for a lakefront location. Beyond the front porch, the living room defines the front of the house. A full kitchen, a dining room and a powder room account for the back of the house. Each of these areas appreciates an abundance of natural lighting and excellent space utilization. Upstairs, two family bedrooms share a full bath. Bedroom 1 enjoys twin closets. Economical construction makes this house even more attractive. You'll find a detached garage with storage space just beyond the back door and arbor making a delightful outdoor living space.

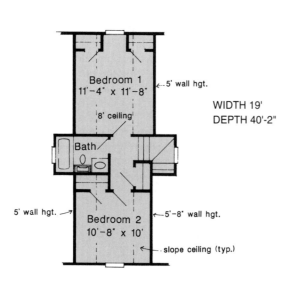

Bedroom 1
11'-4" x 11'-8"

5' wall hgt.

8' ceiling

Bath

5' wall hgt.

5'-8" wall hgt.

Bedroom 2
10'-8" x 10'

slope ceiling (typ.)

WIDTH 19'
DEPTH 40'-2"

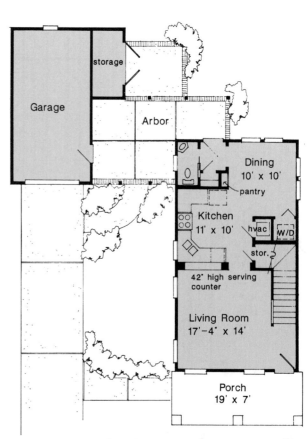

Garage

storage

Arbor

Dining
10' x 10'

pantry

Kitchen
11' x 10'

hvac   W/D

stor.

42" high serving
counter

Living Room
17'-4" x 14'

Porch
19' x 7'

Design AA9117

First Floor: 693 square feet
Second Floor: 342 square feet
Total: 1,035 square feet
Width 27'
Depth 42'-4"

● This quaint, cozy cottage serves a variety of needs. It could be used as a second home or leisure get-away; it could be the perfect guest house or mother-in-law cottage; or it may even make a great primary residence for a single person or a couple. It's fine detailing and traditional features make it a favorite with everyone.

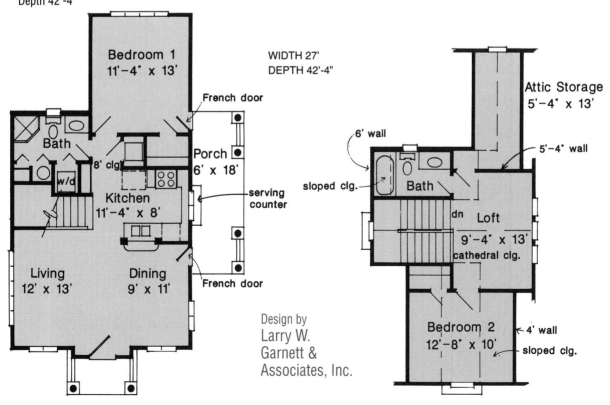

WIDTH 27'
DEPTH 42'-4"

Bedroom 1
11'-4" x 13'

French door

Bath

8' clg.

Porch
6' x 18'

serving counter

Kitchen
11'-4" x 8'

w/d

Living
12' x 13'

Dining
9' x 11'

French door

Design by
Larry W.
Garnett &
Associates, Inc.

Attic Storage
5'-4" x 13'

6' wall

5'-4" wall

sloped clg.

Bath

dn

Loft
9'-4" x 13'
cathedral clg.

Bedroom 2
12'-8" x 10'

4' wall

sloped clg.

Design AA9165

First Floor: 636 square feet
Second Floor: 740 squarefeet
Total: 1,376 square feet
Width 24'-4"
Depth 55'-4"

● An angled staircase puts a new slant in this 1,376-square-foot plan. Two exterior elevation choices, with different roof and window treatments, accommodate the varying tastes of discriminating home builders. Inside, a side entry opens to a two-story foyer with plant shelves flanking the stairway. The living room highlights a fireplace and a built-in cabinet with a bookcase. The dining room has a large window area and a French door leading to the rear patio. The U-shaped kitchen includes a pantry. The first floor also features a powder room, a utility room and a two-car garage with two storage areas. Upstairs, the master suite delights with its ten-foot sloped ceiling, walk-in closet and bath with double-bowl vanity. Two additional family bedrooms share a bath.

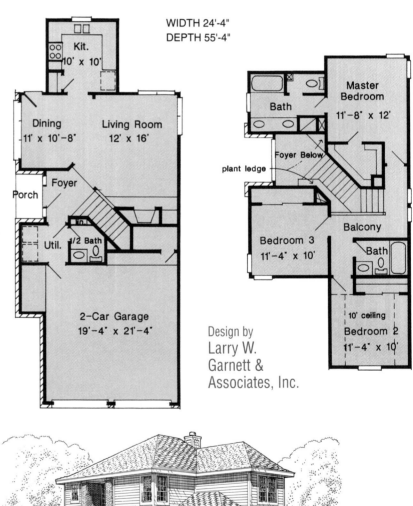

WIDTH 24'-4"
DEPTH 55'-4"

Kit.
10' x 10'

Dining
11' x 10'-8"

Living Room
12' x 16'

Foyer

Porch

1/2 Bath

Util.

2-Car Garage
19'-4" x 21'-4"

Master Bedroom
11'-8" x 12'

Bath

Foyer Below

plant ledge

Balcony

Bedroom 3
11'-4" x 10'

Bath

10' ceiling

Bedroom 2
11'-4" x 10'

Design by
Larry W.
Garnett &
Associates, Inc.

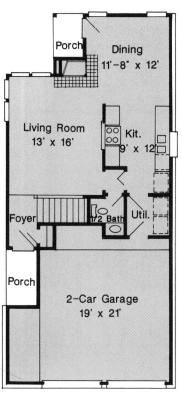

Porch

Dining
11'-8" x 12'

Width 23'-10"
Depth 50'-10"

Living Room
13' x 16'

Kit.
9' x 12'

Foyer

1/2 Bath

Util.

Porch

2-Car Garage
19' x 21'

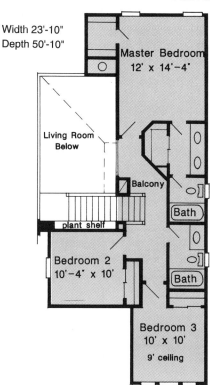

Master Bedroom
12' x 14'-4"

Living Room
Below

Balcony

Bath

plant shelf

Bath

Bedroom 2
10'-4" x 10'

Bedroom 3
10' x 10'

9' ceiling

Design AA9166

First Floor: 642 square feet
Second Floor: 738 square feet
Total: 1,380 square feet
Width 23'-10"
Depth 50'-10"

● With two different exterior elevations to choose from, this 1,380-square-foot plan is sure to please. A porch precedes the entry where you'll find a closet and an open stairwell with a plant ledge. The dramatic living room rises two stories with its sloped ceiling; both the living room and the dining room share a fireplace with a tiled hearth. A French door in the dining room leads to a private rear porch. The corridor-style kitchen has access to the utility room and the two-car garage with its storage space. Upstairs, a balcony overlooks the living room below. The master suite has a ten-foot sloped ceiling and two walk-in closets—one in the bedroom and one in the dressing area. Two more family bedrooms and a hall bath round out the second floor.

Design by
Larry W.
Garnett &
Associates, Inc.

Design AA9167

First Floor: 690 square feet
Second Floor: 962 square feet
Total: 1,652 square feet
Width 19'
Depth 65'-10"

Design AA9168

First Floor: 709 square feet
Second Floor: 1,040 square feet
Total: 1,749 square feet
Width 19'
Depth 65'-10"

Design AA9169

First Floor: 682 square feet
Second Floor: 979 square feet
Total: 1,661 square feet
Width 19'
Depth 65'-10"

● For the builder subdividing a large lot, these homes offer a relationship that's hard to beat. For the builder that's just stumbled upon some prime city or village property, any one of these plans will develop into an outstanding home for generations to come. Each plan, sold separately, begins with front access and a raised foyer. A fireplace adorns each of the plans' living rooms—two of the homes have a wet bar servicing both the living and dining rooms. Design AA9169 features a large breakfast nook off the kitchen; all of the plans have a two-car garage that opens to the rear. Upstairs, gorgeous master suites and utility areas define the modern livability afforded by these plans.

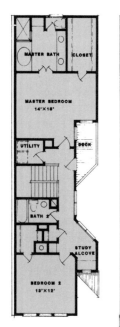

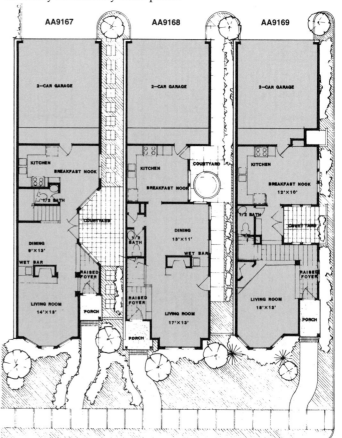

Design by
Larry W.
Garnett &
Associates, Inc.

WIDTH 19'
DEPTH 65'-10"

Houses From 30' to 39' Wide

The last section introduced the starter home; this section on houses from 30' to 39' wide defines it unmistakably. A comfortable plan with room enough for the new family—and amenities enough for the most discerning modern home builder—sets the tone for those building within a more modest budget. These homes fit perfectly in the country or with others in a subdivision. Pages 24-27 illustrate the latter with four different designs that any neighborhood would gladly welcome.

With these new designs comes today's sensibility to fine details. Attention to grandness, both inside and out, extends from stately entryways, varied rooflines, open floor plans, vaulted ceilings, well-placed windows, skylights and master suites. The house on page 26, for example, contains an impressive facade; an 84' depth coupled with added width allows for over 2,600 square feet of living space! The interior of this plan lives up to its exterior: four bedrooms, including a master suite with a luxurious bath; an island kitchen overlooking the dining room; a breakfast room and a family room; a two-car garage; and nine-foot ceilings throughout.

Also in this section, the vacation, retirement or dream home—like those often found on high-priced beachfront or lakefront property—comes into greater play with such plans as the one on page 40. Here, a different sort of floor plan makes itself known with major living areas located to the rear of the house in order to benefit from the views out back. Two-story windows assure that you reap all of the benefits of additional surrounding views.

With added dimension comes increased diversity in design; you'll notice that many of the homes take on a decided regional flair. Good examples of this include the homes on pages 28-31. An emphasis on sun-country living creates delightful adaptations; however, with large windows and covered patios, these homes may very well appeal to home builders in various regions.

Tried and true, many of the more traditional designs make for excellent narrow-lot choices. Page 38 exemplifies this with a quaint Cape Cod; its 1,800 square feet of livability excels with details such as a dual fireplace and a country kitchen. To expand on such traditional styling, the Saltbox design on page 41 introduces a two-car garage and the walk-in closets and master-bath whirlpool that many consider "necessary amenities."

Design AA9430

First Floor: 1,150 square feet
Second Floor: 543 square feet
Total: 1,693 square feet
Width 38'
Depth 50'

● While fitting on some of the smallest lots imaginable, this great 1½-story still encompasses some dynamic features. Check out the dramatic, two-story hearth room that serves as the main living area in the home. Tall windows flank the fireplace and a glass door leads to the outdoor living area. A section of the upper hallway overlooks the hearth room integrating the upper floor with the lower floor. The master bedroom is conveniently located on the main floor overlooking the back yard, with direct access to the full bath serving the lower floor. Two large bedrooms and a bath round out the upper floor.

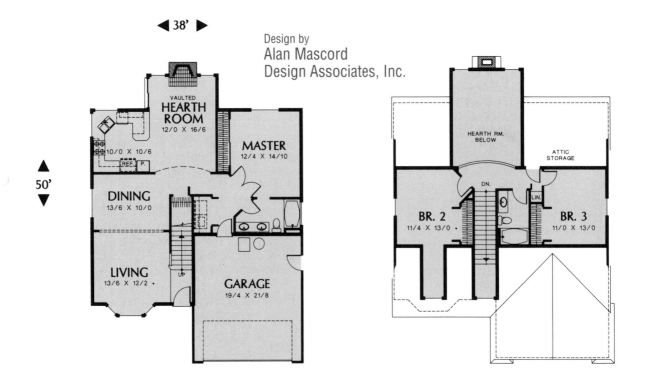

Design by
Alan Mascord
Design Associates, Inc.

Design AA9487

First Floor: 1,175 square feet
Second Floor: 891 square feet
Total: 2,066 square feet
Width 38'
Depth 51'

● Volume ceilings are the choice in this fine two-story home. Note that the den features a vaulted ceiling to complement its half-round window, the living and dining rooms have 11'4" ceilings to complement transom windows and the master suite has a 9' tray ceiling. Other special features include fireplaces in both living and family rooms, columns and plant shelves between the living room and dining room and a whirlpool spa in the master bath.

◄ 38' ►

NOOK
10/4 X 18/6

FAMILY
13/0 X 14/6

LIVING
14/8 X 12/10
(CLG. @ 11'-4")

9/4 X 12/8

PLANT SHELF

R. O. PAN.

DINING
14/8 X 10/0
(CLG. @ 11'-4")

UP

W. D.

▲
51'
▼

GARAGE
20/4 X 21/0

DEN
11/4 X 11/6

Design by
Alan Mascord
Design Associates, Inc.

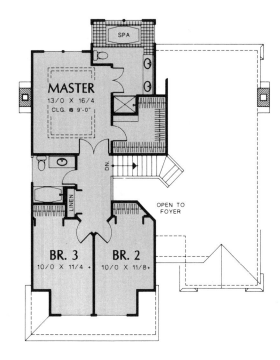

SPA

MASTER
13/0 X 16/4
(CLG. @ 9'-0")

DN.

LINEN

OPEN TO
FOYER

BR. 3
10/0 X 11/4 +

BR. 2
10/0 X 11/8+

Design AA9414

First Floor: 1,007 square feet
Second Floor: 803 square feet
Total: 1,810 square feet
Width 38'
Depth 54'

● This efficient plan is traditionally styled and
just made for narrow lots. Special features
include extra space over the garage for storage
or a workshop, a nook with bay window, a
large family room with fireplace and a kitchen
with expansive corner-window treatment. The
spacious master suite includes a "tray" vaulted
ceiling, spa tub, large shower and double vanity. Two additional bedrooms round out the
upper floor, one featuring a vaulted ceiling and
half-round window.

Design by
Alan Mascord
Design Associates, Inc.

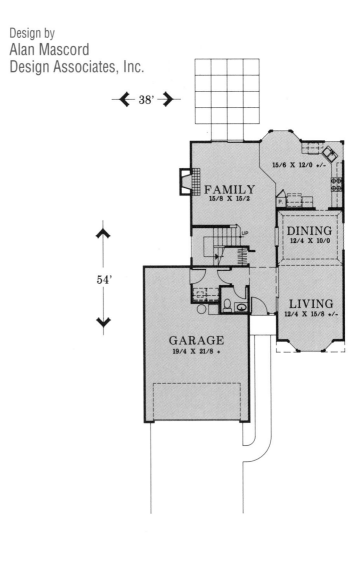

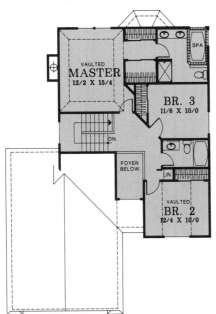

Design AA9505

First Floor: 960 square feet
Second Floor: 968 square feet
Total: 1,928 square feet
Width 38'
Depth 52'

● Multi-level rooflines and a two-story foyer lend interest to this four-bedroom plan. The living room, with its stepped ceiling, serves as an elegant prelude to the dining room at the back of the house. A central kitchen services a bumped-out nook and a large family room with a fireplace. A powder room, with a window for natural light, rests across from the utility room. Access to the two-car garage is gained from this area. The master bedroom dominates the upstairs with a double-door entry, a stepped ceiling and a private bath with a spa tub. Three bedrooms—at the rear of the second floor—share a full hall bath. An open stairwell affords a grand view of the foyer below.

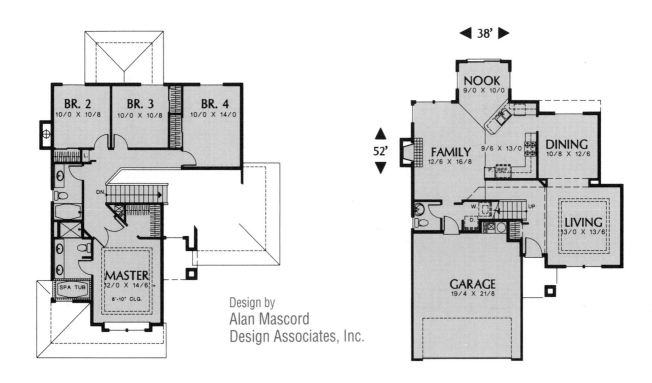

Design by
Alan Mascord
Design Associates, Inc.

17

Design AA3476 First Floor: 1,170 square feet
Second Floor: 838 square feet; Total: 2,008 square feet
Width 36'
Depth 60'

L

CUSTOMIZABLE
Custom Alterations? See page 221
for customizing this plan to your
specifications.

Design by
Home Planners,
Inc.

● A volume ceiling in the living room and a centered fireplace in the family room set the stage for the formal and
casual areas of this home. A hub kitchen boasts a rounded
counter for serving both the family room and the breakfast
area; a pantry in this area offers plenty of storage space. The
utility room, separating the main-floor living areas from the
garage, acquires both light and views from a side window.
Three bedrooms—all with ample closet space, including a
walk-in closet in the master suite—define the second-floor
sleeping quarters. A full hall bath with a double-bowl
vanity serves two of the bedrooms. The master bedroom
utilizes its own bath.

QUOTE ONE
Cost to build? See page 214
to order complete cost estimate
to build this house in your area!

Design AA3477

First Floor: 1,246 square feet
Second Floor: 906 square feet
Total: 2,152 square feet
Width 36'
Depth 54'-2"

L

Cost to build? See page 214 to order complete cost estimate to build this house in your area!

● Brick, wood siding and varied rooflines create a comfortable exterior for this three-bedroom plan. The spacious family room rises into a volume ceiling while featuring a fireplace and both side and rear views—truly an attention-getting room. Open to the family room, the breakfast area contains a convenient snack bar in common with the U-shaped kitchen. Upstairs, the master bedroom pleases with its walk-in closet and private bath with double-bowl vanity. Two accommodating bedrooms make use of an additional full bath.

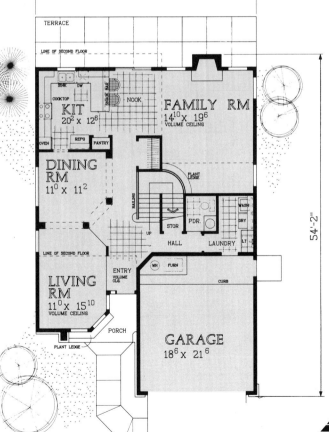

TERRACE

LINE OF SECOND FLOOR

36'-0"

SINK   DW

COOKTOP

KIT
20² x 12⁶

SNACK BAR

NOOK

FAMILY RM
14¹⁰ x 19⁶
VOLUME CEILING

OVEN   REFG   PANTRY

DINING RM
11⁰ x 11²

PLANT LEDGE

RAILINGS

WASH
DRY

PDR.

STOR   UP   HALL   LAUNDRY

LINE OF SECOND FLOOR

54'-2"

LIVING RM
11⁰ x 15¹⁰
VOLUME CEILING

ENTRY
VOLUME CLG.

WH   FURN

CURB

PORCH

PLANT LEDGE

GARAGE
18⁶ x 21⁶

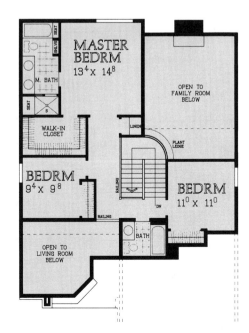

SOLID   SEAT

M. BATH

MASTER BEDRM
13⁴ x 14⁸

SEAT   S

WALK-IN CLOSET

LINEN

OPEN TO FAMILY ROOM BELOW

PLANT LEDGE

BEDRM
9⁴ x 9⁸

RAILING

DN

BEDRM
11⁰ x 11⁰

RAILING

BATH

OPEN TO LIVING ROOM BELOW

CUSTOMIZABLE

Custom Alterations? See page 221 for customizing this plan to your specifications.

Design by
Home Planners,
Inc.

Design AA3481A

Square Footage: 1,901
Width 42'
Depth 63'-6"

L

● In just under 2,000 square feet, this pleasing one-story home bears all the livability of houses twice its size. A combined living and dining room offers elegance for entertaining; with two elevations to choose from, the living room can either support an octagonal bay or a bumped-out nook. The U-shaped kitchen finds easy access to the breakfast nook and rear family room; sliding glass doors lead from the family room to a back stoop. The master bedroom has a quaint potshelf and a private bath with a spa tub, a double-bowl vanity, a walk-in closet and a compartmented toilet. With two additional family bedrooms—one may serve as a den if desired—and a hall bath with dual lavatories, this plan offers the best in accommodations. Both elevations come with the blueprint package.

CUSTOMIZABLE

Custom Alterations? See page 221 for customizing this plan to your specifications.

QUOTE ONE™

Cost to build? See page 214 to order complete cost estimate to build this house in your area!

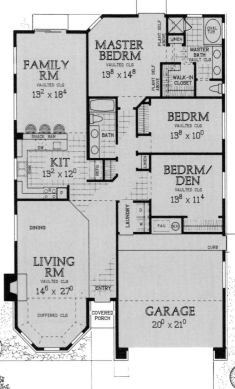

Design AA3481B

Square Footage: 1,908
Width 42'-4"
Depth 63'-10"

L

WIDTH 42'-4"
DEPTH 63'-10"

Design by
Home Planners,
Inc.

Design AA3484 First Floor: 1,139 square feet
Second Floor: 948 square feet; Total: 2,087 square feet
Width 32'
Depth 59'-4"

L **D**

QUOTE ONE™

Cost to build? See page 214
to order complete cost estimate
to build this house in your area!

CUSTOMIZABLE

Custom Alterations? See page 221
for customizing this plan to your
specifications.

● An angled entry offers a new perspective on the formal areas of this house: living room on the left; dining room on the right. Both rooms exchange views through a columned hallway while a potshelf and a niche add custom touches to this already attention-getting arrangement. At the back of the first floor, a family room with built-in bookshelves and

an entertainment-center niche opens to the kitchen and nook where both cooking and dining become a delight. The second floor provides interest with its balcony open to the living and family rooms. Three bedrooms include a master suite with a sloped ceiling, separate closets and a private bath. The two-car garage has direct access to the house.

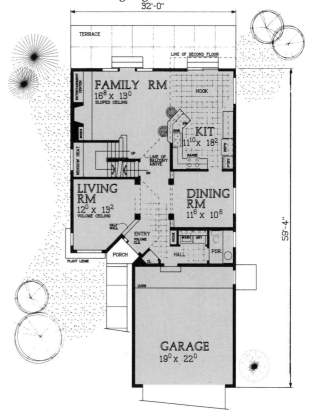

Design by
Home Planners,
Inc.

Design AA3485

First Floor: 1,586 square feet
Second Floor: 1,057 square feet
Total: 2,643 square feet
Width 40'
Depth 64'-6"

L

● A covered porch introduces the foyer of this delightful two-story plan. From here, formal areas open up with the living room on the right and the dining room on the left. Note the pot-shelf that extends around the dining room. A den backs up the formal areas of the house and shares a two-way fireplace with the family room. In the kitchen, an island cooktop facilitates food preparation. A double oven is built-in nearby. Upstairs, three bedrooms include a master suite with its own bath. The secondary bedrooms each partake in a hall bath with dual lavatories.

CUSTOMIZABLE

Custom Alterations? See page 221 for customizing this plan to your specifications.

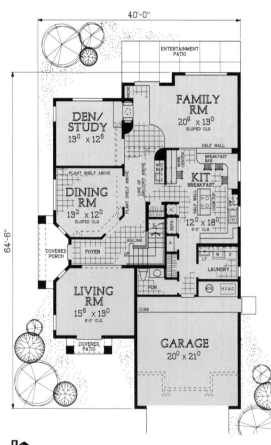

Quote One™

Cost to build? See page 214 to order complete cost estimate to build this house in your area!

Design by
Home Planners,
Inc.

38'-10"

TERRACE

FAMILY RM
15⁸ x 23²
VOLUME CEILING

DINING
RM
15⁴ x 13⁰
8'-0" CEILING

KIT
11² x 23⁴

SNACK BAR

NOOK

ENTRY
VOLUME
CLG.

PORCH

HALL

LAUNDRY

STOR

PDR.

57'-0"

GARAGE
19⁰ x 21⁶

Design AA3494 First Floor: 1,226 square feet
Second Floor: 1,000 square feet; Total: 2,226 square feet
Width 38'-10"
Depth 57'

L

● A bayed breakfast nook adds interest to the interior and exterior of this engaging design—note that the major first-floor living areas occupy the rear of the house. The family room has a number of fine assets including a fireplace, a plant shelf and a volume ceiling. An angled colonnade leads to the dining room with a window bay and passage to the kitchen where a corner sink and a wealth of counter space lend character. All of the upstairs bedrooms find privacy in their staggered locations. The master suite takes advantage of a sloped ceiling, a walk-in closet and an exclusive bath. One of the two family bedrooms features a sloped ceiling; both share a full hall bath with dual lavatories.

CUSTOMIZABLE

Custom Alterations? See page 221 for customizing this plan to your specifications.

MASTER
BEDROOM
14¹⁰ x 15⁴

OPEN TO
FAMILY ROOM
BELOW

SLOPED ⟩⟨ CEILING

M·
BATH

WALK-IN
CLOSET

BEDRM
12¹⁰ x 8¹⁰

OPEN TO
ENTRY
BELOW

BALCONY

RAILING

LINEN

BATH

BEDRM
14⁰ x 13⁶

SLOPED ⟩⟨ CEILING

Design by
Home Planners,
Inc.

QUOTE ONE™

Cost to build? See page 214 to order complete cost estimate to build this house in your area!

23

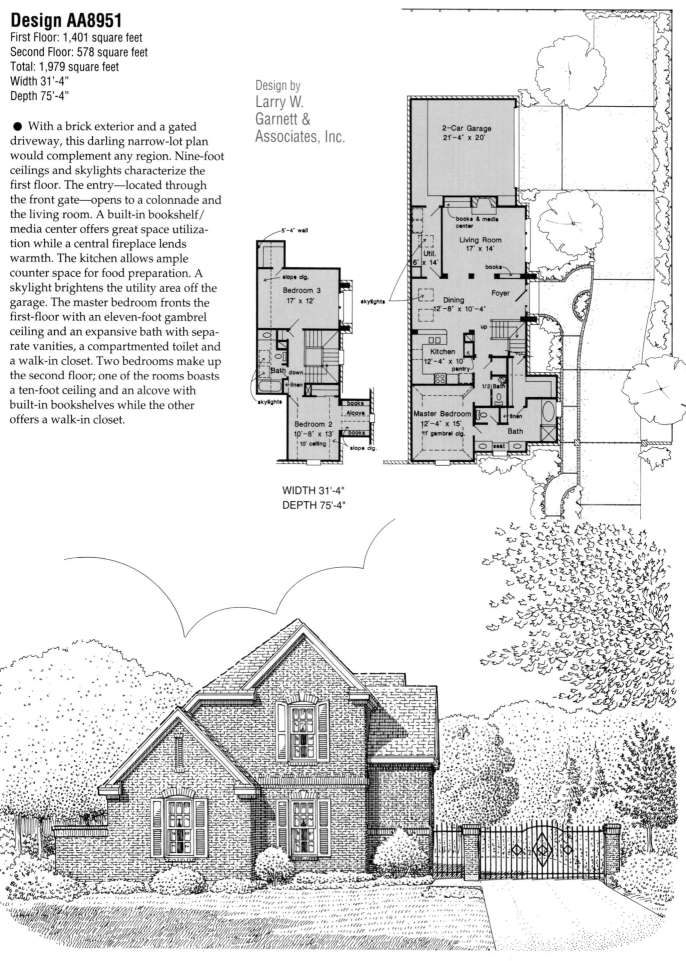

Design AA8951

First Floor: 1,401 square feet
Second Floor: 578 square feet
Total: 1,979 square feet
Width 31'-4"
Depth 75'-4"

● With a brick exterior and a gated driveway, this darling narrow-lot plan would complement any region. Nine-foot ceilings and skylights characterize the first floor. The entry—located through the front gate—opens to a colonnade and the living room. A built-in bookshelf/media center offers great space utilization while a central fireplace lends warmth. The kitchen allows ample counter space for food preparation. A skylight brightens the utility area off the garage. The master bedroom fronts the first-floor with an eleven-foot gambrel ceiling and an expansive bath with separate vanities, a compartmented toilet and a walk-in closet. Two bedrooms make up the second floor; one of the rooms boasts a ten-foot ceiling and an alcove with built-in bookshelves while the other offers a walk-in closet.

Design by
Larry W.
Garnett &
Associates, Inc.

2-Car Garage
21'-4" x 20'

books & media center

Living Room
17' x 14'

Util.
6' x 14'

books

Foyer

Dining
12'-8" x 10'-4"

skylights

up

Kitchen
12'-4" x 10'

pantry

1/2 Bath

linen

Master Bedroom
12'-4" x 15'
11' gambrel clg.

Bath

seat

5'-4" wall

slope clg.

Bedroom 3
17' x 12'

Bath

down

linen

skylights

books

Alcove

books

Bedroom 2
10'-8" x 13'
10' ceiling

slope clg.

WIDTH 31'-4"
DEPTH 75'-4"

Design AA8953

Square Footage: 1,530
Width 30'-6"
Depth 82'

● Bricks and shingles lend a winsome air to this
two-bedroom design. A gated porch brings visitors to
the foyer; a large living room opens from here. A
study backs up the living room with three skylights
and built-in bookshelves. A French door leads from
the dining room to a terrace outside. The kitchen,
with its wet bar to the study, has direct access to the
dining room. With two bedrooms, nothing is spared.
The master suite, with its front-facing window, has a
cathedral ceiling, a walk-in closet and a bath with a
double-bowl vanity. Bedroom 2 remains at the other
end of the house and also features a cathedral ceiling.
A full bath with glass block is located across the hall.

glass block

brick wall

2-Car Garage
21'-4" x 20'-4"

broom clos.

Util.
8' x 5'-4"

niche

Bath

Bedroom 2
12' x 11'-4"
cathedral clg.

Dining
14' x 11'-4"

French doors

Kitchen
11' x 11'-4"

bar sink

pantry

Study
8' x 14'

books

skylights

Living Room
18' x 14'

linen

Bath

Foyer

Porch
8' x 16'

Master Bedroom
12' x 16'
cathedral clg.

6' x 8'

9' ceiling unless otherwise noted

WIDTH 30'-6"
DEPTH 82'

Design by
Larry W.
Garnett &
Associates, Inc.

Design AA8954

First Floor: 1,947 square feet
Second Floor: 695 square feet
Total: 2,642 square feet
Width 35'
Depth 84'

● With a width of only thirty-five feet, this two-story home is able to achieve over 2,600 square feet of living space! The front entry opens to a graceful staircase and a study. This room accesses a full bath and could serve as a guest or family bedroom. A central gallery guides you past built-in bookshelves and cabinets to an open formal area. The living room has a fireplace and a bay window while the dining room finds the kitchen conveniently located directly across the hall. With an island worktop, a walk-in pantry and a utility area a step away, the kitchen aims to please. A sunny breakfast nook and a family room complete the living areas of the house. The bedrooms include a first-floor master suite with a gargantuan bath. Upstairs, two bedrooms with walk-in closets share a Hollywood bath.

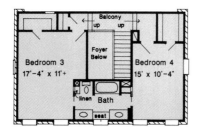

WIDTH 35'
DEPTH 84'

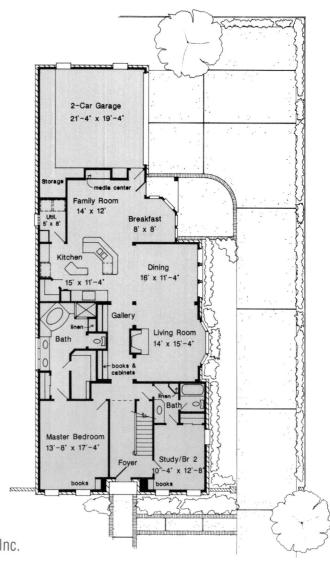

Design by
Larry W.
Garnett &
Associates, Inc.

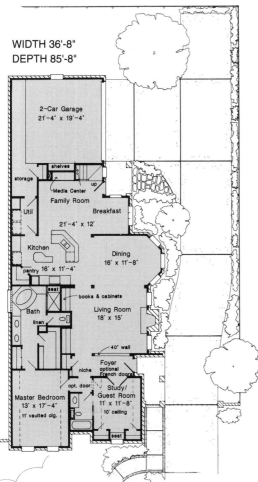

WIDTH 36'-8"
DEPTH 85'-8"

2-Car Garage
21'-4" x 19'-4"

shelves

storage

Media Center
Family Room

up

Breakfast
21'-4" x 12'

Util

Kitchen
16' x 11'-4"

pantry

Dining
16' x 11'-8"

seat

books & cabinets

Bath

Living Room
18' x 15'

linen

40' wall

Foyer
optional
French doors

niche

opt. door

Study/
Guest Room
11' x 11'-8"
10' ceiling

Master Bedroom
13' x 17'-4"
11' vaulted clg.

seat

Design AA8952

Square Footage: 1,973
Optional Second Floor: 344 square feet
Width 36'-8"
Depth 85'-8"

● With a ten-foot ceiling, a window seat, twin closets and
direct access to a full bath, the study of this house could easily
serve as a guest or family bedroom. On the other side of a 40"
wall defining the foyer, the living and dining rooms create a
magnificent space for entertaining. Built-in bookshelves and
cabinets enhance this area. The kitchen overlooks the breakfast
nook and family room where casual living is the focus. The
two-car garage, accessed through the utility area, boasts built-
in shelves and ample storage space. An optional second-floor
bedroom features its own bath. The master bedroom, with an
eleven-foot vaulted ceiling, delights with its private bath.
Here, a corner spa tub gains all the attention.

seat

doors

Balcony

sloped clg.

Bath

Bedroom
16' x 12'
8' ceiling

linen

OPTIONAL SECOND FLOOR 344 sq. ft.

Design by
Larry W.
Garnett &
Associates, Inc.

*Using the preceding four designs as examples, you can see how well
each one works on a narrow-lot and within a neighborhood setting.*

Design AA8611

Square Footage: 1,413
Width 38'
Depth 58'

● An angled side entry to this home allows for a majestic, arched window that dominates its facade. The interior, though small in square footage, holds an interesting and efficient floor plan. Because the breakfast room is placed to the front of the plan, it benefits from two large, multi-paned windows. The dining and family rooms form a single space enhanced by a volume ceiling and an optional fireplace, which is flanked by sets of optional double doors. Both the family room and master bedroom boast access

to the covered patio. A volume ceiling further enhances the master bedroom, which also has a dressing area, walk-in closet and full bath. The plans include options for a family room with corner fireplace, fireplace with French doors or a sliding glass door instead of a fireplace. The package includes plans for three different elevations!

Design by
Home Design
Services, Inc.

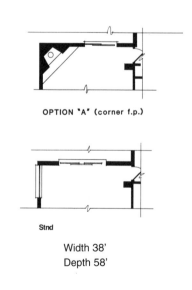

OPTION "A" (corner f.p.)

Stnd

Width 38'
Depth 58'

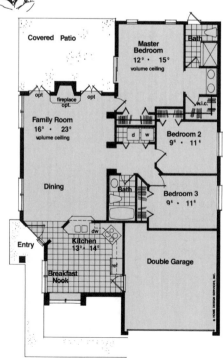

Covered Patio

Master Bedroom
12⁰ · 15⁰
volume ceiling

Bath

opt · fireplace opt. · opt

Family Room
16⁰ · 23⁰
volume ceiling

w.i.c.

d | w

Bedroom 2
9⁶ · 11⁴

Dining

Bath

Bedroom 3
9⁶ · 11⁴

Entry

Kitchen
13⁰ · 14⁰

dw

Double Garage

Breakfast Nook

© HOME DESIGN SERVICES, INC.

Design AA8659

First Floor: 1,230 square feet
Second Floor: 649 square feet
Total: 1,879 square feet
Width 38'
Depth 53'-6"

● The tiled foyer of this two-story home opens to a living and dining space with soaring ceilings. A covered patio invites outdoor livability in a design that is reminiscent of Bermuda architecture. The family-oriented kitchen has an oversized breakfast area with a volume ceiling and a view to the front yard. The master bedroom occupies the rear of the first floor and offers privacy with its sumptuous bath; a corner soaking tub, dual lavatories and a compartmented toilet lend character to the room. Upstairs, a loft overlooking the living spaces below could become a third bedroom. One of the family bedrooms features a walk-in closet. Both bedrooms utilize a generous hall bath.

Design by
Home Design
Services, Inc.

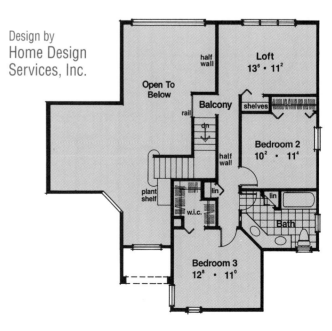

29

● This volume-look home's angled entry opens to a wealth of living potential with a media room to the right and formal living and dining rooms to the left. Remaining exposed to the dining room, the living room pleases with its marbled hearth and sliding glass doors to the back terrace. A covered porch, accessed from both the dining and breakfast rooms, adds outdoor dining possibilities. The kitchen utilizes a built-in desk and a snack bar pass-through to the breakfast area. A large pantry and closet lead to the laundry area near the garage. Upstairs, four bedrooms accommodate the large family well. In the master suite, amenities such as a sitting area and a balcony add definition. The master bath sports a whirlpool and a walk-in closet.

Design AA3456

First Floor: 1,130 square feet
Second Floor: 1,189 square feet
Total: 2,319 square feet
Width 40'-7"
Depth 57'-8"

L

Width 40'-7"
Depth 57'-8"

Design by
Home Planners, Inc.

Design AA3463

First Floor: 1,163 square feet
Second Floor: 1,077 square feet
Total: 2,240 square feet
Width 36'
Depth 63'

● Fine family living takes off in this grand two-story plan. The tiled foyer leads to a stately living room with sliding glass doors to the back terrace and columns separating it from the dining room. Additional accents include a corner curios niche and access to a covered porch. For casual living, look no further than the family room/breakfast room combination. Even more interesting, the kitchen supplies an island counter in the midst of its accommodating, angled layout. On the second floor, the master bedroom draws attention to itself by offering a fireplace, access to a deck and a spoiling bath. A smart addition, the study niche in the hallway shares the outside deck. Two family bedrooms wrap up the sleeping facilities.

Design by
Home Planners,
Inc.

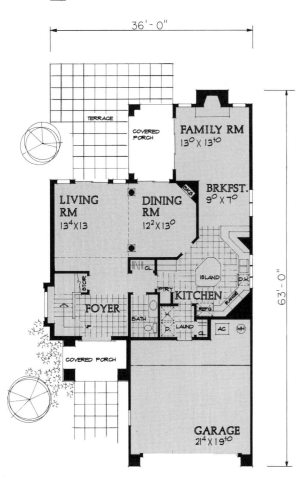

QUOTE ONE™

Cost to build? See page 214
to order complete cost estimate
to build this house in your area!

Design AA9148

First Floor: 838 square feet
Second Floor: 453 square feet
Total: 1,291 square feet
Width 35'-8"
Depth 45'-2"

● Small but exceedingly comfortable, this two-story, split-bedroom plan works well for families and empty-nesters alike. The open living/dining area features a ten-foot ceiling and is complemented by a U-shaped kitchen. A warming fireplace in the living room is flanked by bright windows. The master bedroom is found on the first floor and has its own bath plus plenty of closet space and a ten-foot ceiling. Upstairs there are two additional bedrooms and a full bath. Space is available for a fourth bedroom, adding 164 square feet to the plan.

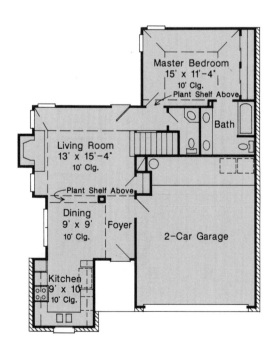

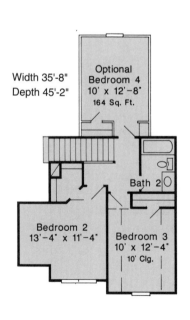

Design by
Larry W.
Garnett &
Associates, Inc.

Design AA8910

First Floor: 1,163 square feet
Second Floor: 540 square feet
Total: 1,703 square feet
Width 38'-8"
Depth 61'-2"

● With a brick and wood siding exterior, this home takes on a comfortable, traditional air. The family will love the breakfast room and its front-yard views; the kitchen, open to this area, boasts a corner sink with dual windows overlooking the side yard. A plant shelf graces the dining and living rooms as well as the tiled entry. The living room offers a fireplace and a vaulted ceiling—a sophisticated feature for modern living. To round out the first floor, a grand master suite with a ten-foot vaulted ceiling offers a private bath with dual lavatories and a compartmented toilet. With a walk-in closet, this bedroom can't be beat. Upstairs, two family bedrooms each sport a walk-in closet. A loft or game area facilitates family fun.

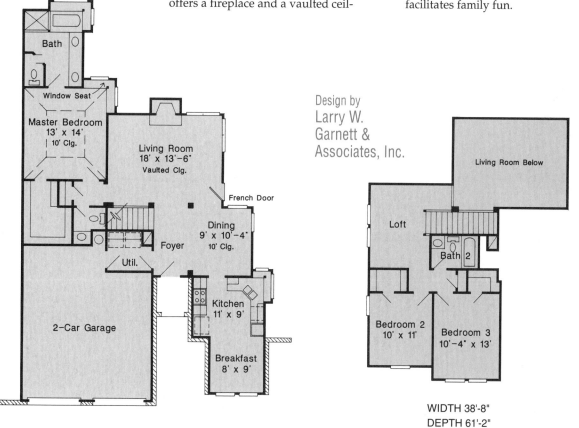

Design by
Larry W.
Garnett &
Associates, Inc.

WIDTH 38'-8"
DEPTH 61'-2"

Design AA8944

Square Footage: 1,505
Width 33'-4"
Depth 65'-10"

● An octagonal dining area lends character to this charming one-story home. Inside, the kitchen shares a 42" bar pass-through with the dining room, assuring ease in serving meals—formal or casual. From the kitchen, there's direct access to the two-car garage. Here, space for a washer and dryer rests in a comfortable nook. The living area showcases a ten-foot ceiling and a walk-in wet bar for entertaining. The well-zoned sleeping quarters—located at the back of the house—include two family bedrooms. Each has a set of corner windows and generous closet space. The master bedroom, with a full wall of closet space, sports its own bath. In it, a double-bowl vanity, a separate tub and shower and a compartmented toilet ensure the best in modern convenience.

Design by
Larry W.
Garnett &
Associates, Inc.

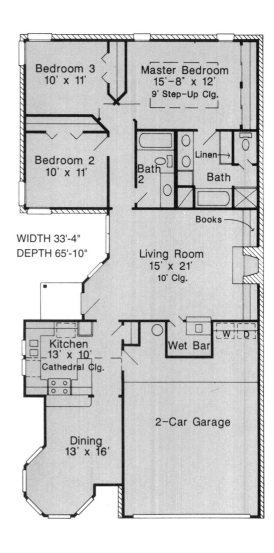

Bedroom 3
10' x 11'

Master Bedroom
15'-8" x 12'
9' Step-Up Clg.

Bedroom 2
10' x 11'

Bath 2

Linen

Bath

Books

WIDTH 33'-4"
DEPTH 65'-10"

Living Room
15' x 21'
10' Clg.

W D

Kitchen
13' x 10'
Cathedral Clg.

Wet Bar

2-Car Garage

Dining
13' x 16'

Design AA8894

First Floor: 846 square feet

Second Floor: 400 square feet

Total: 1,246 square feet

Width 36'-8"

Depth 38'-8"

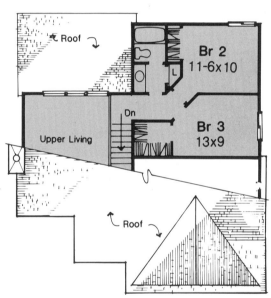

Roof

Br 2
11-6x10

Dn

Br 3
13x9

Upper Living

Roof

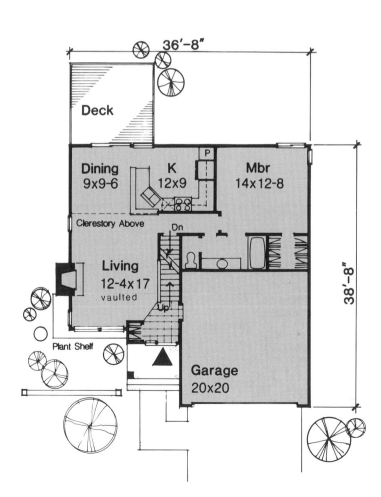

36'-8"

Deck

Dining
9x9-6

K
12x9

P

Mbr
14x12-8

Clerestory Above

Dn

Living
12-4x17
vaulted

Up

Plant Shelf

38'-8"

Garage
20x20

● A sloping roofline and wood siding lend a fresh look to this stunning starter home. Inside options include a second floor that can be built unfinished and completed as budgets allow. On the first floor, a tiled entryway reveals a vaulted living room with a fireplace. A rear kitchen serves a dining room that accesses a rear deck for outside enjoyments. Master-suite enhancements include corner windows, a walk-in closet and private passage to a full bath. Two bedrooms on the second floor include one with a walk-in closet and share a full hall bath.

Design by

LifeStyle
HomeDesigns

Design AA8946

Square Footage: 1,119
Width 39'-4"
Depth 47'-10"

● At just a bit over 1,100 square feet, this house is surprising with its wealth of livability. The tiled foyer opens to a living room with a ten-foot ceiling. A fireplace also contributes to this room's charm. A plant shelf stretches between the living and dining room to add definition. In line with great space utilization, the U-shaped kitchen remains open to the dining room. The master bedroom claims privacy at the back of the house. A skylight illuminates the master bath where a walk-in closet is just a step away. The kids will find their favorite bedroom: one boasts a large closet while the other basks in the light offered by an elegant set of windows. Nearby, the two-car garage leaves room for a laundry area.

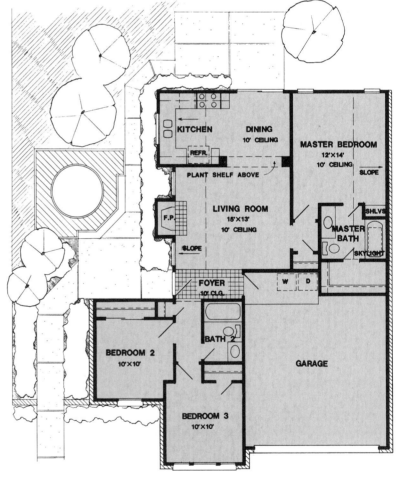

WIDTH 39'-4"
DEPTH 47'-10"

Design by
Larry W.
Garnett &
Associates, Inc.

Design AA9037

Square Footage: 1,048
Width 39'-4"
Depth 46'

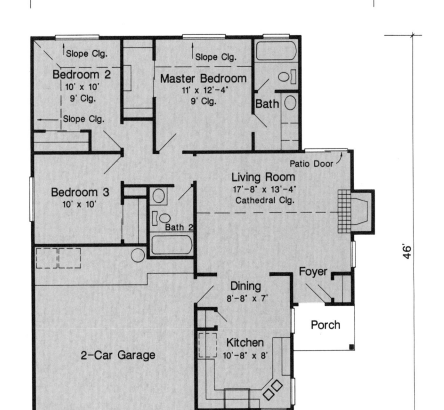

39'-4"

Slope Clg.

Bedroom 2
10' x 10'
9' Clg.

Slope Clg.

Master Bedroom
11' x 12'-4"
9' Clg.

Bath

Slope Clg.

Patio Door

Bedroom 3
10' x 10'

Living Room
17'-8" x 13'-4"
Cathedral Clg.

Bath 2

Foyer

2-Car Garage

Dining
8'-8" x 7'

Porch

Kitchen
10'-8" x 8'

46'

Design by
Larry W.
Garnett &
Associates, Inc.

● Scaled-down living need not necessarily mean feature-less floor planning, and this compact plan proves it. It provides many of the same special details that are expected in much larger and grander homes. Note, for example, the wealth of storage space: large closets in all three bedrooms, space in the garage, ample pantry in the kitchen, hall closet in the foyer. Counter space abounds in the U-shaped kitchen and corner windows here light up the work area. The master bedroom features a large master bath with a compartmented stool and tub. This bedroom and one family bedroom have sloped ceilings. Don't miss the cathedral ceiling in the living room and the cozy hearth here as well.

Design AA2661

First Floor: 1,020 square feet
Second Floor: 777 square feet
Total: 1,797 square feet
Width 34'
Depth 30'

 L **D**

● Any other starter house or retirement home couldn't have more charm than this design. Its compact frame houses a very livable plan. An outstanding feature of the first floor is the large country kitchen. Its fine attractions include a beam ceiling, a raised-hearth fireplace, a built-in window seat and a door leading to the outdoors. A living room is in the front of the plan and has another fireplace which shares the single chimney. The rear dormered second floor houses the sleeping and bath facilities.

California Engineered Plans and California Stock Plans are available for this home. Call 1-800-521-6797 for more information.

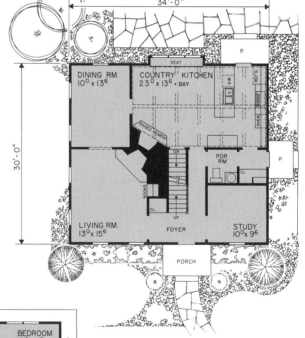

QUOTE ONE™

Cost to build? See page 214 to order complete cost estimate to build this house in your area!

Design by
Home Planners, Inc.

CUSTOMIZABLE

Custom Alterations? See page 221 for customizing this plan to your specifications.

Design AA3501 First Floor: 960 square feet
Second Floor: 733 square feet; Total: 1,693 square feet
Width 32'
Depth 30'

L **D**

● This efficient Saltbox design includes three bedrooms and two full baths plus a handy powder room on the first floor. A large living room in the front of the home features a fireplace. The rear of the home is left open, with room for a kitchen with snack bar, breakfast area with fireplace and dining room with outdoor access. If you wish, use the breakfast area as an all-purpose dining room and turn the dining room into a library or sitting room.

Design by
Home Planners,
Inc.

QUOTE ONE™
Cost to build? See page 214
to order complete cost estimate
to build this house in your area!

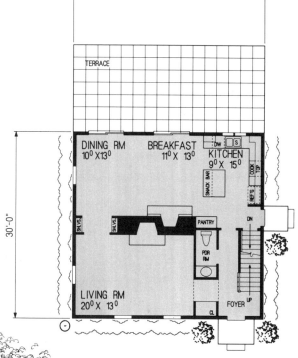

32'-0"

TERRACE

DINING RM 10⁰ X13⁰   BREAKFAST 11⁰ X 13⁰   KITCHEN 9⁰ X 15⁰

30'-0"

SNACK BAR

PANTRY

PDR RM

DN

LIVING RM 20⁰ X 13⁰

FOYER   UP

BEDROOM 13⁰ X 9⁰   BEDROOM 13⁰ X 9⁰

RAILING   DN

BATH

BEDROOM 12⁰ X 14⁰

MASTER BATH

ROOF

Photo by Andrew D. Lautman

Design AA2493

First Floor: 1,387 square feet
Second Floor: 929 square feet
Total: 2,316 square feet
Width 30'
Depth 51'-8"

Design by
Home Planners,
Inc.

● Perfect for a narrow lot, this shingle- and stone-sided Nantucket Cape caters to the casual lifestyle. The side entrance gives direct access to the wonderfully open living areas: gathering room with fireplace; kitchen with angled, pass-through snack bar; dining area with sliding glass doors to a covered eating area. Note also the large deck that further extends the living potential. Also on this floor is a large master suite. Upstairs is a convenient guest suite with private balcony. It is complemented by two smaller bedrooms.

Design AA3379 First Floor: 1,086 square feet
Second Floor: 902 square feet; Total: 1,988 square feet
Width 34'
Depth 56'-4"

L **D**

● Colonial styling is perfect in this two-story, narrow-lot plan. With the garage facing toward the front, the home is protected from street noise and works well on a lot that allows very little clearance on the sides. Living areas are concentrated in the formal living and dining rooms and the media room with nearby powder room. The kitchen holds a large snackbar counter through to the breakfast room. Sliding glass doors here allow easy access to the rear terrace. The bedrooms are on the second floor and include a master with fireplace and garden whirlpool and two family bedrooms. One of the secondary bedrooms includes a large walk-in closet.

Design by
Home Planners,
Inc.

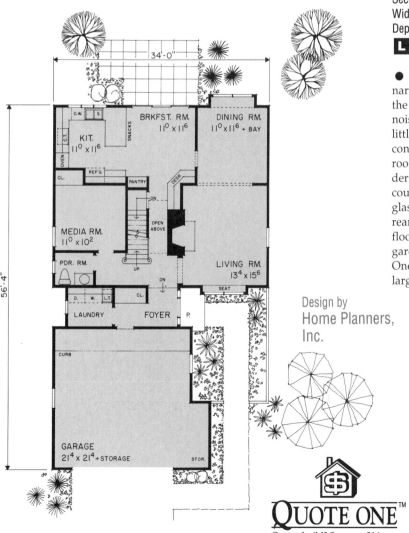

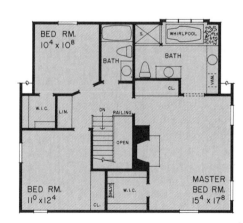

Quote One™

Cost to build? See page 214
to order complete cost estimate
to build this house in your area!

41

Design AA2974

First Floor: 911 square feet
Second Floor: 861 square feet
Total: 1,772 square feet
Attic: 1,131 square feet
Width 38'
Depth 52'

L

● Victorian houses are well known for their orientation on narrow building sites. And when this occurs nothing is lost to the captivating exterior styling. This house is 38 feet wide, but its narrow width belies the tremendous amount of livability found inside. And, of course, the ubiquitous porch/veranda contributes mightily to style as well as to livability. The efficient, U-shaped kitchen is flanked by the informal breakfast room and the formal dining room. The rear living area is spacious and functions in an exciting manner with the outdoor areas. Bonus recreational, hobby and storage space is offered by the basement and the attic.

California Engineered Plans and California Stock Plans are available for this home. Call 1-800-521-6797 for more information.

ATTIC
26⁰ x34⁰
(HEADROOM 21⁰ x 29⁰)
ROOF

RAILING

UPPER BEDROOM

ROOF

MASTER BEDROOM
12⁰ x 17⁰

VANITY

DRESSING RM

WALK-IN CLOSET

BATH

ROOF

ATTIC

BEDROOM
12⁰ x 11⁰

LINEN

BEDROOM
10⁴ x 12⁰

SLOPED CEILING

ROOF

38'-0"

VERANDA

RAILING

SCREENED PORCH
11² x 11⁶

LIVING RM.
13⁴ x 17⁰

DINING RM.
11⁸ x 11⁰

RANGE

STORAGE

KITCHEN
12⁰ x 9⁴

CURB

PDR RM

FOYER

SNACK BAR

BRKFST. RM
12⁰ x 8⁴ BAY

GARAGE
11⁸ x 23⁴

LAUND

52'-0"

COVERED PORCH

QUOTE ONE™
Cost to build? See page 214 to order complete cost estimate to build this house in your area!

Design by
Home Planners, Inc.

Design by
Home Planners,
Inc.

QUOTE ONE™

Cost to build? See page 214
to order complete cost estimate
to build this house in your area!

Design AA3316 First Floor: 1,111 square feet
Second Floor: 886 square feet; Total: 1,997 square feet
Width 34'-1"
Depth 50'

L

● Don't be fooled by a small-looking exterior. This
plan offers three bedrooms and plenty of living space.
Notice that the screened porch leads to a rear terrace
with access to the breakfast room. A living room/dining
room combination adds spaciousness to the first floor.

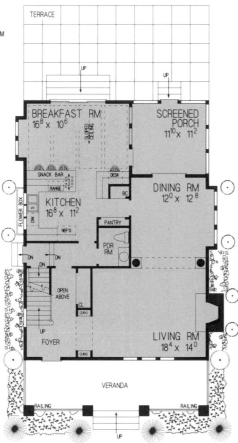

Width 34'-1"
Depth 50'

Design AA9374

First Floor: 879 square feet
Second Floor: 945 square feet
Total: 1,824 square feet
Width 38'
Depth 44'-8"

● This two-story home recalls an earlier time through its use of brick and glass block accents and a wood-railed porch. Inside, the formal dining room offers ample space for formal dinners while the family room, with its raised-hearth fireplace, provides a space that's suited for formal and casual living. In the kitchen, a snack bar serves the bumped-out breakfast nook. Close to the garage door, the laundry room finds natural light from a side window. Four bedrooms create the upstairs sleeping quarters. The master suite boasts a nine-foot ceiling and a spacious dressing area; the master bath includes separate vanities, a step-up whirlpool and a private toilet. All of the family bedrooms have double windows and share a full hall bath.

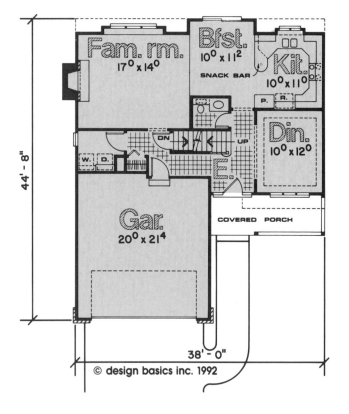

© design basics inc. 1992

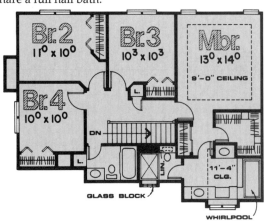

Design by
Design
Basics,
Inc.

44

One-Story Houses From 40' to 49' Wide

To increase narrow-lot choices, this next section expands a bit on the narrow lot itself. In just one story, many of the homes featured here offer over 1,500 square feet of living space; some expand to 2,200 square feet and over! The larger floor plans include added features such as dens and studies. You'll also notice that entrances will now either face to the front or will have a front-facing porch leading to a side-door entry. In any case, grander entrances become a key design feature: front porches boast columns, arches and volume-looks; foyers often unfold commanding perspectives on open living areas.

For those looking to build in a suburban setting, many of these designs make very appropriate candidates. On page 53, for example, this charming brick home will be a welcome addition to any neighborhood. The unique layout of this house presents an open outdoor space toward the back. Take the liberty to do some gardening here or use the area to construct a safe play area for the kids. Inside, a grand entry is brought to life by a raised foyer and columns—these columns also lend formality to the living and dining areas.

For those interested in something different, the innovative design on page 80, with its rustic air, will make a rural site complete. You'll find all the creature comforts inside including a formal living room and den with a shared dual fireplace, a family room with a corner hearth and a vaulted master bedroom with all of today's amenities.

Open floor plans and high ceilings in the designs on pages 60 and 61 belie the smaller widths, creating instead a larger feeling of space inside the narrow frames. These homes are ideal for entertaining family and friends. On page 60, the attractive facade presents a contemporary view with a large, sunny window in the vaulted living room.

See pages 64-69 for super home-building alternatives with a choice of exterior elevations that epitomizes all the best in narrow-lot designing. On page 69, the front-facing double garage easily accesses the street, while the central entry provides an interesting introduction to the layout of the plan. This "H" pattern provides bumped-out rooms and nooks that enjoy quiet due to their private walls. In this design, casual and formal living areas are drawn together via a serpentine wall and a plant shelf. A dual fireplace adds spice to the family room and the living room. On the left side of the plan, away from the traffic of the main living areas, the sleeping quarters are comprised of well-separated bedrooms.

Design AA9175

Square Footage: 1,399
Width 40'-4"
Depth 60'

● Exceptional floor planning provides all of today's amenities in a home just under 1,400 square feet. The tiled foyer acts as a pivot for access to the living room and main living areas, the laundry room and garage and the secondary bedroom. A delightful courtyard rests in view of the living room where a fireplace and built-in bookshelves lend charm. The dining room gains passage to this courtyard through a side door. The bright and efficient kitchen leaves room for a large pantry. Nearby, the master bedroom delights with its large private bath. Here you'll find a separate soaking tub and a shower as well as a generous walk-in closet.

Design by
Larry W.
Garnett &
Associates, Inc.

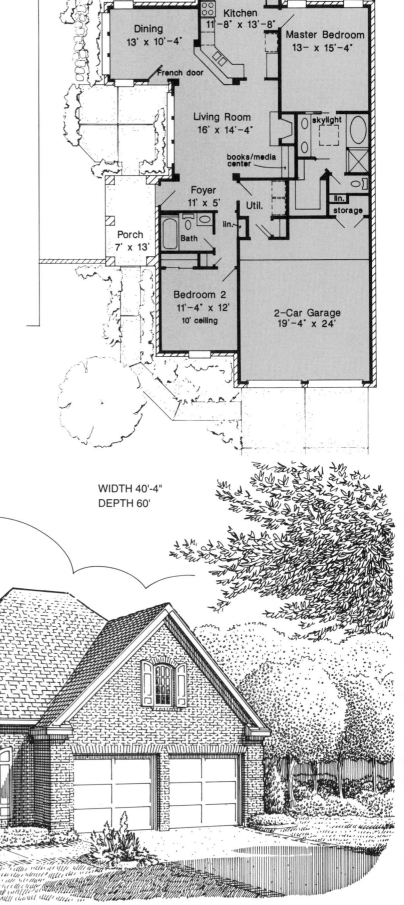

WIDTH 40'-4"
DEPTH 60'

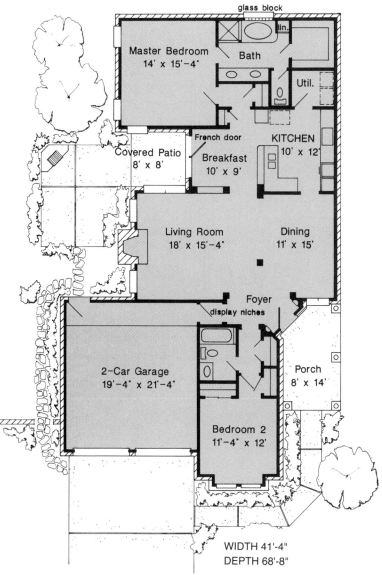

glass block

Master Bedroom
14' x 15'-4"

Bath

lin.

Util.

Covered Patio
8' x 8'

French door

Breakfast
10' x 9'

KITCHEN
10' x 12'

Living Room
18' x 15'-4"

Dining
11' x 15'

Foyer

display niches

2-Car Garage
19'-4" x 21'-4"

Porch
8' x 14'

Bedroom 2
11'-4" x 12'

WIDTH 41'-4"
DEPTH 68'-8"

Design AA9176

Square Footage: 1,594
Width 41'-4"
Depth 68'-8"

● Make great first impressions with this two-bedroom plan. A columned porch introduces an angled foyer, also defined by columns. A fireplace resides at one end of the living room—this room expands into the dining room. For ease in entertaining, the kitchen easily services the dining room and also accommodates a breakfast room. Enjoy your morning coffee here or on the patio just outside. As an added luxury, the laundry room is located near the kitchen. The master bedroom, at the rear of the plan for privacy, makes use of a bath with dual lavatories, a compartmented commode, a soaking tub, a separate shower and a walk-in closet.

Design by
Larry W.
Garnett &
Associates, Inc.

Design AA9178

Square Footage: 1,706
Width 42'
Depth 67'-8"

● With a width of only 42 feet, this house achieves
over 1,700 square feet in living space! Its pleasing
exterior, with a volume roof and shuttered windows,
provides a perfect introduction to the interior. The
open living and dining rooms offer a nice atmosphere
for formal entertaining. With a columned foyer as a
prelude, guests won't help but be impressed. The
breakfast room overlooks a side courtyard where
there's room enough for outdoor dining. A utility
area adjacent to the kitchen leaves room for a folding
counter. Sleeping accommodations include a front
secondary bedroom with a walk-in closet and convenient access to a full bath. The master bedroom offers
a fine bath and a large walk-in closet.

Design by
Larry W.
Garnett &
Associates, Inc.

glass block

Master Bedroom
14' x 15'-4"

lin.

Util.

French door

Covered Patio
5' x 9'

Kitchen
11' x 12'-8"

Breakfast
12' x 10'

pantry

Living Room
18' x 14'-8"

Dining
11' x 13'-4"

Foyer

display niches

Porch
7' x 14'

2-Car Garage
19'-4" x 21'-4"

Bedroom 2
13'-4" x 12'
10' ceiling

WIDTH 42'
DEPTH 67'-8"

48

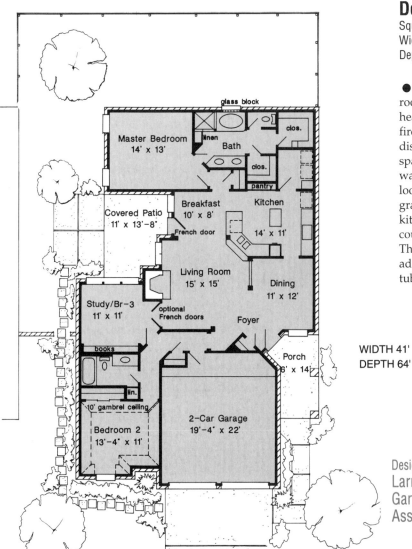

Design AA9177

Square Footage: 1,710
Width 41'
Depth 64'

● To meet all of your needs and wants, this two-bedroom plan offers a wealth of livability. Acting as the heart of the home, the living room delights with its fireplace and French doors to the study. Here you'll discover a full wall of built-in bookshelves—adequate space for your reading collection—and an exquisite wall of windows looking out on the courtyard. Before looking too much further, notice the closet space that graces the front entry as well as the garage entry. The kitchen remains large and even features an island countertop for additional ease in food preparation. The master bedroom utilizes two walk-in closets in addition to a bath with dual lavatories and a separate tub and shower.

WIDTH 41'
DEPTH 64'

Design by
Larry W.
Garnett &
Associates, Inc.

49

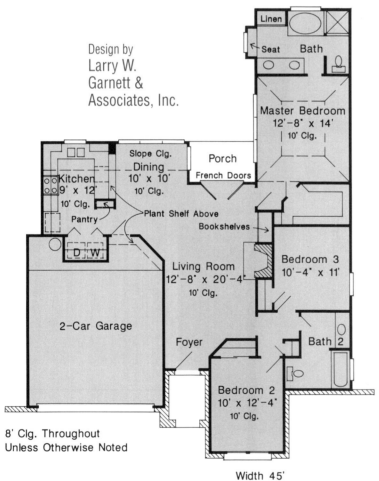

Design by
Larry W.
Garnett &
Associates, Inc.

Linen

Seat   Bath

Master Bedroom
12'-8" x 14'
10' Clg.

Slope Clg.
Dining
10' x 10'
10' Clg.

Porch
French Doors

Kitchen
9' x 12'
10' Clg.

Pantry

Plant Shelf Above
Bookshelves

D W

Living Room
12'-8" x 20'-4"
10' Clg.

Bedroom 3
10'-4" x 11'

2-Car Garage

Foyer

Bath 2

Bedroom 2
10' x 12'-4"
10' Clg.

8' Clg. Throughout
Unless Otherwise Noted

Width 45'
Depth 59'-6"

Design AA9158
Square Footage: 1,396
Width 45'
Depth 59'-6"

● Effective floor planning
makes this home appear to
be much larger than it really
is. From the foyer, views
flow all the way through
French doors to a rear porch.
The living room, with a fireplace and built-in bookcases,
is open to the dining room
and kitchen. A plant shelf
aids in tying all of these areas
together—a lovely design
feature. Note the alcove in
the kitchen where you'll find
room enough for a washer
and a dryer. The two sec-
ondary bedrooms find a full
bath between them. Bedroom
2 will delight with its ten-
foot ceiling. The master suite,
with a complete bath, is
tucked away to the rear of
the home for privacy.

Design AA9149

Square Footage: 1,468
Width 42'
Depth 54'-10"

● Compact and comfortable
are the by-words of this cozy
one-story design. Start with
the recessed entry that leads to
a raised tile foyer opening to
all areas of the home. The living room acts as the hub and
is graced with plant shelves,
built-ins and warming fireplace. The large kitchen area
features plenty of counter
space and has a light-filled
dining space for formal or
casual meals. A lovely master
suite with gambrel ceiling is
separated from secondary
bedrooms. Its adjoining bath
has linen storage, dual lavatories, a skylight and compartmented toilet. One of the secondary bedrooms functions
well as a study or guest room
if needed.

Design by
Larry W.
Garnett &
Associates, Inc.

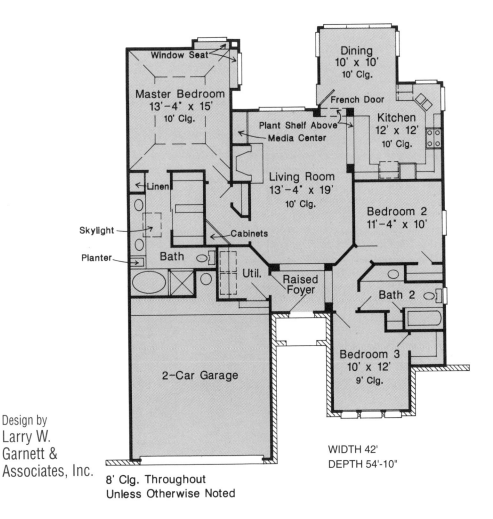

Window Seat

Dining
10' x 10'
10' Clg.

Master Bedroom
13'-4" x 15'
10' Clg.

French Door

Plant Shelf Above
Media Center

Kitchen
12' x 12'
10' Clg.

Linen

Living Room
13'-4" x 19'
10' Clg.

Bedroom 2
11'-4" x 10'

Skylight

Cabinets

Planter

Bath

Util.

Raised
Foyer

Bath 2

2-Car Garage

Bedroom 3
10' x 12'
9' Clg.

WIDTH 42'
DEPTH 54'-10"

8' Clg. Throughout
Unless Otherwise Noted

Design AA8948

Square Footage: 1,394
Width 44'-8"
Depth 60'-6"

● Three bedrooms and formal living and dining rooms grace this lovely brick home. A step
down from the foyer, the living room rises to a
twelve-foot ceiling, and has a built-in media
center, a fireplace and a corner window seat.
With a plant shelf above, the dining room dis-
tinguishes itself from the living room. It boasts
a ten-foot ceiling and overlooks the back courtyard. The neat kitchen will serve the house
gourmet with its pantry and cupboard space.
French doors open off the kitchen and lead to
the courtyard—you may decide to set up summer breakfasts here. The kitchen also accesses
an efficient utility area. In Bedroom 2, a ten-
foot ceiling lends appeal, while Bedroom 3
makes use of a walk-in closet. The master bedroom, located at the very rear of the house,
delights with its vaulted ceiling, corner window seat and luxurious bath.

Design by
Larry W.
Garnett &
Associates, Inc.

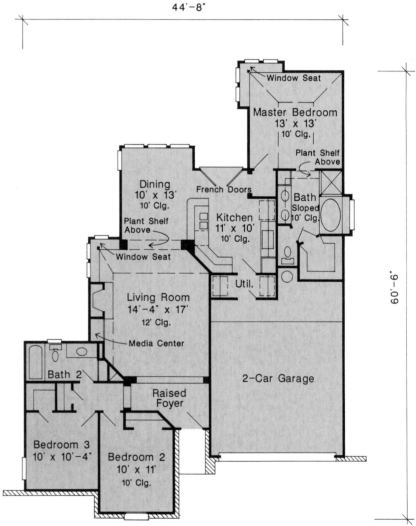

Design AA9114

Square Footage: 1,529
Width 44'
Depth 75'-10"

● This quaint design delivers the best in floor plans and beautifully incorporates outdoor living spaces. The entry foyer opens to the central living area with attached dining room. The uniquely shaped kitchen has an open counter that overlooks this area. To the left of the plan are three bedrooms; family bedrooms are cleverly separated from the master suite. The front bedroom could be used as a study and contains a lovely bay window. Two French doors (one in the dining room and one in the master bath) lead to the rear patio.

Design by
Larry W.
Garnett &
Associates, Inc.

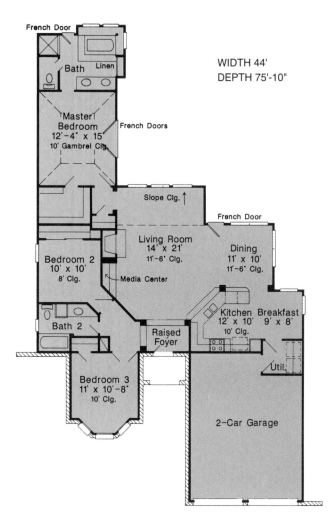

WIDTH 44'
DEPTH 75'-10"

53

Design AA9506

Square Footage: 1,463
Width 40'
Depth 53'

● A combination of shingles and wood siding
adds interest to this three-bedroom home. The
skylit foyer offers a commanding view of the
great room where a fireplace demands attention. Columns add definition to the living
areas. The kitchen extends to an island cooktop
and has convenient access to the dining room.
Here, sliding glass doors open to the rear yard.
For added convenience, a utility room opens
off the garage while providing passage to the
house. Closets separate Bedrooms 2 and 3, thus
allowing for more quiet; the rooms share a full
hall bath. The vaulted master suite takes
advantage of its front location and features a
private bath with dual lavatories and a walk-in
closet.

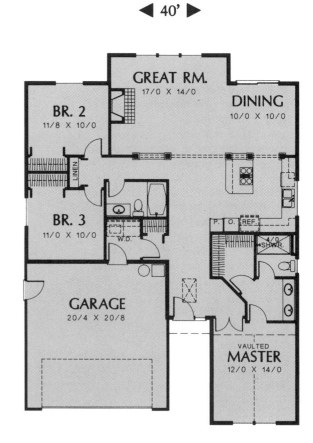

Design by
Alan Mascord
Design Associates, Inc.

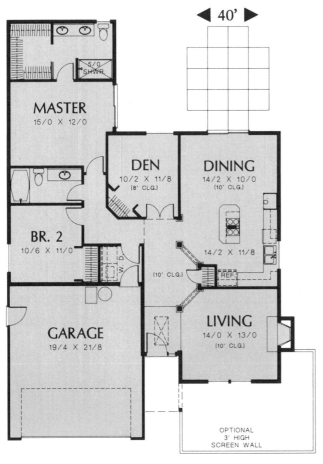

OPTIONAL
3' HIGH
SCREEN WALL

Design AA9507

Square Footage: 1,401
Width 40'
Depth 60'

● Vertical siding succeeds in moving the eye up in this compact one-story plan. For added interest, an optional three-foot-high screen wall encloses the area just outside the living room window. The foyer unfolds with a skylight and a ten-foot ceiling. Columns lend an air of formality to the living and dining rooms and the kitchen. A den is found straight ahead in the foyer and offers privacy for studies or the occasional out-of-town guest. The kitchen showcases an island cooktop and ample counter space. The dining room, with its ten-foot ceiling, has sliding glass doors that lead to a back terrace. The master bedroom also features sliding glass doors to this outdoor area.

Design by
Alan Mascord
Design Associates, Inc.

Design AA9431

Square Footage: 1,316
Width 46'
Depth 50'

● An exceptional use of
cedar shingles, horizontal
cedar siding and brick highlights the exterior of this one-
story home. And the floor
plan is bursting with amenities found normally on much
larger homes. Note, for
example, the dramatically
vaulted great room with the
plant shelf floating across the
entry. The master bedroom is
also vaulted. The covered
patio lends itself to great outdoor living even in inclement
weather. Opening off the
entry with a pair of French
doors is a den which could
be used as a third bedroom.

◀ 46' ▶

50'

Design by
Alan Mascord
Design Associates, Inc.

56

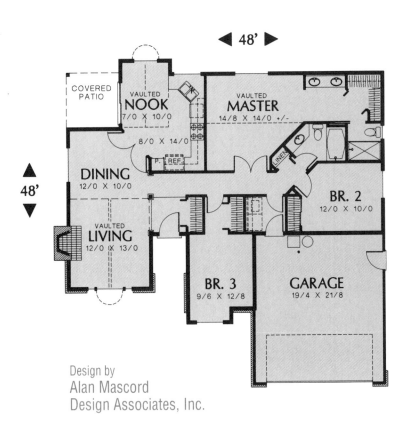

Design AA9439

Square Footage: 1,338
Width 48'
Depth 48'

● This classic single-story home invites a second look— particularly for those who are planning to build for affordability. Special features make it attractive while budget-worthy: the living room, nook and master suite all contain vaulted ceilings; the covered patio provides outdoor enjoyment even in inclement weather. Notice that the living and dining areas remain open to each other—this creates a friendly atmosphere for entertaining. Of course, the fireplace in the living room adds additional warmth to the setting. Each of the family bedrooms enjoys ample closet space as well as lots of privacy. The master bedroom, opening through double doors, spotlights its own bath.

Design by
Alan Mascord
Design Associates, Inc.

◄ 42' ►

MASTER
11/0 X 15/0 +/-

DEN/BR. 3
10/0 X 10/4

VAULTED
LIVING
12/0 X 14/0

BR. 2
12/0 X 10/0

LINEN

DINING
13/0 X 10/0
(11' CLG.)

PANTRY

GARAGE
19/4 X 21/8

13/6 X 14/0 +/-

▲
50'
▼

Design AA9429

Square Footage: 1,367
Width 42'
Depth 50'

● Featuring a combination of cedar shingles and vertical cedar siding, this ranch home has a compact, convenient floor plan. Both kitchen and nook face the front where a courtyard wall provides privacy for outdoor relaxation. The entry and dining room both have eleven-foot ceilings, allowing for attractive transom windows. This area is also enhanced by a series of columns separating the vaulted living room from the dining room. Opening off the hallway with a pair of French doors is a den which could be used as a third bedroom.

Design by
Alan Mascord
Design Associates, Inc.

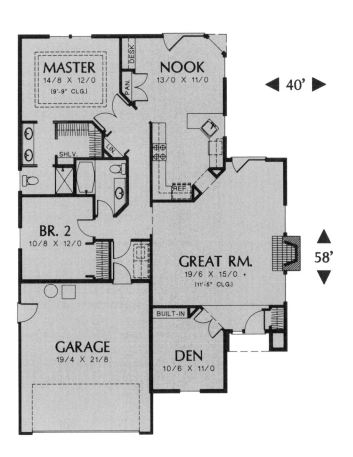

Design AA9508

Square Footage: 1,523
Width 40'
Depth 58'

● The repeated roof treatments and varying exterior materials add interest to this darling home. Inside, the great room commands attention with its fireplace, high ceiling and overall spaciousness. Double doors lead to a den where built-ins enhance an already attractive room—perfect for quiet getaways. A built-in desk adds to the inviting character of the kitchen and breakfast nook. The great room could easily support a formal dining area serviced by the angular kitchen passageway. The sleeping quarters consist of a master suite with a private bath and a walk-in closet, and a secondary bedroom for family or guests. A utility area ties the house and garage together well.

Design by
Alan Mascord
Design Associates, Inc.

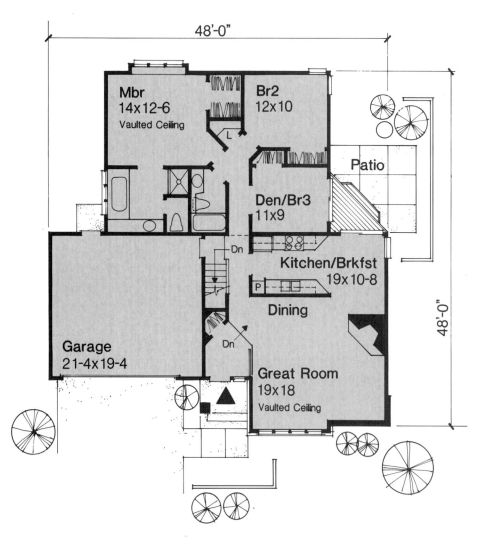

Design AA8893

Square Footage: 1,368
Width 48'
Depth 48'

● The modern flair of this one-story home offers great curb appeal. Inside, flexible living patterns accommodate the growing family. The raised foyer leads to a vaulted great room. A fireplace and dining space make this a cozy area. The galley-style kitchen opens to a breakfast nook. Sliding glass doors here lead to a private patio. The sleeping zone includes two secondary bedrooms—one could easily serve as a den. The master bedroom features a vaulted ceiling, bumped-out windows, a walk-in closet and a spacious bath with a separate shower.

Design by
LifeStyle
HomeDesigns

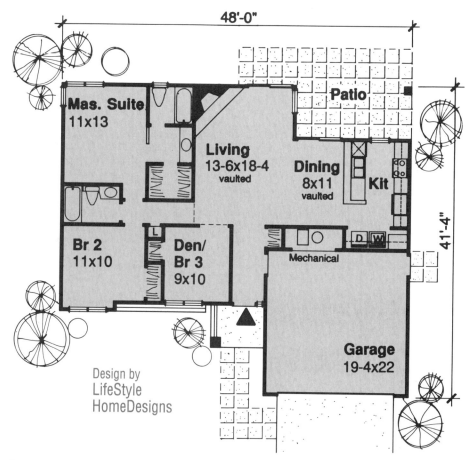

48'-0"

41'-4"

Mas. Suite
11x13

Living
13-6x18-4
vaulted

Patio

Dining
8x11
vaulted

Kit

Br 2
11x10

Den/
Br 3
9x10

Mechanical

D W

Garage
19-4x22

Design by
LifeStyle
HomeDesigns

Design AA8895

Square Footage: 1,159
Width 48'
Depth 41'-4"

● Fine starter livability is present in this handsome ranch home. At the heart of the home is the vaulted living room with a corner fireplace and views of the rear patio. The dining room connects to this area and is easily serviced by the efficient kitchen. You'll find a washer and dryer tucked into a neat kitchen alcove. Three bedrooms include one that could double as a den. In the master suite, a walk-in closet and a compartmented bath gain attention. A basement stairway can be built in place of the laundry/mechanical space.

Design AA3460

Square Footage: 1,389
Width 44'-8"
Depth 54'-6"

L

Design by
Home Planners,
Inc.

● A double dose of charm, this special farmhouse plan offers two elevations in its blueprint package—one showcases a delightful wraparound porch. Though rooflines and porch options are different, the floor plan is the same and very livable. A formal living room/dining room combination has a warming fireplace and a delightful bay window. The kitchen separates this area from the more casual family room. In the kitchen, you'll find an efficient snack bar that services the family room, as well as a pantry for additional storage space. Three bedrooms include two family bedrooms served by a full bath and a lovely master suite with its own private bath. Notice the location of the washer and dryer—convenient to all of the bedrooms.

California Engineered Plans and California Stock Plans are available for this home. Call 1-800-521-6797 for more information.

QUOTE ONE™

Cost to build? See page 214 to order complete cost estimate to build this house in your area!

CUSTOMIZABLE

Custom Alterations? See page 221 for customizing this plan to your specifications.

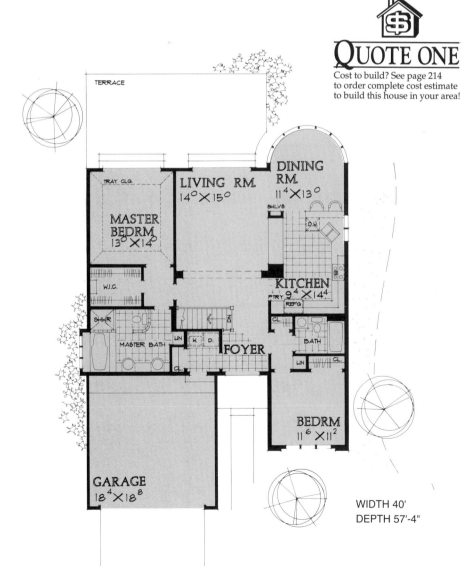

TERRACE

TRAY CLG.

MASTER
BEDRM
13⁰ × 14⁰

LIVING RM.
14⁰ × 15⁰

DINING
RM.
11⁴ × 13⁰

SHLVS

D.W.

W.I.C.

KITCHEN
9⁴ × 14⁴

SHWR

PTRY

REFG

MASTER BATH

LIN

W. D.

FOYER

CL.

BATH

CL.

LIN

BEDRM
11⁶ × 11²

GARAGE
18⁴ × 18⁸

WIDTH 40'
DEPTH 57'-4"

Quote One™

Cost to build? See page 214
to order complete cost estimate
to build this house in your area!

Design AA3453

Square Footage: 1,442
Width 40'
Depth 57'-4"

L

● This volume home impresses
with its stately rooflines and stucco
exterior. The front porch opens to
an eleven-foot ceiling in the foyer.
Straight ahead, an elegant living
room serves as a prelude to the
dramatic circular dining bay. Here,
family and guests alike will revel in
the fine views out the back of the
house. The kitchen, with its advan-
tageous snack bar, offers an abundance of counter and cabinet space.
The media room, with its closet
space and access to a full hall bath,
could easily convert to a bedroom.
In the master bedroom you'll find a
lengthy closet in addition to a stunning bath. Glass block provides
privacy to the toilet and shower
while the spa tub delights in its
well-illuminated nook. Dual lavatories complete the amenities in
this room.

Design by
Home Planners,
Inc.

63

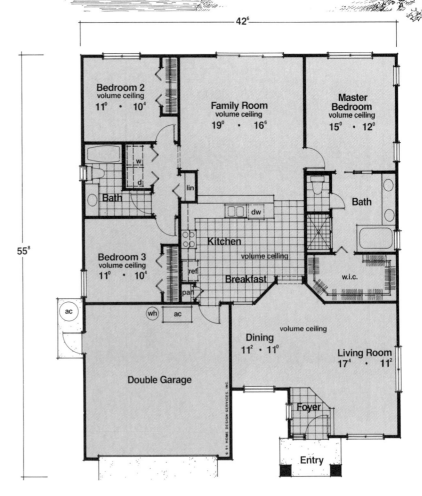

Design by
Home Design
Services, Inc.

Design AA8632

Square Footage: 1,750
Width 42'-6"
Depth 55'-8"

● This dapper design boasts two exterior elevation choices—both with true good looks. Inside, a volume ceiling enlivens the combined living and dining rooms. Interestingly, the kitchen acts as the heart of the home, both in location and style. A tiled floor and a volume ceiling set the mood of the room while ample counter space lends to its practicality. Casual living takes precedence in the spacious family room. In the master bedroom, you'll find a private bath that includes dual lavatories, a private commode and an expansive walk-in closet. The secondary bedrooms find privacy by design as well as convenience in the full bath that separates them. Also noteworthy, the washer and dryer location rests in a tidy alcove by these bedrooms.

42⁶

Bedroom 2
volume ceiling
11⁰ • 10⁴

Family Room
volume ceiling
19⁰ • 16⁶

Master Bedroom
volume ceiling
15⁰ • 12⁰

Bath

w
d

lin

dw

Bath

55⁸

Bedroom 3
volume ceiling
11⁰ • 10⁴

ref

Kitchen
volume ceiling

Breakfast

w.i.c.

ac

wh ac

pan

Double Garage

Dining
11² • 11⁰

volume ceiling

Living Room
17⁴ • 11²

Foyer

Entry

Design AA8633

Square Footage: 1,865
Width 45'
Depth 66'

● This innovative plan takes advantage of an angled entry to the home, maximizing visual impact and making it possible to include four bedrooms. The joining of the great room and dining space makes creative interior decorating possible. The master suite also takes advantage of angles in creating long vistas into the space. The master bath is designed with all the amenities usually found in much larger homes. The kitchen and breakfast nook overlook the outdoor living space where you can even have an outdoor kitchen area—great for entertaining. The traditional feel of the exterior and the up-to-date interior make this house the perfect design for the nineties.

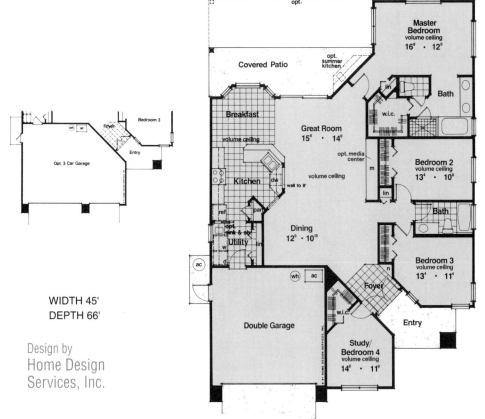

WIDTH 45'
DEPTH 66'

Design by
Home Design
Services, Inc.

© 91 HOME DESIGN SERVICES, INC.

J.N. HANSEN

Design AA8610
Square Footage: 1,280
Width 40'
Depth 48'

● This plan is ideal for the young family that needs a house that's small but smart. As in larger plans, this home boasts a private master's retreat with double closets, soaking tub and shower. The living area embraces the outdoor living space. The family eat-in kitchen design allows for efficient food preparation. Note the interior laundry closet included in the home. This plan comes with three options for Bedroom 2 and one option for the master bath. It also includes blueprints for three elevation choices!

Design by
Home Design
Services, Inc.

Covered Patio

Family Room
14⁰ • 12⁰
volume ceiling

Bedroom 2
13⁰ • 9⁰
volume ceiling

Breakfast

Bedroom 3
10⁰ • 9⁰
volume ceiling

Bath

Kitchen
14⁰• 9⁰

Dining
11⁰ • 12⁰

w d

Bath

Foyer

Double Garage

Master
Bedroom
13⁰ • 12⁰
volume ceiling

© 91 HOME DESIGN SERVICES, INC.

WIDTH 40'
DEPTH 48'

© 91 HOME DESIGN SERVICES, INC.

Design AA8631

Square Footage: 1,697
Width 45'
Depth 68'-4"

● Great great-room design!
This exciting plan features a
main gathering space bordered
on the left by the formal dining
area with decorative built-in
wall for a custom touch. The
unobstructed view of the rear
outdoor space is maximized
from the gathering space as well
as the kitchen and breakfast
room. The placement of secondary bedrooms toward the
front of the home gives a sense
of privacy. The master suite
compares favorably to much
larger homes, boasting a huge
walk-in shower, private toilet
and oversized vanity and closet.
Space for a media center and
fireplace are also allowed for in
the design. The blueprints for
this design include options for
two different exteriors.

Width 45'
Depth 68'-4"

Design by
Home Design
Services, Inc.

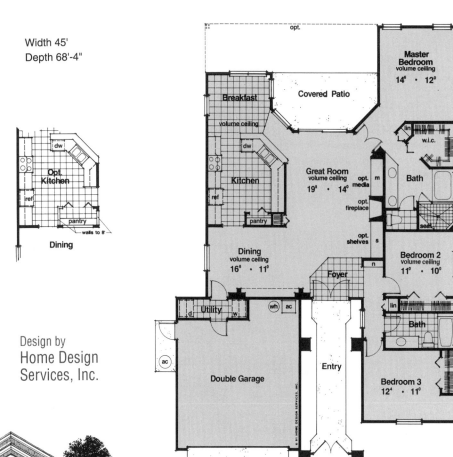

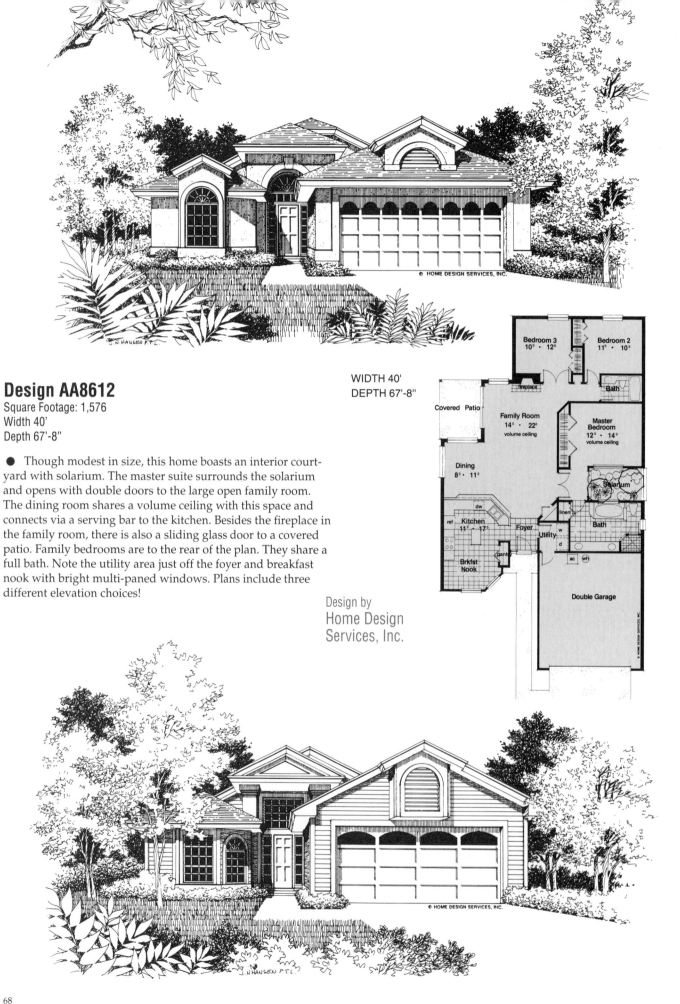

© HOME DESIGN SERVICES, INC.

Design AA8612

Square Footage: 1,576
Width 40'
Depth 67'-8"

● Though modest in size, this home boasts an interior court-yard with solarium. The master suite surrounds the solarium and opens with double doors to the large open family room. The dining room shares a volume ceiling with this space and connects via a serving bar to the kitchen. Besides the fireplace in the family room, there is also a sliding glass door to a covered patio. Family bedrooms are to the rear of the plan. They share a full bath. Note the utility area just off the foyer and breakfast nook with bright multi-paned windows. Plans include three different elevation choices!

WIDTH 40'
DEPTH 67'-8"

Design by
Home Design
Services, Inc.

Bedroom 3
10⁰ • 12⁰

Bedroom 2
11⁰ • 10⁰

Bath

Covered Patio

Family Room
14⁰ • 22⁰
volume ceiling

fireplace

Master Bedroom
12⁵ • 14⁰
volume ceiling

Dining
8⁰ • 11⁰

Solarium

Kitchen
11⁰ • 17⁰

linen

Bath

ref

dw

Foyer

Utility

w
d

Brkfst Nook

pant

ac wft

Double Garage

© HOME DESIGN SERVICES, INC.

© HOME DESIGN SERVICES, INC.

© HOME DESIGN SERVICES, INC.

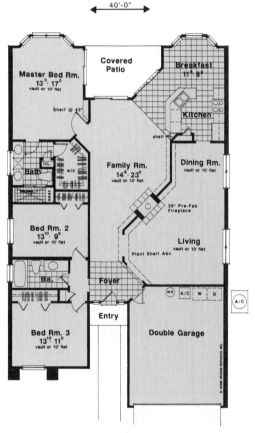

40'-0"

66'-8"

Master Bed Rm.
13⁰· 17⁰
vault or 10' flat

Covered Patio

Breakfast
11⁸· 8⁶

Kitchen

Shelf @ 42"

shelf

Bath

lin.

wic

seat

Family Rm.
14⁸· 23⁰
vault or 10' flat

Dining Rm.
vault or 10' flat

36" Pre-Fab Fireplace

Bed Rm. 2
13¹⁰· 9⁸
vault or 10' flat

Living
vault or 10' flat

Plant Shelf Abv.

Ba.

Foyer

wh   A/C   W   D

A/C

Entry

Bed Rm. 3
13¹⁰· 11⁰
vault or 10' flat

Double Garage

Design AA8613

Square Footage: 1,872
Width 40'
Depth 66'-8"

● Vaulted ceilings throughout this home suggest the innovative touches that add interest in a single-level plan. Sidelight and overhead windows brighten a foyer that opens to the family and living rooms. A plant shelf spans the entry into the living room, which is united with the dining room under a high ceiling. A vaulted ceiling also augments the family room. Notice the two-way fireplace and access to a covered patio here. The kitchen is convenient to the dining room and to a bayed breakfast nook. The master bedroom also has a bay window plus a full bath with oversized shower. Two additional bedrooms share a full bath. Plans include two different elevation choices!

Design by
Home Design
Services, Inc.

© HOME DESIGN SERVICES, INC.

Design AA9113

Square Footage: 1,496
Width 43'-8"
Depth 74'-8"

● This great one-story design fits well on a narrow lot. From the covered front porch, the foyer opens to living areas on the left. These areas include a living room with a fireplace and a pass-through bar to the kitchen, as well as a glass-surrounded dining area with a French door. A utility area leads to the two-car garage out back. Three bedrooms complete the living space and include a master bedroom that fancies its own bath: a garden tub, dual vanities and a separate shower set the stage in this bath. Note, too, the French door that leads to the tiled courtyard. Two family bedrooms share a full hall bath. Bedroom 2 even has a walk-in closet. Bedroom 3 features a built-in desk.

Design by
Larry W.
Garnett &
Associates, Inc.

WIDTH 43'-8"
DEPTH 74'-8"

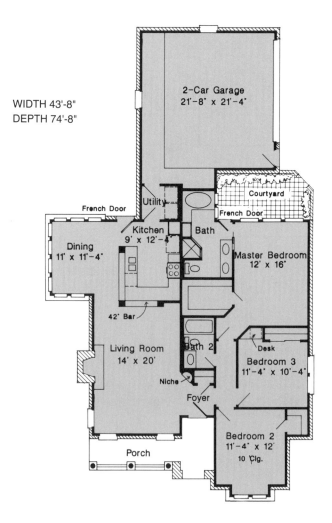

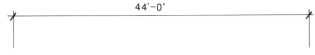

44'-0"

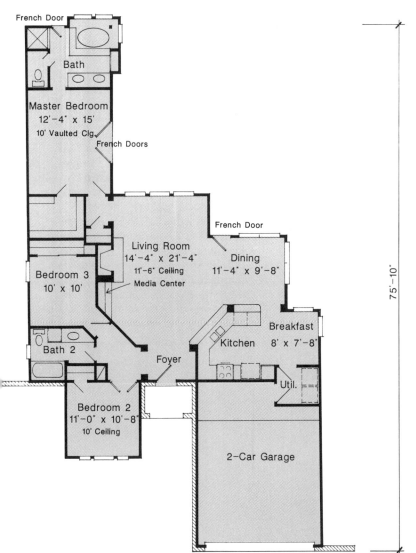

French Door

Bath

Master Bedroom
12'-4" x 15'
10' Vaulted Clg.

French Doors

French Door

Living Room
14'-4" x 21'-4"
11'-6" Ceiling
Media Center

Dining
11'-4" x 9'-8"

Bedroom 3
10' x 10'

Breakfast

Kitchen
8' x 7'-8"

Bath 2

Foyer

Util.

Bedroom 2
11'-0" x 10'-8"
10' Ceiling

2-Car Garage

75'-10"

Design AA8955

Square Footage: 1,507
Width 44'
Depth 75'-10"

● A wonderful narrow-lot choice, this three-bedroom home offers all the best in modern livability. The unique layout allows natural light infiltration on the inside, and space for a back yard or garden on the outside. The living room showcases a raised ceiling, a fireplace and a built-in media center. Just off this room, the dining room takes advantage of a French door at the rear. A breakfast nook remains in a sunny corner of the kitchen and will serve well for quiet mornings. For convenience, the two-car garage finds passage to the house through a utility area off the kitchen. A must-see, the master bedroom features complete privacy in its wing of the house. A vaulted ceiling adds depth while French doors open to the outdoors. The master bath supports a corner spa tub.

Design by
Larry W.
Garnett &
Associates, Inc.

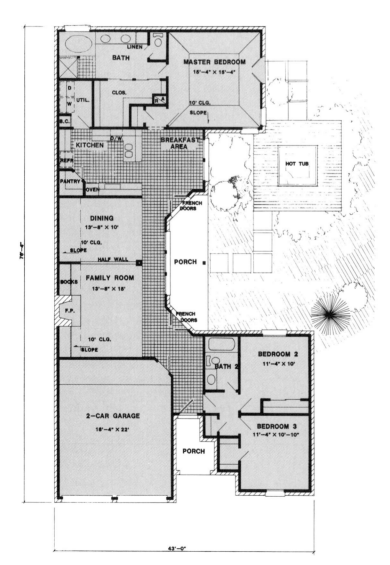

LINEN

BATH

MASTER BEDROOM
15'-4" X 15'-4"

CLOS.

D
W   UTIL.

B.C.

10' CLG.

R

SLOPE

D/W

BREAKFAST
AREA

KITCHEN

REFR

PANTRY   OVEN

HOT TUB

FRENCH
DOORS

DINING
13'-8" X 10'

10' CLG.

SLOPE

HALF WALL

PORCH

BOOKS   FAMILY ROOM
13'-8" X 15'

F.P.

FRENCH
DOORS

10' CLG.

SLOPE

BATH 2

BEDROOM 2
11'-4" X 10'

2-CAR GARAGE
18'-4" X 22'

BEDROOM 3
11'-4" X 10'-10"

PORCH

76'-4"

43'-0"

Design AA9170

Square Footage: 1,908
Width 43"
Depth 76'-4"

● A gated front porch introduces the
unique layout of this house. A lengthy
tiled hall ties together the major living
areas. The family room shares perspectives with the dining room by
way of a half wall. Bookshelves and a
central fireplace lend to this room's
character. The kitchen finds itself on
the other side of the dining room. A
walk-in pantry and an attached breakfast area define this space. Two sets of
French doors lead to a side porch
overlooking the side yard. You may
decide to fit a hot tub into the scope of
this quaint outdoor area. The master
bedroom takes advantage of a ten-foot
sloped ceiling and French doors leading to the yard. Two additional bedrooms remain at the front of the
house. One utilizes a walk-in closet.

Design by
Larry W.
Garnett &
Associates, Inc.

Design AA9171

Square Footage: 2,218
Width 49'
Depth 76'

● With an air of elegance, this home
boasts a most livable floor plan. The
tiled foyer extends into a hallway
passing by the living and dining
rooms. A raised-hearth fireplace in the
living room and a planter shelf
between this room and the dining
room will surely delight family and
friends. A covered porch adds interest
to these areas, as well as to the breakfast area—you'll find access to it
through a set of French doors. In the
kitchen, a spacious pantry will delight
the house gourmet. A window illuminates the very thoughtful utility
room—with counter space and cabinets—that is found off the breakfast
area. Well-segregated sleeping quarters include a glorious master suite. A
sitting area acts as a pleasant prelude
to the bedroom itself. French doors
and another covered porch open to
the side yard. You may decide to
install a hot tub in this yard.

Design by
Larry W.
Garnett &
Associates, Inc.

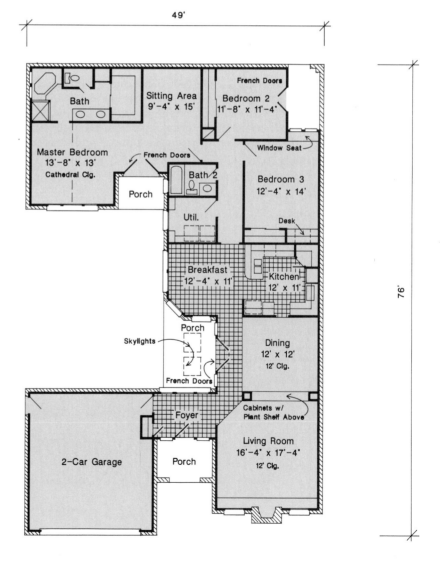

Design AA8949
Square Footage: 2,229
Width 47'-4"
Depth 80'-8"

● Come home to this beautiful one-story! Inside, the foyer leads to an elegant angled living room with built-in bookshelves and French doors opening to the rear patio. The dining room takes advantage of a covered porch—perfect for entertaining guests while dinner

cooks. An octagonal breakfast nook completes the kitchen area and offers ample space for a dinette set. Three bedrooms accommodate the family. These include a bountiful master suite with its bayed sitting area and private bath—don't miss the walk-in closet

located here. The secondary bedrooms share a compartmented hall bath. Bedroom 3 enjoys a walk-in closet while Bedroom 2 allows for interesting angles on furniture placement.

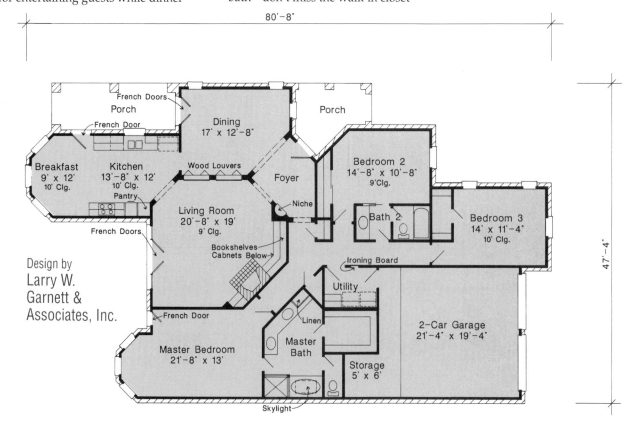

Design by
Larry W.
Garnett &
Associates, Inc.

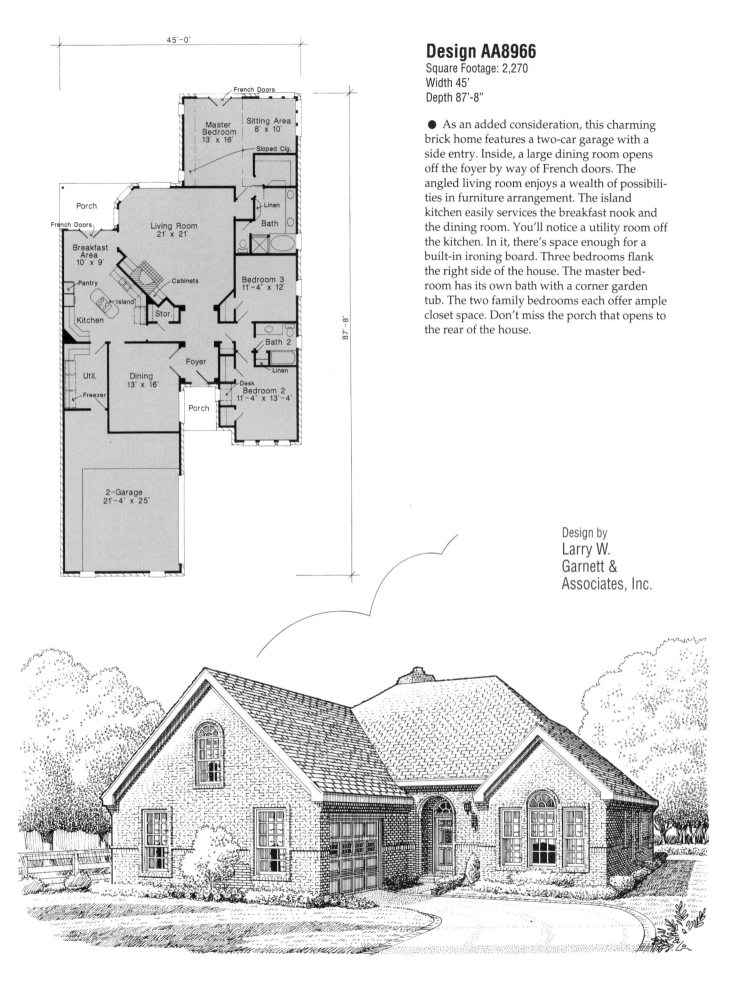

Design AA8966

Square Footage: 2,270
Width 45'
Depth 87'-8"

● As an added consideration, this charming brick home features a two-car garage with a side entry. Inside, a large dining room opens off the foyer by way of French doors. The angled living room enjoys a wealth of possibilities in furniture arrangement. The island kitchen easily services the breakfast nook and the dining room. You'll notice a utility room off the kitchen. In it, there's space enough for a built-in ironing board. Three bedrooms flank the right side of the house. The master bedroom has its own bath with a corner garden tub. The two family bedrooms each offer ample closet space. Don't miss the porch that opens to the rear of the house.

Design by
Larry W.
Garnett &
Associates, Inc.

45'-0"

French Doors

Master Bedroom
13' x 16'

Sitting Area
8' x 10'

Sloped Clg.

Porch

French Doors

Living Room
21' x 21'

Linen

Bath

Breakfast Area
10' x 9'

Pantry

Cabinets

Bedroom 3
11'-4" x 12'

Island

Stor.

Kitchen

Bath 2

Util.

Dining
13' x 16'

Foyer

Linen

Freezer

Desk
Bedroom 2
11'-4" x 13'-4"

Porch

87'-8"

2-Garage
21'-4" x 25'

Design AA9147

Square Footage: 1,078
Width 41'-8"
Depth 50

● You'll find three bedrooms
within this darling Victorian adaptation. The front porch introduces a
fine place for taking in summer
breezes. Step inside and find a living room with sliding glass doors
to the back yard and a fireplace to
cozy up to. The kitchen extends a
pantry and a corner sink with dual
views. The two family bedrooms
define the right side of the plan.
Both are equal in size and share a
full bath. The master bedroom,
located on the left side of the plan,
extends a private bath and a walk-
in closet. Note the space in the
garage for a washer and dryer set.

Design by
Larry W.
Garnett &
Associates, Inc.

41'-8"

50'

Bedroom 3
10' x 10'

Patio Door

Bath 2

Slope Clg.

Slope Clg.

Master Bedroom
13' x 11'-4"
9' Clg.

Living Room
15' x 17'-4"
11' Clg.

Bedroom 2
10' x 10'

Bath

Foyer

Dining
9' x 10'
Cath. Clg.

Kitchen
10' x 10'

2-Car Garage

Porch

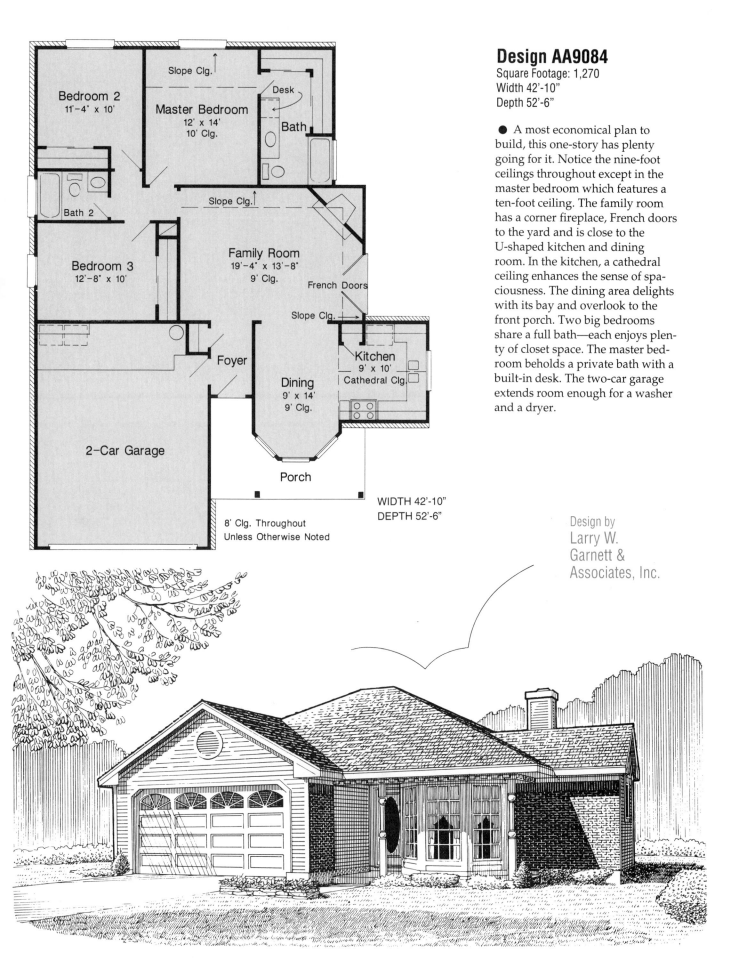

Design AA9084

Square Footage: 1,270
Width 42'-10"
Depth 52'-6"

● A most economical plan to build, this one-story has plenty going for it. Notice the nine-foot ceilings throughout except in the master bedroom which features a ten-foot ceiling. The family room has a corner fireplace, French doors to the yard and is close to the U-shaped kitchen and dining room. In the kitchen, a cathedral ceiling enhances the sense of spaciousness. The dining area delights with its bay and overlook to the front porch. Two big bedrooms share a full bath—each enjoys plenty of closet space. The master bedroom beholds a private bath with a built-in desk. The two-car garage extends room enough for a washer and a dryer.

Design by
Larry W.
Garnett &
Associates, Inc.

Bedroom 2
11'-4" x 10'

Master Bedroom
12' x 14'
10' Clg.

Slope Clg.

Desk

Bath

Bath 2

Slope Clg.

Bedroom 3
12'-8" x 10'

Family Room
19'-4" x 13'-8"
9' Clg.

French Doors

Slope Clg.

Foyer

Kitchen
9' x 10'
Cathedral Clg.

Dining
9' x 14'
9' Clg.

2-Car Garage

Porch

WIDTH 42'-10"
DEPTH 52'-6"

8' Clg. Throughout
Unless Otherwise Noted

Design AA9144

Square Footage: 1,198
Width 43'-4"
Depth 50'

● The elegant bay window and porch detailing combine to create a cozy home that is actually economical to construct. A 42"-high wall separates the dining area from the living room with its 9' sloped ceiling and expansive corner windows. The efficient kitchen has plenty of cabinets, along with a pantry and a corner sink. The master bedroom has a 9' sloped ceiling and a bath with a large walk-in closet.

Design by
Larry W.
Garnett &
Associates, Inc.

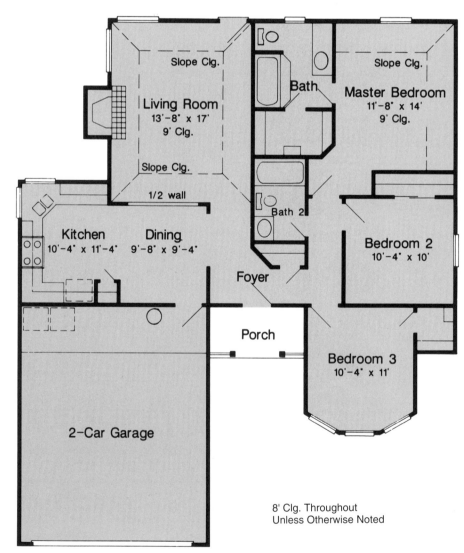

WIDTH 43'-4"
DEPTH 50'

8' Clg. Throughout
Unless Otherwise Noted

Slope Clg.

Living Room
13'-8" x 17'
9' Clg.

Slope Clg.

1/2 wall

Bath

Master Bedroom
11'-8" x 14'
9' Clg.

Slope Clg.

Bath 2

Kitchen
10'-4" x 11'-4"

Dining
9'-8" x 9'-4"

Bedroom 2
10'-4" x 10'

Foyer

Porch

Bedroom 3
10'-4" x 11'

2-Car Garage

Design AA9036

Square Footage: 1,236
Width 42'-4"
Depth 52'

● The openness of this home's floor plan gives it a feel of more square footage than it actually has. Notice how the family room flows freely into the dining area. Also nice is the use of sloped ceilings throughout and the cathedral ceiling in the kitchen. The plan is designed for three bedrooms with two full baths or for Bedroom 3 to be used as a study to complement the family room. The two-car garage allows for a generous workshop or a storage space.

Design by
Larry W.
Garnett &
Associates, Inc.

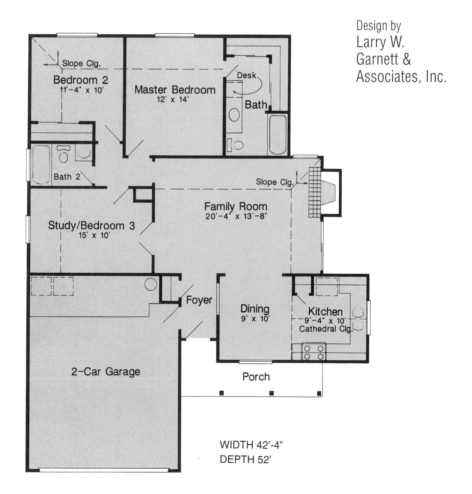

Slope Clg.

Bedroom 2
11'-4" x 10'

Master Bedroom
12' x 14'

Desk

Bath

Bath 2

Slope Clg.

Family Room
20'-4" x 13'-8"

Study/Bedroom 3
15' x 10'

Foyer

Dining
9' x 10'

Kitchen
9'-4" x 10'
Cathedral Clg.

2-Car Garage

Porch

WIDTH 42'-4"
DEPTH 52'

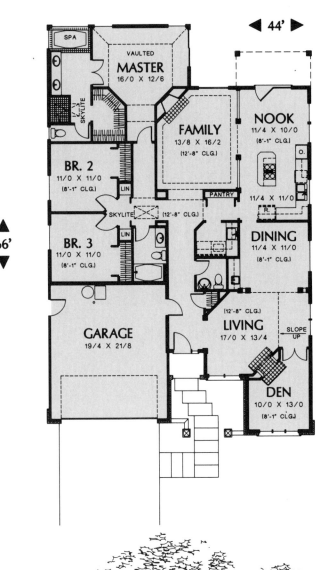

SPA

VAULTED

MASTER
16/0 X 12/6

SKYLITE

NOOK
11/4 X 10/0
(8'-1" CLG.)

FAMILY
13/8 X 16/2
(12'-8" CLG.)

BR. 2
11/0 X 11/0
(8'-1" CLG.)

LIN

PANTRY

11/4 X 11/0

SKYLITE X (12'-8" CLG.)

O.

R.

BR. 3
11/0 X 11/0
(8'-1" CLG.)

LIN

DINING
11/4 X 11/0
(8'-1" CLG.)

66'

GARAGE
19/4 X 21/8

(12'-8" CLG.)

LIVING
17/0 X 13/4

SLOPE
UP

44'

DEN
10/0 X 13/0
(8'-1" CLG.)

Design AA9451

Square Footage: 2,089
Width 44'
Depth 66'

● This one-story design gives a sense of space with dramatic raised ceilings in the entry, master suite, living room and family room. Formal living dominates the front of the plan but flows gracefully to more casual family living at the rear. The living room and the den share a dual fireplace, thus creating a cozy atmosphere for quiet living. The dining room finds a wet bar for entertaining—the kitchen takes pleasure in easy access to this area. Enjoy family interludes in the family room located at the rear of the house. Three bedrooms include two twin secondary bedrooms—each with a linen closet just outside the door. A skylight brightens the hallway here. The master suite sports a skylight in its private, luxurious bath.

Design by
Alan Mascord
Design Associates, Inc.

Two-Story Houses From 40' to 49' Wide

If you're looking to accommodate a growing family or if you're interested in scoping out greater variety in designs, you'll take pleasure in knowing your narrow lot can support both of these interests and more. With the addition of a second story to an already enlarged lot, square footages address these added livability concerns. In a manner of speaking, the addition of a second story allows for a design to reach new heights! Of course, all the interior "musts" introduced in preceding narrow-lot designs abound, including details to make fabulous first impressions and well-integrated living areas. As an example of this, the Neo-classic design featured on page 103 greets its occupants with a fanciful front entrance court. The floor plan creates an exceptional traffic pattern with formal areas commanding central interest and casual areas set to one side. With this design, the extra square footage afforded by a second story translates into four upstairs bedrooms; each one assures privacy by design.

Find your niche with something old, something new. The Queen Anne Victorian on page 90 will serve as a stunning addition to any historical neighborhood of like houses. But, by building such a house new, there's every opportunity to incorporate the walk-in closets, the island kitchen, the utility room and the outdoor amenities—all the things today's home builder looks for in a design. Note the developed deck—wrapping around a sun room—that supports space for a hot tub. The second floor consists of four bedrooms, including a master suite that acts as a true escape. A fireplace, study and compartmented bath all contribute to this feeling.

To reap all of these same modern benefits from an "Old World" perspective, take note of the house featured on page 123. A stunning exterior with stonework and spires introduces an interior that guarantees satisfaction. Like the design on page 90, the master suite acts as a true respite with a sitting area and double doors leading to a secluded bath and walk-in closet. The kids may profit from some of the same modern courtesies: each secondary bedroom has a walk-in closet. Not only attention-getting as a design feature, but wonderfully practical, a large storage area opens off the two-car garage, again proof that narrow doesn't mean a lack of depth in design.

Choices abound! For the more contemporary-minded, the home on page 118 comes full circle with an interior brimming with the best of today's amenities. Under 50 feet wide, this house has a two-car garage, full utility room, breakfast room plus formal dining room, sun room, enormous great room and more. The second floor is comprised solely of the master bedroom; you may decide to build the optional bedroom/study.

Design AA9312

First Floor: 1,150 square feet
Second Floor: 1,120 square feet
Total: 2,270 square feet
Width 46'
Depth 48'

● Lap siding, special windows and a covered porch enhance the elevation of this popular style. The spacious two-story entry surveys the formal dining room with hutch space. An entertainment center, through-fireplace and bayed windows add appeal to the great room. Families will love the spacious kitchen, breakfast and hearth room. Enhancements to this casual living area include a through-fireplace, gazebo dinette, wrapping counters, an island kitchen and planning desk. An efficient U-shaped staircase routes traffic throughout. Comfortable secondary bedrooms and a sumptuous master suite feature privacy by design. Bedroom 3 is highlighted by a half round window, volume ceiling and double closets while Bedroom 4 features a built-in desk. The master suite has a vaulted ceiling, large walk-in closet, His and Hers vanities, compartmented stool/shower area and an oval whirlpool tub.

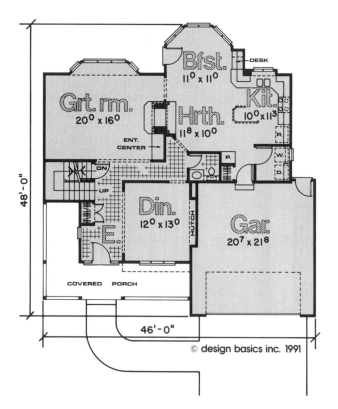

© design basics inc. 1991

Design by
Design
Basics,
Inc.

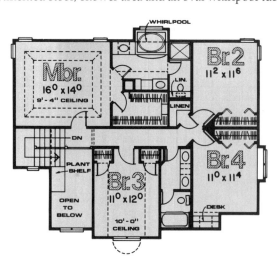

Design AA9386

First Floor: 964 square feet

Second Floor: 877 square feet

Total: 1,841 square feet

Width 40'

Depth 46'

● The front elevation of this attractive two-story home presents a smart application of brick and siding accents. Inside, formal entertaining takes off in the living room with its cathedral ceiling and openness to the dining room. The kitchen enjoys a shared snack bar with the breakfast nook—the family room joins this area with its wooden floors. A warming fireplace and built-in bookshelves highlight this casual living area. Also notice the utility room located on the other side of the wall from the family room. An end window illuminates the handy sink located here. Four bedrooms accommodate the growing family well. Bedroom 3, as an added bonus, extends to a ten-foot ceiling. In the master suite, a nine-foot boxed ceiling sets a dramatic mood. The private bath, opening through double doors, will delight with its whirlpool and double-bowl vanity.

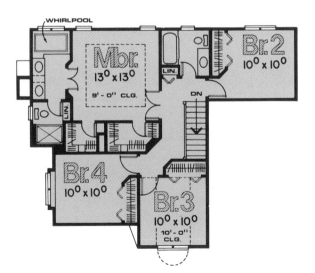

Design by
Design
Basics,
Inc.

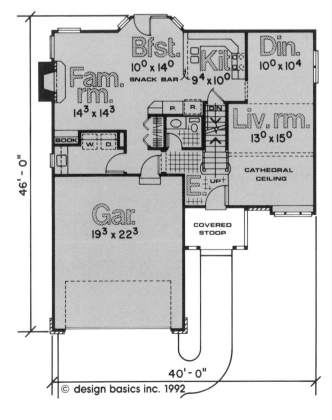

Design AA9259

First Floor: 1,224 square feet
Second Floor: 950 square feet
Total: 2,174 square feet
Width 48'
Depth 48'

● Abundant windows throughout this home add light and a feeling of openness. The front entry separates formal from informal living patterns: living room and dining room on the left, den and family room on the right. If desired, the den can be made to open up to the family room with French doors. To the rear is the kitchen which opens to the bayed breakfast room. Notice the fireplace in the family room. Upstairs there are four bedrooms. Three secondary bedrooms share a full bath. Bedroom 2 has a volume ceiling and half-round window. The master suite features a plant shelf, whirlpool, skylight above the vanity and a walk-in closet.

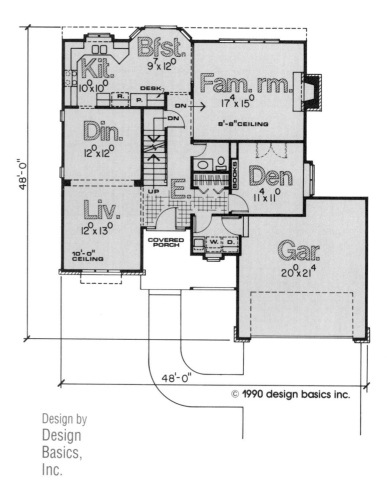

© 1990 design basics inc.

Design by
Design
Basics,
Inc.

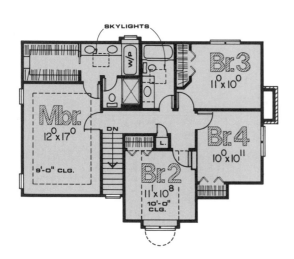

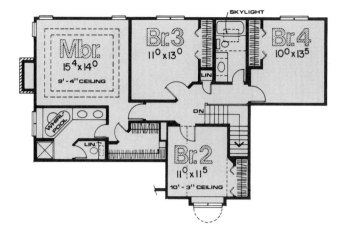

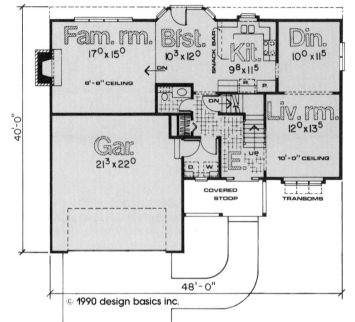

© 1990 design basics inc.

48'-0"

40'-0"

Design AA9391

First Floor: 1,042 square feet
Second Floor: 1,051 square feet
Total: 2,093 square feet
Width 48'
Depth 40'

● The quaint front porch on this handsome home serves as a nice prelude to what's inside. The living room, located to the right of the entry, features a ten-foot ceiling and a transom window. Open to the living room, the dining room accommodates formal meals well. The kitchen carries a snack bar that's convenient to the breakfast room, a pantry and a window over the sink. A step down from the breakfast room, the large family room, with a fireplace and rear-facing windows, demands attention. You'll find the second floor very accommodating: three family bedrooms—including one with a volume ceiling—share a skylit hall bath while the master bedroom exudes elegance with its tiered ceiling and private bath.

Design by
Design
Basics,
Inc.

Design AA9385

First Floor: 1,195 square feet
Second Floor: 1,034 square feet
Total: 2,229 square feet
Width 40'
Depth 52'

● This majestic-looking home offers a delightful floor plan. The foyer reveals a winding staircase and double doors to the den. In this versatile room, a spider-beamed ceiling and built-in bookshelves lend style and appeal. The great room rises into a sixteen-foot ceiling and also supports a fireplace flanked by built-in media centers. The kitchen features a snack bar to the breakfast area where a door opens to the covered stoop outside. Double doors connect this whole area to the dining room. Upstairs, the master bedroom showcases a built-in dresser and entertainment center. The master bath offers a unique angle on luxury with its fabulous whirlpool and walk-in closet. A delightful loft overlooks the great room below; you may decide to build a bedroom in its place.

Design by
Design
Basics,
Inc.

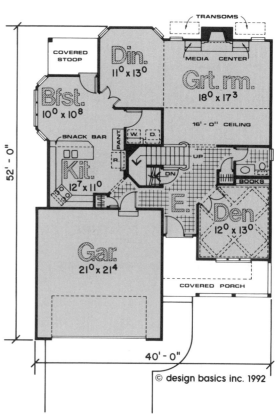

© design basics inc. 1992

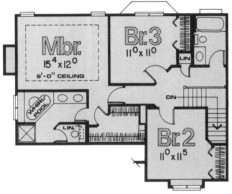

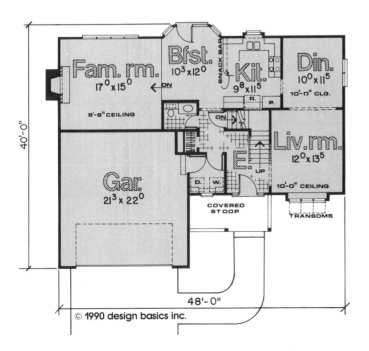

Design AA9282

First Floor: 1,042 square feet
Second Floor: 803 square feet
Total: 1,845 square feet
Width 48'
Depth 40'

● At 1,845 square feet, this classic two-story home is perfect for a variety of lifestyles. Upon entry from the covered front porch, the thoughtful floor plan is immediately evident. To the right of the entry is a formal volume living room with ten-foot ceiling. Nearby is the formal dining room with bright window. Serving the dining room and bright bayed dinette, the kitchen features a pantry, Lazy Susan and window sink. Off the breakfast area, step down into the family room with a handsome fireplace and wall of windows. Upstairs, two secondary bedrooms share a hall bath. The private master bedroom has a boxed ceiling, walk-in closet and a pampering dressing area with double vanity and whirlpool.

Design by
Design
Basics,
Inc.

Design AA9642

First Floor: 1,378 square feet
Second Floor: 468 square feet
Total: 1,846 square feet
Width 49'-8"
Depth 63'

● This well-proportioned, compact house provides for a lifestyle that is cozy and inviting. The two-level entrance foyer has windows at the second level, allowing natural light to flood the area. Both the great room and the dining room boast tray ceilings as well as round columns at their entrances. In the kitchen, a smart breakfast bay takes precedence. Note the deck that backs up the plan with room enough for a spa. The large master suite is located on the main level and has a gracious master bath with a double-bowl vanity, shower and whirlpool tub. Two family bedrooms share a full bath. The plan includes a crawl-space foundation.

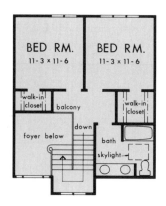

Design by
Donald A.
Gardner,
Architect, Inc.

Design AA9711

First Floor: 1,271 square feet
Second Floor: 665 square feet
Total: 1,936 square feet
Width 41'-6"
Depth 44'-8"

● Wood siding and a wraparound porch set the stage for a very charming country home. The great room features dormers that allow an influx of natural light. Both formal and family gatherings will be a joy in this room with its attention-getting center fireplace. The kitchen opens up into a bayed breakfast nook with back-porch access. A deck extends from the porch and supports a spa. The dining room is nestled off the kitchen and living room. You'll find even more livability in this design—it incorporates four bedrooms! One, at the front of the house, could serve as a study. Upstairs, the master bedroom acts as a nice retreat with its balcony overlooking the great room, and its full bath containing a whirlpool tub, a double-bowl vanity and a walk-in closet.

Design by
Donald A.
Gardner,
Architect, Inc.

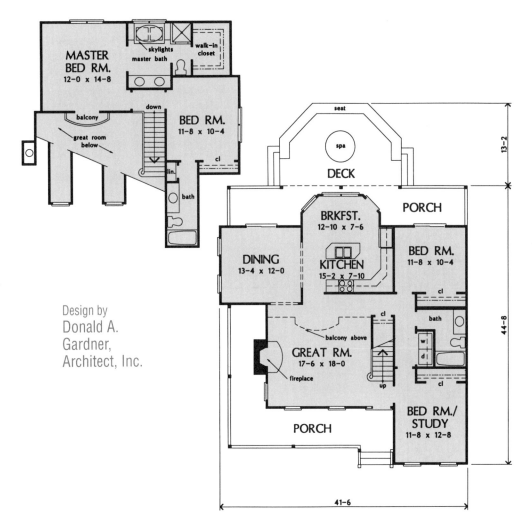

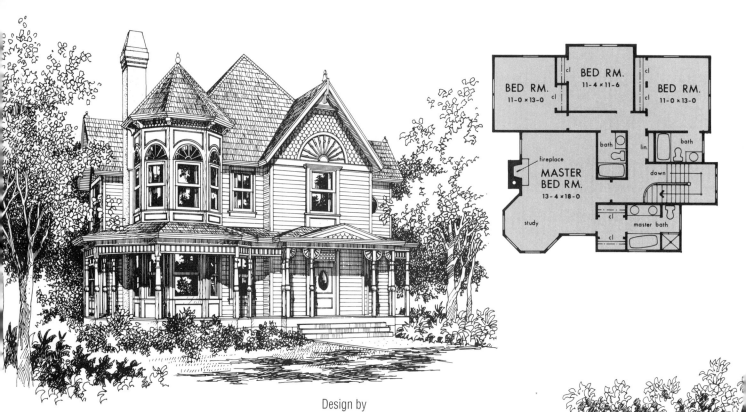

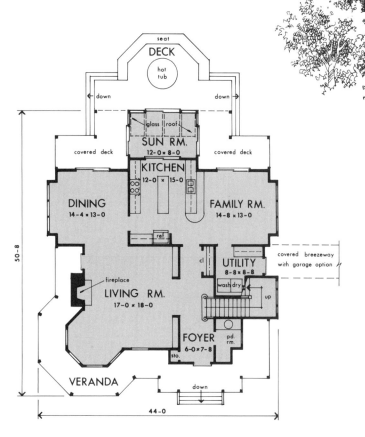

Design AA9678

First Floor: 1,393 square feet
Second Floor: 1,195 square feet
Total: 2,588 square feet
Width 44'
Depth 50'-8"

Design by
Donald A.
Gardner,
Architect, Inc.

● This elegant Victorian of the Queen Anne era features an exterior of distinctive decorative detailing consistent with its time, yet offers an interior plan that satisfies today's standards. A spacious living room incorporates a large bay-windowed area and a fireplace. The generous kitchen with island counter is centrally located to the dining and family rooms and to the sun room. The partially covered rear deck with hot tub is accessible from the living areas as well. On the second level, the master suite has a fireplace, walk-in closet and bay-windowed area which can serve as a study. Of the three additional bedrooms, one enjoys a private bath; the others share a full bath. Plans for a separate garage are available if specified.

Design AA9621

First Floor: 1,325 square feet
Second Floor: 453 square feet
Total: 1,778 square feet
Width 48'-4"
Depth 51'-10"

● For the economy-minded family desiring a wraparound covered porch, this compact design has all the amenities available in larger plans with little wasted space. In addition, a front Palladian window, dormer and rear arched windows provide exciting visual elements to the exterior. The spacious great room has a fireplace, a cathedral ceiling and clerestory windows. A second-level balcony overlooks this gathering area. The kitchen is centrally located for maximum flexibility in layout and features a pass-through to the great room. Besides the generous master suite with its well-appointed full bath, there are two family bedrooms located on the second level sharing a full bath with double vanity. Note the ample attic storage space. For a crawl-space foundation, order Design AA9621; for a basement foundation, order Design AA9621-A.

FRONT

REAR

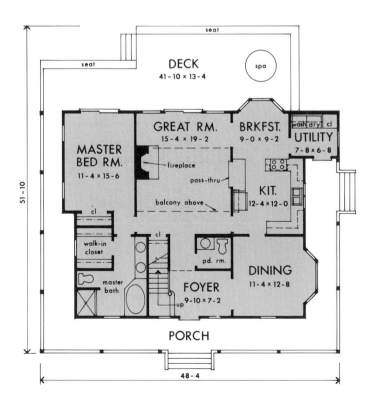

Design by
Donald A.
Gardner,
Architect, Inc.

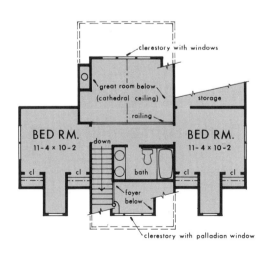

Design AA9493

First Floor: 944 square feet
Second Floor: 832 square feet
Total: 1,776 square feet
Width 40'
Depth 40'

● This darling traditional design extends many of the fine features you'd expect to find in larger homes. Upon entry, the formal living and dining areas open up with columns for definition. The L-shaped kitchen boasts an island cooktop and a built-in desk. Enjoy a morning cup of coffee in the breakfast nook—from here, sliding glass doors open to a rear terrace. The vaulted family room provides a warming hearth and will surely delight all. On the second floor, three bedrooms combine to offer excellent sleeping quarters. The vaulted master bedroom has its own skylit bath. Don't miss the utility area that adds so much to the upstairs.

Width 40'
Depth 40'

Design by
Alan Mascord
Design Associates, Inc.

Design AA9475

First Floor: 1,085 square feet
Second Floor: 1,110 square feet
Total: 2,195 square feet
Width 49'
Depth 47'

● Farmhouse design is popular throughout the country—this plan is an outstanding example. The corner entry leads to a formal parlor on the left and dining room on the right. To the rear of the first floor are the family room with fireplace and island kitchen with nook. The stairs are centrally located and a nearby powder room will be appreciated by guests. Upstairs are four bedrooms (or three and a den). The master bedroom has a vaulted ceiling and lovely private bath.

Design by
Alan Mascord
Design Associates, Inc.

◀ 49' ▶

▲
47'
▼

VAULTED
FAMILY
13/0 X 13/6

NOOK
9/6 X 13/6

8/6 X 13/6

DESK

GARAGE
21/8 X 21/4

DINING
10/8 X 12/0 +

UP

PARLOR
13/0 X 11/10 +

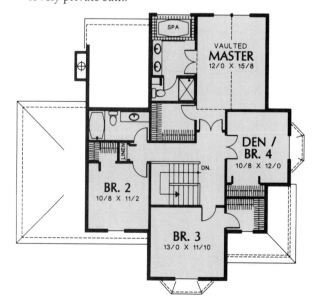

SPA

VAULTED
MASTER
12/0 X 15/8

LINEN

DEN /
BR. 4
10/8 X 12/0

BR. 2
10/8 X 11/2

DN.

BR. 3
13/0 X 11/10

Design AA9425

First Floor: 1,062 square feet
Second Floor: 838 square feet
Total: 1,900 square feet
Width 46'
Depth 48'

● This is one efficient plan for narrow lots that features Tudor-adaptation styling. Indoors resides a most compelling floor plan. The main gathering area, the family room, will invite cozy conversation in front of its warming hearth. The eating nook overlooks this area and is adjacent to an island kitchen with expansive corner window treatment. The formal living and dining rooms are to the front and open invitingly to one another. Besides two family bedrooms, there is a wonderful master suite with spa tub, glass-block screened wall and a walk-in closet.

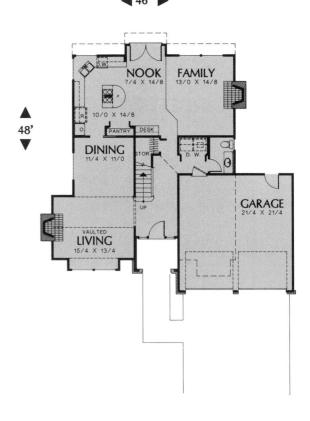

Design by
Alan Mascord
Design Associates, Inc.

Design AA9464

First Floor: 1,166 square feet
Second Floor: 1,019 square feet
Total: 2,185 square feet
Width 40'
Depth 50'

● This home, designed to fit on a 50' lot, provides an abundance of features due to its efficient use of space. The two-story foyer forms a central core providing convenient access to any part of the home. The comfortable master suite includes a walk-in closet and double vanity as well as a shower and spa tub. The informal area of the home stretches across the rear and features a bayed-out nook with a sliding patio door providing convenient access to the outdoor living spaces. A more attractive four-bedroom home with these features and compact footprint would be hard to find!

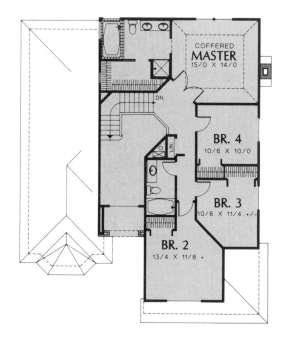

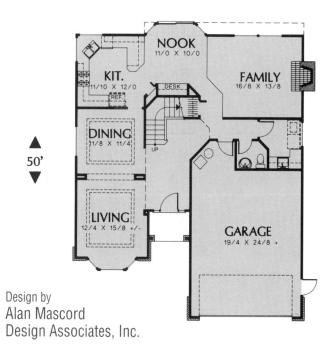

Design by
Alan Mascord
Design Associates, Inc.

95

Design AA8897

First Floor: 834 square feet
Second Floor: 722 square feet
Total: 1,556 square feet
Width 40'-4"
Depth 41'-8"

● In this contemporary interpretation of the traditional cottage, wood and stone accents create a homey feel. The foyer leads to a vaulted living room with a three-sided fireplace, which can be viewed from the dining room. The country kitchen across the rear gives a great family focus on outdoor living with a nearby deck. The kitchen utilizes an efficient layout to maximize counter and cupboard space. On the second floor, three bedrooms comfortably accommodate the family. The master bedroom enjoys a private bath with two lavatories. A walk-in closet will also gain appreciation.

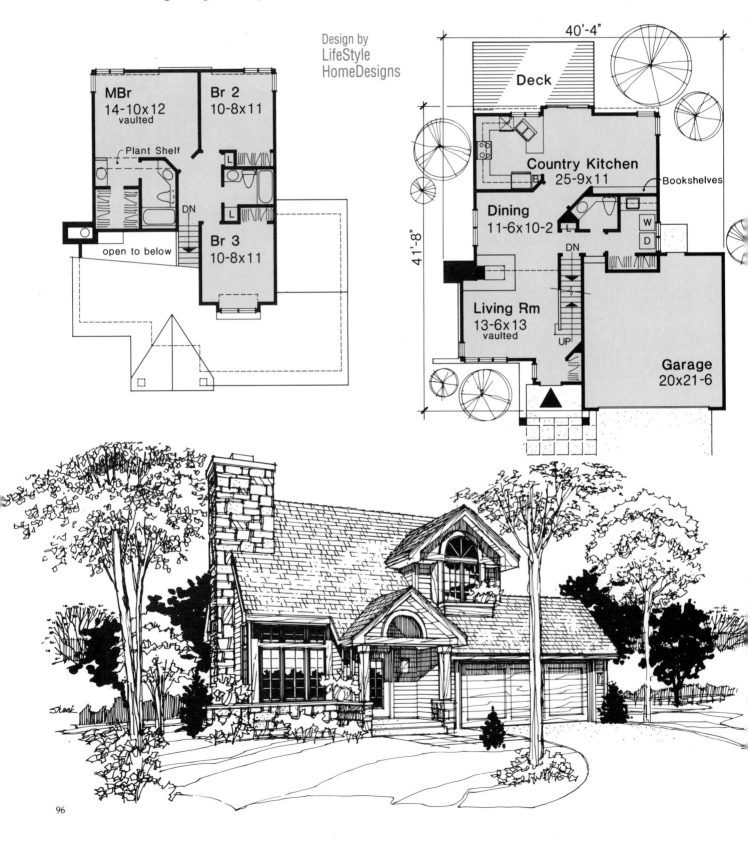

Design by
LifeStyle
HomeDesigns

MBr
14-10x12
vaulted

Br 2
10-8x11

Plant Shelf

DN

open to below

Br 3
10-8x11

40'-4"

Deck

Country Kitchen
25-9x11

Bookshelves

Dining
11-6x10-2

41'-8"

Living Rm
13-6x13
vaulted

DN

UP

W
D

Garage
20x21-6

Design AA8896

First Floor: 668 square feet
Second Floor: 691 square feet
Total: 1,359 square feet
Width 48'
Depth 29'-10"

● A raised foyer gives the inside of this home added dimension. A bright, vaulted living room includes a fireplace and easy access to the rear dining room—perfect for entertaining. The kitchen and breakfast room offer efficiency in meal preparation and serving. A coat closet and a powder room are situated near the two-car garage. The master bedroom suite is removed from two bedrooms—or one bedroom and a loft.

Design by
LifeStyle
HomeDesigns

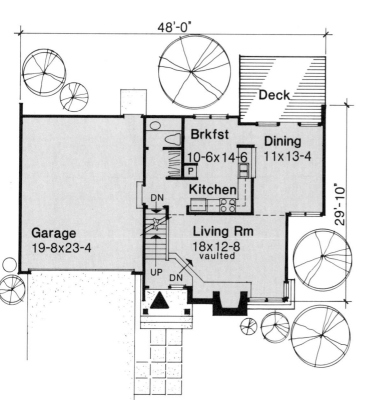

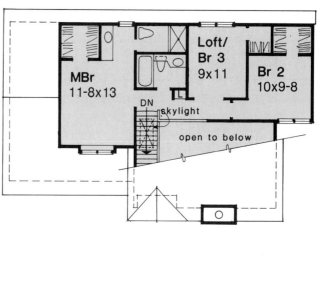

Design AA3562

First Floor: 1,182 square feet
Second Floor: 927 square feet
Total: 2,109 square feet
Width 40'
Depth 54'

L **D**

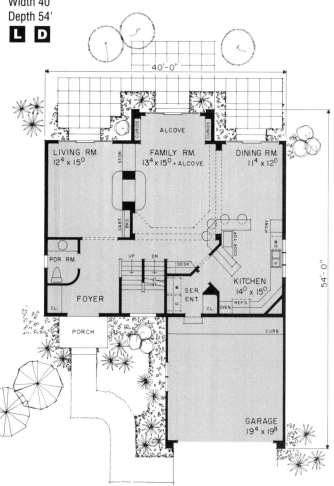

● Interesting detailing marks the exterior of this home as a beauty. Its interior makes it a livable option for any family. Entry occurs through double doors to the left side of the plan. A powder room with curved wall is handy to the entry. Living areas of the home are open and well-planned. The formal living room shares a through fireplace with the large family room. The dining room is adjoining and has a pass-through counter to the L-shaped kitchen. Special details on this floor include a wealth of sliding glass doors to the rear terrace and built-ins throughout. Upstairs are three bedrooms with two full baths.

Design by
Home Planners,
Inc.

Cost to build? See page 214
to order complete cost estimate
to build this house in your area!

Design AA3561 First Floor: 1,006 square feet
Second Floor: 990 square feet; Total: 1,996 square feet
Width 40'
Depth 50'

L **D**

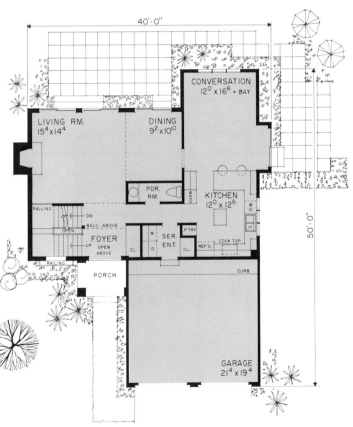

QUOTE ONE ™
Cost to build? See page 214
to order complete cost estimate
to build this house in your area!

● Great style demands an equally great floor plan—this home has both! The front-facing garage allows room for the home to be built on just about any size lot and keeps street noise to a minimum. Living areas are on the first floor and include a living room/dining combination and a conversation area just off the island kitchen. Note the fireplace in the living area and the sliding glass doors to the rear terrace. You'll also enjoy the fact that the living room rises to two stories. Upstairs are three bedrooms including a master suite with a tray ceiling and a private bath. Here, amenities include a whirlpool tub, dual lavatories and a compartmented toilet and shower.

Design by
Home Planners,
Inc.

Design AA3457
First Floor: 1,252 square feet
Second Floor: 972 square feet; Total: 2,224 square feet
Width 48'
Depth 58'

QUOTE ONE™
Cost to build? See page 214
to order complete cost estimate
to build this house in your area!

● For family living, this delightful three-bedroom plan scores big. Stretching across the back of the plan, casual living areas take precedence. The family room focuses on a fireplace and enjoys direct access to a covered porch. The breakfast room allows plenty of space for friendly meals—the island kitchen remains open to this room thus providing ease in serving meals and, of course, conversations with the cook. From the two-car garage, a utility area opens to the main-floor living areas. Upstairs, the master suite affords a quiet retreat with its private bath; here you'll find a whirlpool tub set in a sunny nook. A balcony further enhances this bedroom. The two secondary bedrooms share a full hall bath with a double-bowl vanity.

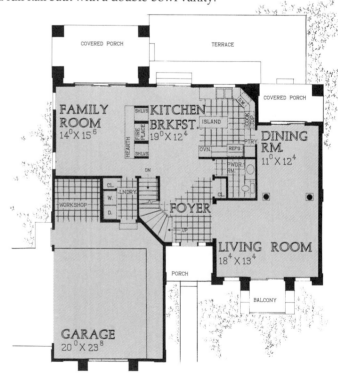

WIDTH 48'
DEPTH 58'

Design by
Home Planners,
Inc.

Cost to build? See page 214
to order complete cost estimate
to build this house in your area!

QUOTE ONE™

Design AA3459

First Floor: 1,392 square feet
Second Floor: 1,178 square feet
Total: 2,570 square feet
Width 46'
Depth 50'

L

● This innovative, compact plan affords over 2,500 square feet in living space! A central, angled staircase provides an interesting pivot with which to admire the floor plan. To begin with, the living room rises to two stories and even sports a front porch. The dining room, with its bumped-out nook, enjoys the use of a china alcove. The island kitchen finds easy access to the dining room and blends nicely into the airy breakfast room. A large pantry and a built-in desk also grace the kitchen and the breakfast room, respectively. In the family room, relaxed living comes through with the introduction of a fireplace and access to a covered patio and a terrace. The second floor will please all your family members with its four bedrooms, including a master suite with a private bath.

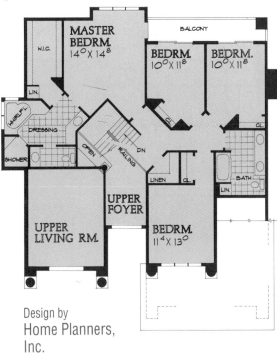

Design by
Home Planners, Inc.

Quote One™

Cost to build? See page 214
to order complete cost estimate
to build this house in your area!

Design AA3464 First Floor: 1,776 square feet

Second Floor: 876 square feet; Total: 2,652 square feet
Width 42'
Depth 72'-8"

L **D**

● If you're looking for something a little different from the rest,
this dramatic home may end your search. A two-story foyer
introduces an open formal area consisting of a volume living
room and a dining room separated by columns. The kitchen sits
to the rear of the plan and shares space with the breakfast room.
Here, a curved wall adds interest—sliding glass doors take you
out to a covered porch and a connecting terrace. The family room
enjoys access to this terrace while maintaining great indoor livability with its see-through fireplace and volume ceiling. Also on
the first floor, the master bedroom offers to its lucky occupants a
pampering bath. The sleeping accommodations are complete
with three upstairs bedrooms.

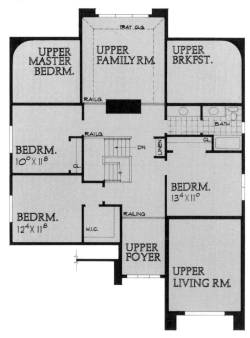

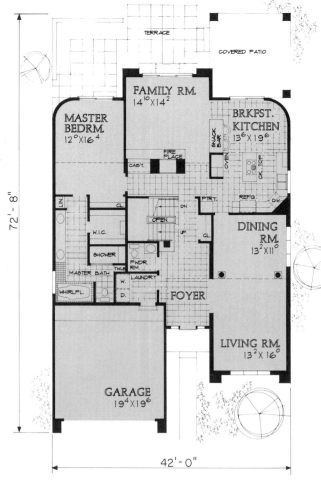

Design by
Home Planners,
Inc.

Design AA3574 First Floor: 1,488 square feet; Second Floor: 1,590 square feet
Total: 3,078 square feet; Bonus Room: 264 square feet
Width 46'
Depth 70'

L **D**

● An elongated entrance court complements the graceful exterior of this home. The two-story foyer introduces a magnificent open space made up of a gathering room—with a fireplace—and a dining room. Both areas access the back porch and terrace. For family pursuits, a rear family room provides a pleasant hearth and passage to the porch. Nearby, the U-shaped island kitchen enjoys a breakfast room and a nearby laundry room. On the second floor, four bedrooms accommodate family and guests alike. The master suite utilizes a private bath with a whirlpool tub while another bedroom also features its own bath. Also notable about this design is the bonus room which may be built in place of the one-car garage.

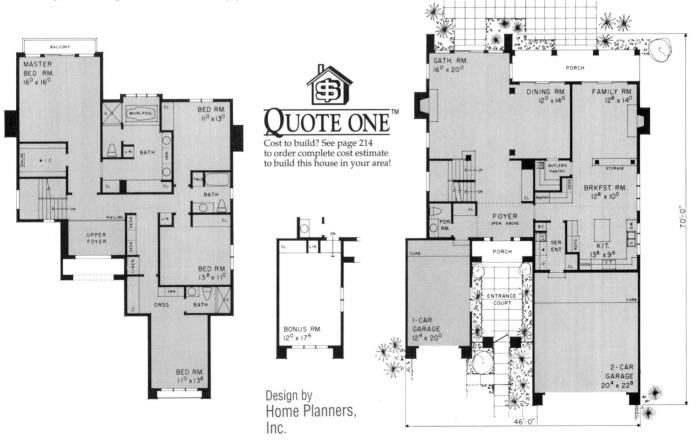

Quote One™

Cost to build? See page 214 to order complete cost estimate to build this house in your area!

Design by
Home Planners, Inc.

Design AA8640

First Floor: 1,485 square feet
Second Floor: 697 square feet
Total: 2,182 square feet
Width 42'-4"
Depth 58'-4"

● This two-story home has everything for the young family or the empty nester. The double-door entry foyer has a seemingly unlimited view of the huge great room. This living area comes complete with fireplace and media center. The formal dining room, tucked away in the front of the home, is perfect for quiet candlelight dinners. The kitchen and nook areas overlook the outdoor living space and the great room. The master suite on the first floor features a California closet plan for best use of space. Other amenities include a soaking tub, adjacent shower and private toilet. The stairs to the second floor have a free-floating design with open rails. Bedrooms on the second floor are ample; Bedroom 4 can be used as a loft area or activity room for the kids. Blueprints come with options for two different exteriors.

Design by
Home Design
Services, Inc.

Design AA8660

First Floor: 1,766 square feet
Second Floor: 880 square feet
Total: 2,646 square feet
Width 40'
Depth 68'-4"

● A striking use of keystone banding helps to create the majestic elevation of this home. Inside, versatility is the operative word for this plan and its large spaces: formal entertaining, casual family living—all take off with the expansive dining, family and game rooms. Access to the covered patio is found in the master bedroom, the game room and off the breakfast area. The master bedroom, with its vaulted ceiling, features His and Hers closets and a bath with a soaking tub and a large shower. Upstairs, three bedrooms share a loft space perfect for the kids. A cleverly arranged hall bath offers a double-bowl vanity. If desired, Bedroom 2 may support a private full bath.

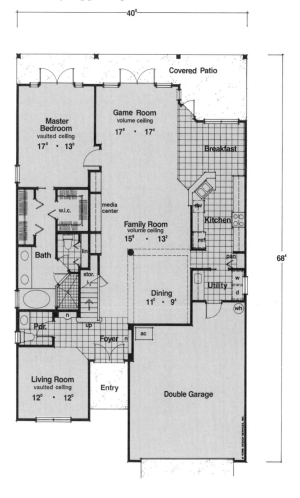

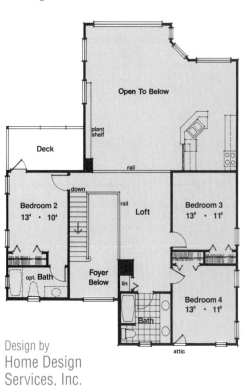

Design by
Home Design
Services, Inc.

105

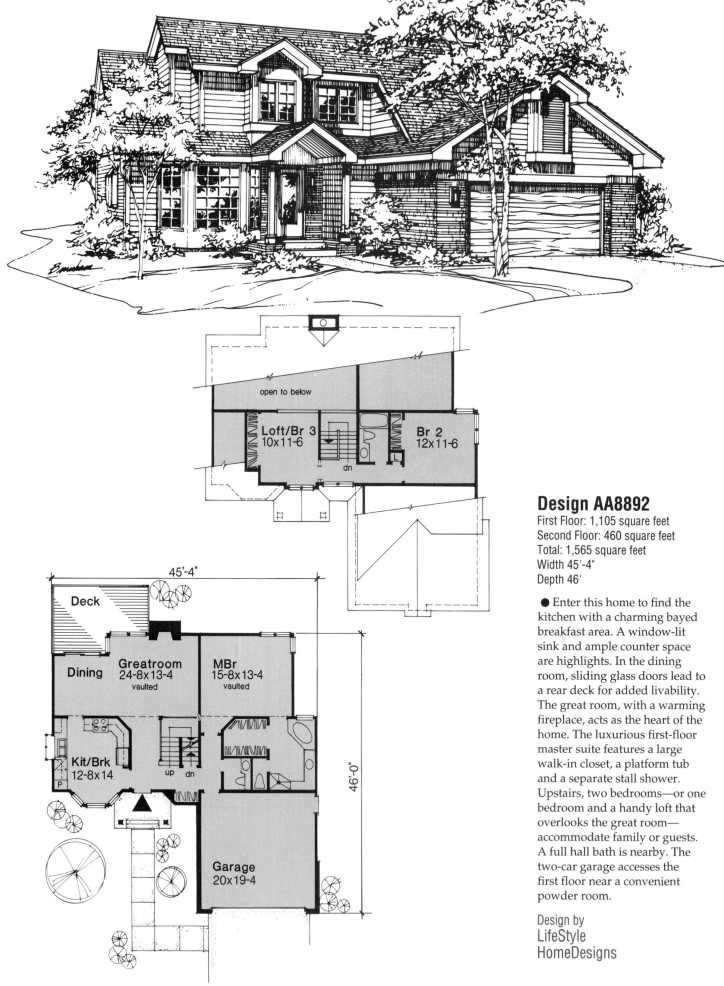

open to below

Loft/Br 3
10x11-6

Br 2
12x11-6

dn

Design AA8892

First Floor: 1,105 square feet
Second Floor: 460 square feet
Total: 1,565 square feet
Width 45'-4"
Depth 46'

● Enter this home to find the
kitchen with a charming bayed
breakfast area. A window-lit
sink and ample counter space
are highlights. In the dining
room, sliding glass doors lead to
a rear deck for added livability.
The great room, with a warming
fireplace, acts as the heart of the
home. The luxurious first-floor
master suite features a large
walk-in closet, a platform tub
and a separate stall shower.
Upstairs, two bedrooms—or one
bedroom and a handy loft that
overlooks the great room—
accommodate family or guests.
A full hall bath is nearby. The
two-car garage accesses the
first floor near a convenient
powder room.

Design by
LifeStyle
HomeDesigns

45'-4"

Deck

Dining

Greatroom
24-8x13-4
vaulted

MBr
15-8x13-4
vaulted

Kit/Brk
12-8x14

up dn

46'-0"

Garage
20x19-4

Design AA9341

First Floor: 1,401 square feet
Second Floor: 891 square feet
Total: 2,292 square feet
Width 40'
Depth 56'

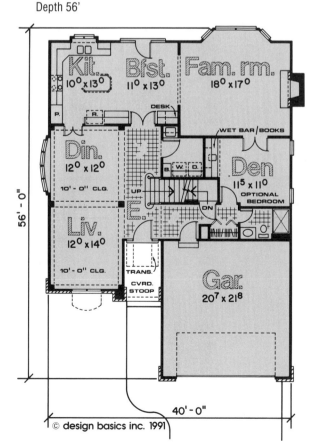

● At 40 feet wide, this 1½-story home is perfect for a narrow lot line. Inside, elegant window details highlight the dining and family rooms where French doors access an optional den with a wet bar. A gourmet island kitchen has wrapping counters, a pantry and a planning desk to serve the sunny breakfast area. Homeowners will appreciate the second level configuration, designed to offer privacy. Each secondary bedroom enjoys handy access to a pampering compartmented bath with dual lavs. Bedroom 2 includes a built-in bookcase. Attractions in the master suite include an arched transom window, two walk-in closets and French doors to a balcony overlook. Special touches in the master bath are dual vanities, corner windows and a sparkling glass block wall between the shower stall and whirlpool tub.

Design by
Design
Basics,
Inc.

Design AA9384

First Floor: 1,486 square feet
Second Floor: 441 square feet
Total: 1,927 square feet
Width 42'
Depth 55'

● French doors off the entry of this house reveal a charming den—or use this room to accommodate guests. The lofty, open great room features a raised-hearth fireplace flanked by two large windows. A wet bar, placed in the breakfast room near the great room, makes a nice entertaining feature. In the breakfast room, extensive windows and a volume ceiling lend a bright, elevated feeling to the whole kitchen area. The staircase leading to the second level is conveniently located at the back of the house for greater traffic control. Two bedrooms constitute the second level—one sports a walk-in closet. The master bedroom—on the first level for privacy—enjoys the use of a luxurious private bath.

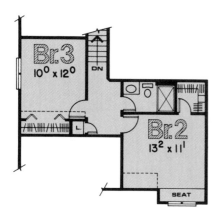

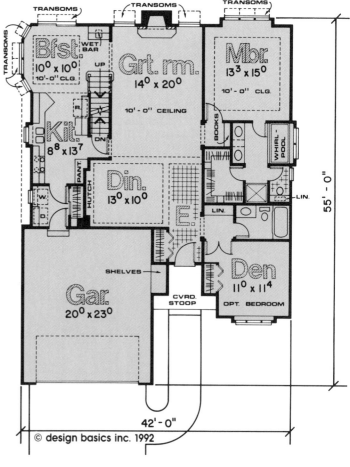

© design basics inc. 1992

Design by
Design
Basics,
Inc.

Design AA9338

First Floor: 1,509 square feet
Second Floor: 661 square feet
Total: 2,170 square feet
Width 44'
Depth 60'

● Alluring! The exterior of this compact four bedroom, 1½-story home gracefully combines brick details and siding. Elegant columns enhance the open feeling of the formal dining room. Bright windows and the raised-hearth fireplace combine with a ceiling that soars to 16 feet, heightening the drama of the spacious great room. A generous kitchen with pantry and snack bar serves a sunny, bayed breakfast area. In the main floor master suite, be sure to savor the elegance of its tiered ceiling. Homeowners will enjoy the pampering master bath/dressing area with a whirlpool, His and Hers vanities, make-up counter and a large walk-in closet. Upstairs, three secondary bedrooms were designed to accommodate young adults and house guests. Bedroom 2 may be converted to an optional den/loft with a built-in desk and bookshelves. At 2,170 square feet, this home suits a variety of lifestyles!

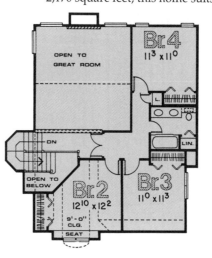

Design by
Design
Basics,
Inc.

© design basics inc. 1991

Design AA2622

First Floor: 624 square feet
Second Floor: 624 square feet
Total: 1,248 square feet
Width 46'
Depth 26'

L **D**

● This Colonial adaptation
provides a functional design
that allows for expansion in
the future. A cozy fireplace
in the living room adds
warmth to this space as well
as to the adjacent dining area.
The roomy L-shaped kitchen
features a breakfast nook and
an over-the-sink window.
Upstairs, two secondary
bedrooms share a full bath
with double vanity. The master
bedroom is on this floor as
well. Its private bath contains
access to attic storage. An additional storage area over the
garage can become a bedroom,
office or study in the future.

CUSTOMIZABLE

Custom Alterations? See page 221
for customizing this plan to your
specifications.

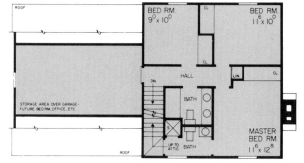

QUOTE ONE™

Cost to build? See page 214
to order complete cost estimate
to build this house in your area!

Design by
**Home Planners,
Inc.**

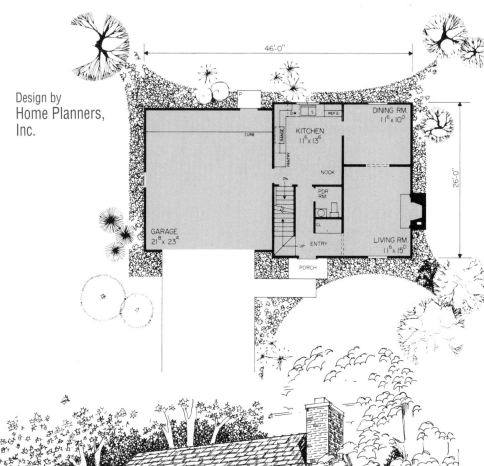

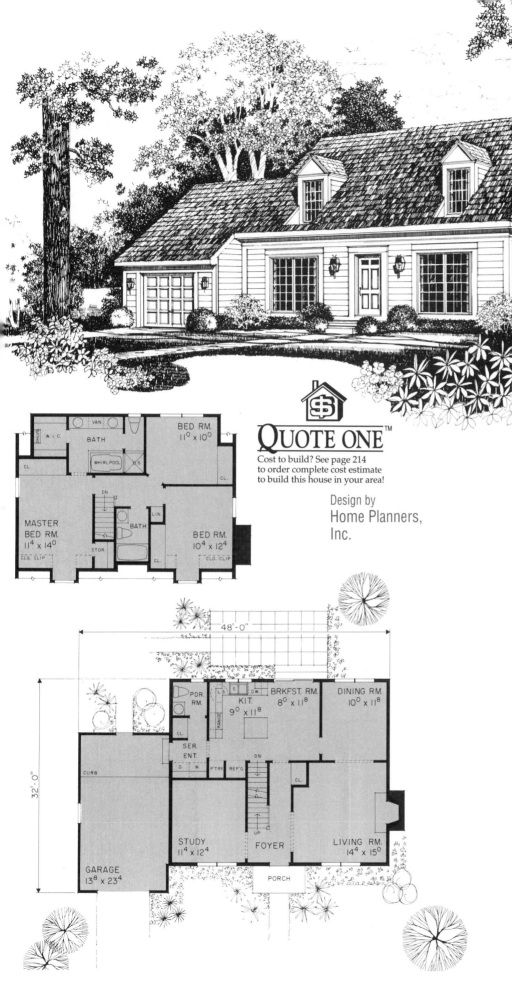

BED RM.
11⁰ x 10⁰

BATH

VAN.

W.I.C.

CL.

CL.

WHIRLPOOL

DN

MASTER
BED RM.
11⁴ x 14⁰

BATH

LIN.

BED RM.
10⁴ x 12⁴

STOR.

CLG. CLIP

CLG. CLIP

QUOTE ONE™

Cost to build? See page 214
to order complete cost estimate
to build this house in your area!

Design by
Home Planners,
Inc.

Design AA3571

First Floor: 964 square feet
Second Floor: 783 square feet
Total: 1,747 square feet
Width 48'
Depth 32'

L **D**

● For those interested in both
traditional charm and modern
convenience, this Cape Cod
fits the bill. Enter the foyer
and find a quiet study to the
left, a living room with a fireplace to the right. Straight
ahead: the kitchen and breakfast room with terrace access.
The island countertop affords
lots of room for meal preparation. A lazy Susan guarantees
easy storage and access of
kitchenware. The dining room
is conveniently located off the
breakfast room and enjoys formal space with the living
room. The service entry introduces a laundry and powder
room. Upstairs, the master
bedroom spoils with its
secluded bath—a whirlpool
tub is just one of the amenities
found here. Two additional
bedrooms complete the second floor. Each one partakes
in a full hall bath.

48'-0"

32'-0"

PDR. RM.

KIT.
9⁰ x 11⁸

BRKFST. RM.
8⁰ x 11⁸

DINING RM.
10⁰ x 11⁸

RANGE

CL.

SER. ENT.

D.W.

P'TRY

REF'G.

DN

CL.

CURB

GARAGE
13⁸ x 23⁴

STUDY
11⁴ x 12⁴

FOYER

UP

LIVING RM.
14⁴ x 15⁰

PORCH

Photo by Andrew D. Lautman

Design AA1956

First Floor: 990 square feet
Second Floor: 728 square feet
Total: 1,718 square feet
Width 48'
Depth 34'-10"

D

● The blueprints for this home include details for both the three-bedroom and the four-bedroom options. The first-floor livability does not change. The foyer leads to a large living room on the right. The formality of this room extends to the dining room in back. The U-shaped kitchen utilizes a convenient snack-bar pass-through to the breakfast area. The family room impresses with its raised-hearth fireplace, built-in bookshelves and exposed beam ceiling.

QUOTE ONE™
Cost to build? See page 214
to order complete cost estimate
to build this house in your area!

Design by
Home Planners, Inc.

OPTIONAL 3-BEDROOM PLAN

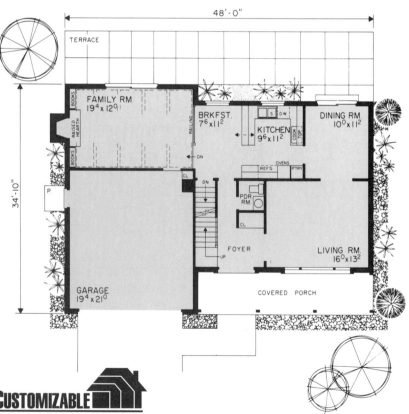

CUSTOMIZABLE
Custom Alterations? See page 221
for customizing this plan to your
specifications.

112

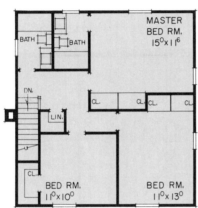

MASTER
BED RM.
15⁰x11⁶

BATH   BATH

DN.

LIN.

CL.   CL. CL.   CL.

CL.

BED RM.
11⁰x10⁰

BED RM.
11⁰x13⁰

Design AA1361

First Floor: 965 square feet
Second Floor: 740 square feet
Total: 1,705 square feet
Width 46'-5"
Depth 34'-3"

L **D**

● An abundance of livability is offered by this charming, traditional adaptation. It will be most economical to build. The entry hall gives way to a central, L-shaped kitchen. The formal dining room opens to the right. The spacious living room affords many different furniture arrangements. In the family room, casual living takes off with direct access to the rear terrace. Note the first-floor laundry conveniently located between the kitchen and family room. Upstairs, three bedrooms include a master bedroom with a private bath. Double closets guarantee ample space for wardrobes. One of the secondary bedrooms features a walk-in closet. Don't forget the handy broom closet and pantry located just off the kitchen.

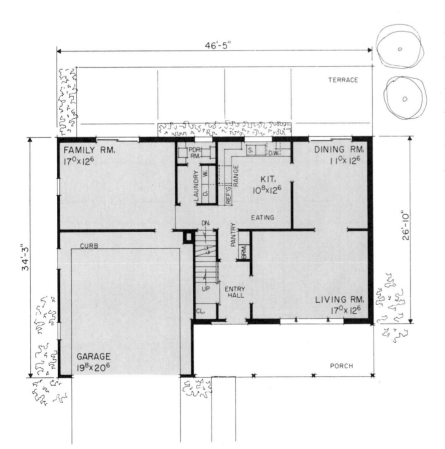

46'-5"

TERRACE

FAMILY RM.
17⁰x12⁶

PDR.
RM.

LAUNDRY
D. W.

REFG'.

RANGE

S.

D.W.

DINING RM.
11⁰x12⁶

KIT.
10⁸x12⁶

EATING

34'-3"

CURB

DN.

PANTRY

BRM.

26'-10"

UP   ENTRY
HALL

CL.

LIVING RM.
17⁰x12⁶

GARAGE
19⁸x20⁶

PORCH

Design by
Home Planners,
Inc.

113

Design AA2657

First Floor: 1,217 square feet
Second Floor: 868 square feet
Total: 2,085 square feet
Width 49'-8"
Depth 44'

L

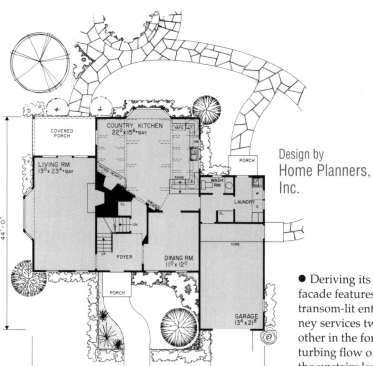

Design by
Home Planners,
Inc.

● Deriving its design from the traditional Cape Cod style, this facade features clapboard siding, small-paned windows and a transom-lit entrance flanked by carriage lamps. A central chimney services two fireplaces, one in the country-kitchen and the other in the formal living room which is removed from the disturbing flow of traffic. The master suite is located to the left of the upstairs landing. A full bathroom services two additional bedrooms on the second floor.

Design AA8898

First Floor: 1,075 square feet
Second Floor: 816 square feet
Total: 1,891 square feet
Width 43'-4"
Depth 46'

● The vaulted entry area of this home will impress visitors. The great room features a vaulted ceiling shared with the dining room. The U-shaped kitchen serves the family room with a pass-through. A bay window and deck access make the family room extra special, as does a warming hearth. A utility room and a powder room lead to the two-car garage. Upstairs, three bedrooms include a master bedroom suite with an efficient, private bath and two closets. The secondary bedrooms share a full hall bath.

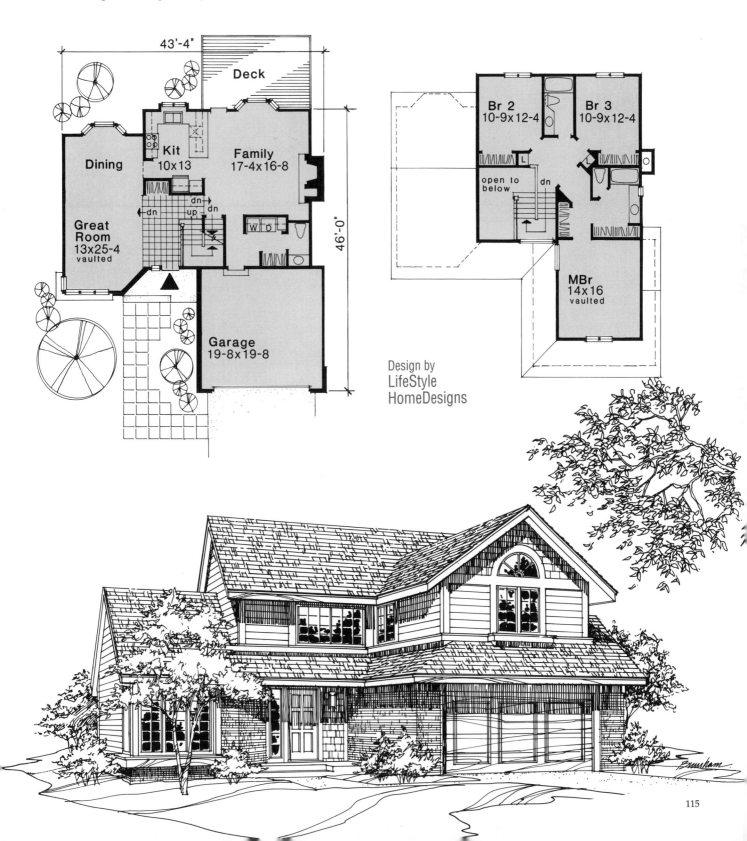

Design by
LifeStyle
HomeDesigns

Design AA2711

First Floor: 975 square feet
Second Floor: 1,024 square feet
Total: 1,999 square feet
Width 40'-4"
Depth 52'

L **D**

● Sleek, affordable style is the hallmark of this design. The large dining area, the efficient U-shaped kitchen, the mudroom off the garage and the spacious bedrooms are key selling points for a young family. Also notice the private balcony off the master suite, the cozy study with lots of storage space, the terrace to the rear of the house and the sizable snack bar.

California Engineered Plans and California Stock Plans are available for this home. Call 1-800-521-6797 for more information.

Design by
Home Planners, Inc.

CUSTOMIZABLE

Custom Alterations? See page 221 for customizing this plan to your specifications.

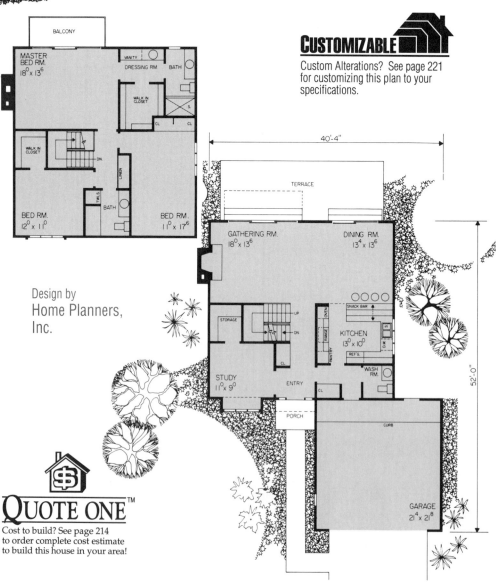

Quote One™

Cost to build? See page 214 to order complete cost estimate to build this house in your area!

Photo by Laszlo Regos

Design AA2488

First Floor: 1,113 square feet
Second Floor: 543 square feet
Total: 1,656 square feet
Width 44'
Depth 32'

D

QUOTE ONE™

Cost to build? See page 214
to order complete cost estimate
to build this house in your area!

Design by
Home Planners,
Inc.

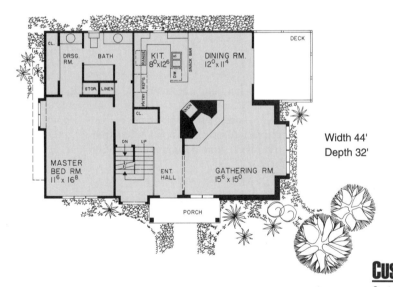

Width 44'
Depth 32'

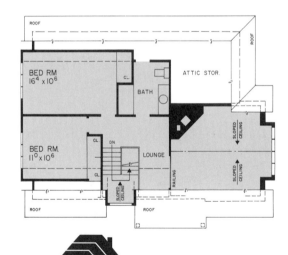

CUSTOMIZABLE

Custom Alterations? See page 221
for customizing this plan to your
specifications.

● This is truly a cozy cottage for the young at heart! Whether called upon to serve the young active family as a leisure-time retreat at the lake, or the retired couple as a quiet haven in later years, this charming design will perform well. As a year round second home, the upstairs, with its two sizable bedrooms, full bath and lounge area looking down into the gathering room below, will ideally accommodate the younger generation. When called upon to function as a retirement home, the second floor will cater to the visiting family members and friends. Also, it will be available for use as a home office, study, sewing room, music area, hobby area, etc. Of course, as an efficient, economical home for the young, growing family, this design will function well.

California Engineered Plans and California Stock Plans are available for this home. Call 1-800-521-6797 for more information.

Design AA9635

First Floor: 1,564 square feet (includes sun room)
Second Floor: 746 square feet
Total: 2,310 square feet
Width 47'-4"
Depth 69'

● Bold contemporary lines strike an elegant chord in this two-story plan. The entry foyer leads to a multi-purpose great room with a fireplace and sliding glass doors to a rear deck. The formal dining room is attached and there is a connecting sun room. A nearby kitchen has an attached breakfast room and a large walk-in pantry. Two bedrooms on this floor share a full bath. The master suite dominates the second floor. It features a large walk-in closet, double lavatories, a corner tub and spiral stairs to the sun room. The upstairs balcony connects it to a study or optional bedroom. For a crawl-space foundation, order Design AA9635; for a basement foundation, order Design AA9635-A.

47-4

DECK
29-8 x 10-0

SUN RM.
13-4 x 9-0
balcony above

GREAT RM.
15-4 x 27-0

fireplace

BED RM.
10-4 x 11-4

cl

DINING
13-4 x 12-0

balcony above

bath

window garden

KITCHEN
13-4 x 8-0

down

FOYER
6-0 x 5-0 cl

lin.

ref

up

BED RM.
10-4 x 11-4

cl

BRKFST.
11-4 x 8-0

pantry

UTILITY

dry wash cl

sto

69-0

GARAGE
20-4 x 21-0

Design by
Donald A.
Gardner,
Architect, Inc.

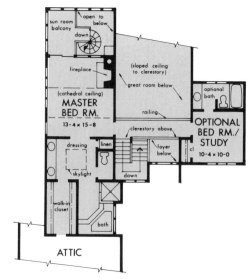

sun room balcony

open to below

down

fireplace

(sloped ceiling to clerestory)

great room below

(cathedral ceiling)

MASTER BED RM.
13-4 x 15-8

railing

clerestory above

optional bath

OPTIONAL BED RM./ STUDY
10-4 x 10-0

dressing

linen

foyer below

cl

skylight

down

walk-in closet

bath

ATTIC

FRONT

Design AA9613

First Floor: 1,340 square feet
Second Floor: 504 square feet
Total: 1,844 square feet
Width 45'-4"
Depth 60'

● Because this home's sun room is a full two stories high, it acts as a solar collector when oriented to the south. Enjoying the benefits of this warmth are the dining and great rooms on the first floor, and the master suite on the second floor. A spacious deck further extends the outdoor living potential. Special features to be found in this house include: sloped ceiling with exposed wood beams and a fireplace in the great room; cathedral ceiling, fireplace, built-in shelves and ample closet space in the master bedroom; clerestory windows and a balcony overlook in the upstairs study; and convenient storage space in the attic over the garage. Order Design AA9613 for a crawl-space foundation; order Design AA9613-A for a basement foundation.

DECK
27-8 × 12-0

balcony above

SUN RM.
13-4 × 8-0

GREAT RM.
13-4 × 25-0

BED RM.
10-4 × 11-4

DINING
11-4 × 12-4

fireplace

study above

cl

storage

bath

window planter

KITCHEN
11-4 × 8-0

down

FOYER
6-0 × 5-0

up

lin.

cl

ref.

SERVICE

dry wash cl

pantry

BED RM.
10-4 × 11-4

cl

GARAGE
20-2 × 21-4

45-4

60-0

open to below

balcony
(in sun room)

down

shelves

(sloped ceiling
to clerestory)

MASTER
BED RM.
(cathedral ceiling)
11-4 × 14-4
fireplace

great room below

railing

clerestory above

dressing

cl

STUDY
8-4 × 8-4

lin.

down

up

walk-in
closet

bath

ATTIC

Design by
Donald A.
Gardner,
Architect, Inc.

REAR

119

Design AA9614

First Floor: 1,345 square feet
Second Floor: 536 square feet
Total: 1,881 square feet
Width 45'
Depth 69'-4"

● An elegant exterior combines with a functional interior to offer an exciting design for the contemporary-minded. Notice the cheery sun room that captures the heat of the sun. The master suite and the great room both have access to this bright space through sliding glass doors. A U-shaped kitchen has a window garden, a breakfast bar and ample cabinet space. Note how the great-room ceiling with exposed wood beams slopes from the deck up to operable clerestory windows at the study/play area on the second level. Also notice the bonus storage space in the attic over the garage. Order Design AA9614 for a crawl-space foundation; order Design AA9614-A for a basement foundation.

Design by
Donald A.
Gardner,
Architect, Inc.

FRONT

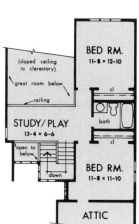

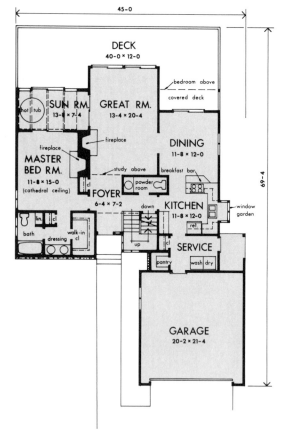

REAR

120

Design AA9617

First Floor: 1,340 square feet
Second Floor: 651 square feet
Total: 1,991 square feet
Width 45'-4"
Depth 60'

● What a grand plan for contemporary family living! Beyond the handsome exterior are some excellent features that complement today's lifestyles. Of special note: the two-story sun room with access to the great room, the dining room and the master bedroom; a sloped-ceilinged great room with clerestory windows; two first-floor bedrooms and a third, second-floor bedroom that could double as a study; a delightful rear deck; and ample storage space over the garage. If contemporary living is your style, this may be the plan for you. Order Design AA9617 for a crawl-space foundation; order Design AA9617-A for a basement foundation.

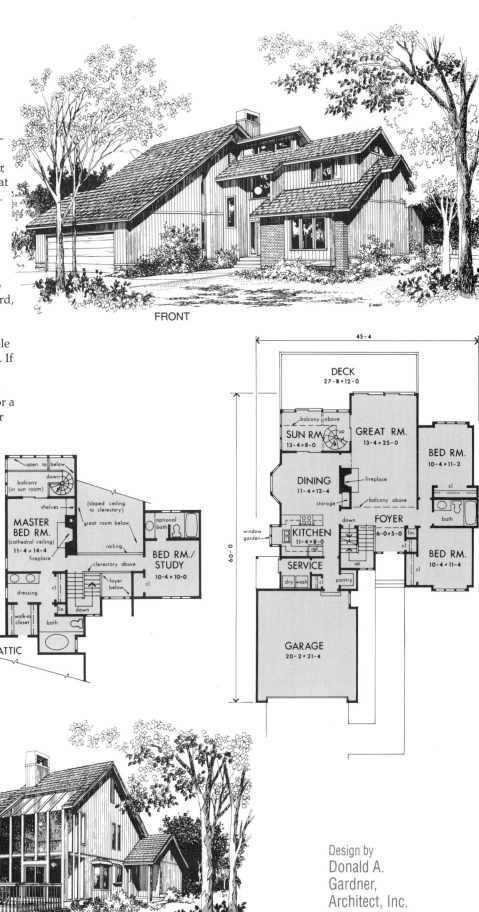

FRONT

REAR

Design by
Donald A.
Gardner,
Architect, Inc.

Design AA9813

First Floor: 1,724 square feet
Second Floor: 700 square feet
Total: 2,424 square feet
Width 47'-10"
Depth 63'-10"

● This cozy English cottage might be found hidden away in a European garden. To the left of the foyer you will see the sunlit dining room, highlighted by a dramatic tray ceiling and expansive windows with transoms. This room and the living room flow together to form one large entertainment area. In the gourmet kitchen are a work island, an oversized pantry and a bright adjoining octagonal breakfast room with a gazebo ceiling. The great room features a pass-through wet bar, a fireplace and bookcases or an entertainment center. The master suite enjoys privacy at the rear of the home. An open-rail loft above the foyer leads to additional bedrooms with walk-in closets, private vanities and a shared bath. This home is designed with a basement foundation.

Design by
Design Traditions

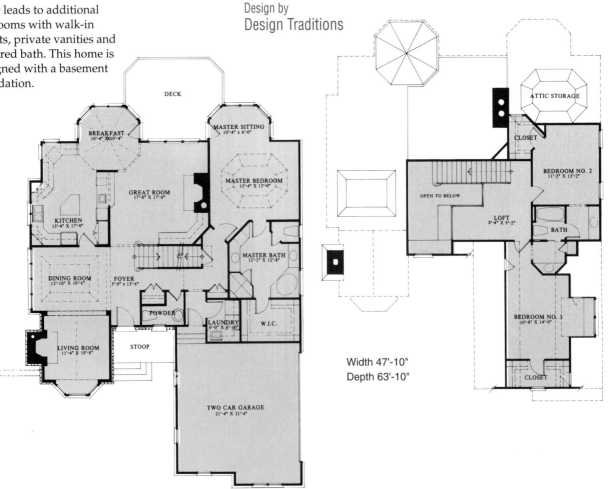

Width 47'-10"
Depth 63'-10"

Family Room Perspective

Design AA9800

First Floor: 1,231 square feet
Second Floor: 1,154 square feet
Total: 2,385 square feet
Width 44'
Depth 47'-9"

● All the Old World elements of gables, dormer windows, stone work, multi-level roof and spires combine to create this charming cottage. The main focal point of the foyer is the large formal dining room with its beautiful triple window combination. The family room features a beamed ceiling, fireplace, and convenient back staircase. The breakfast area has a bay window and a door to the back deck, ideal for outdoor entertaining. The master suite has extended space with its own bay sitting area, roomy bath with whirlpool tub, and spacious closet. Other bedrooms share a bath. There is also a bonus room over the garage.

WIDTH 44'
DEPTH 47'-9"

Design by
Design Traditions

Design AA8969

First Floor: 1,395 square feet
Second Floor: 543 square feet
Total: 1,938 square feet
Width 40'
Depth 62'-6"

WIDTH 40'
DEPTH 62'-6"

● An emphasis on elegance prevails in this design. With volume looks and a brick exterior, it'll be the talk of the neighborhood. The front porch gives way to a tiled foyer that leads back to the living room/dining room combination. A sloped ceiling, a fireplace and French doors leading outside lend character to this area. The kitchen maximizes efficiency and easily services the roomy breakfast area where a ten-foot ceiling adds dramatic appeal. The master bedroom completes the first floor. Charm comes across with this room's vaulted ceiling, French door and expansive bath. The latter introduces a walk-in closet fit for a king. Upstairs, two family bedrooms each enjoy a vaulted ceiling and the quiet of a hall reading area flanked by bookshelves.

Design by
Larry W.
Garnett &
Associates, Inc.

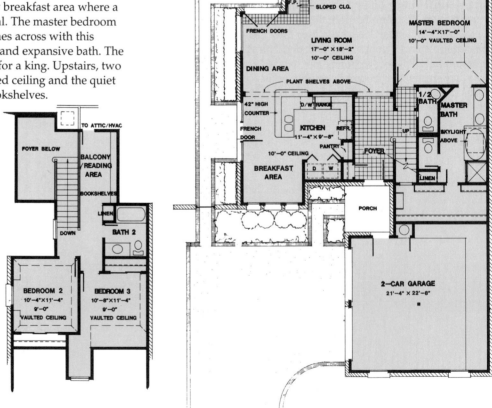

Design AA9172

First Floor: 2,066 square feet
Second Floor: 601 square feet
Total: 2,667 square feet
Width 44'-8"
Depth 77'-4"

● A family room backs up the first floor of this plan and delights with its abundant windows and central fireplace. Use it for impressive entertaining or as a cozy getaway. There's also a living room with a fireplace that shares an interesting formal relationship with the dining room. The kitchen expands into a breakfast room and finds ease in all aspects of meal preparation with its center island. Locate your washer and dryer in the utility room off the garage. Sleeping accommodations excel with an excellent master suite situated at the rear of the first floor. Upstairs, two bedrooms offer plenty of room for creative furniture arrangements. The hall bath allows added space for storage with its dormer window.

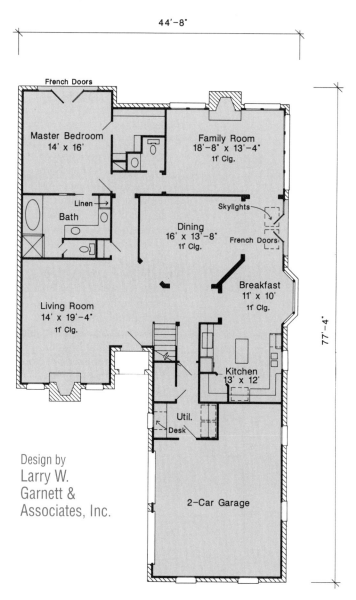

44'-8"

French Doors

Master Bedroom
14' x 16'

Family Room
18'-8" x 13'-4"
11' Clg.

Linen

Bath

Skylights

Dining
16' x 13'-8"
11' Clg.

French Doors

Breakfast
11' x 10'
11' Clg.

Living Room
14' x 19'-4"
11' Clg.

Kitchen
13' x 12'

Util.
Desk

77'-4"

Design by
Larry W.
Garnett &
Associates, Inc.

2-Car Garage

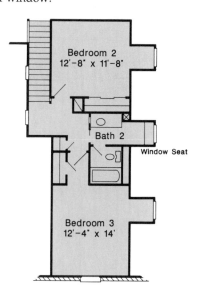

Bedroom 2
12'-8" x 11'-8"

Bath 2

Window Seat

Bedroom 3
12'-4" x 14'

125

Design by
Larry W.
Garnett &
Associates, Inc.

Design AA9173

First Floor: 1,715 square feet
Second Floor: 806 square feet
Total: 2,521 square feet
Width 43'-4"
Depth 62'-4"

● With a stately appearance, this two-story home would make a fine addition to both city and suburban neighborhoods. The foyer opens to a spacious living room as well as to French doors leading to the banquet-sized dining room. Here, French doors lead to a back porch and courtyard. The kitchen delights with its interesting arrangement and attached breakfast nook. The master bedroom, located on the other side of the first floor, extends a romantic air with its fireplace and French doors to a back walkway. The master bath spoils with a separate tub and shower, a compartmented toilet and a large walk-in closet. Upstairs, two secondary bedrooms each have a private bath—one room even has a private deck. A library alcove finishes off this floor.

43'-4"

French Doors
French Door

Master Bedroom
19'-8" x 15'

Breakfast
11'-4" x 9'-4"

Porch
French Doors

Bath

Kitchen
11'-4" x 14'
Pantry

Skylight
Linen

Dining
13' x 16'-8"

Util.

Up

French Doors

Stor.   Foyer

Porch

2-Car Garage
19'-4" x 23'-4"

Living Room
16' x 17'-4"

62'-4"

Balcony/
Deck

Bath 3

Study/
Guest Room
13' x 16'-8"

Books

Foyer
Below

Library

Window Seat

Down

Balcony

Bath 2

Linen

Bedroom 2
16' x 11'
9' Clg.

Houses From 50' to 59' Wide

With so many narrow-lot choices behind you, it may seem astounding that more lie ahead. In this last width-defined section, we examine houses from 50' to 59' wide. This translates into very suburban settings with designs that emphasize affordability without sacrificing style. A good illustration of this is the exemplary plan on page 160. Rivaling similar designs of greater size, this 2,000+ square-foot plan sets a pattern to serve the most demanding occupants. An attention-getting facade with multiple windows encloses a well-arranged floor plan. The first floor extends an air of formality: living room, dining room, front study. Three bedrooms await upstairs. Surely this house will delight generations to come.

Win big with the home featured on page 148—elegant Georgian detailing and everyday living co-exist beautifully in this plan. The first floor opens with a columned dining room and great room that stretches to a huge back porch. Family and company alike will relax in the keeping room with its cozy corner hearth. The second story is also sure to delight. As a result of the bumped-out garage with upstairs livability, the second-story sleeping quarters take on an L-shaped, winged arrangement. Bedrooms 3 and 4 share a Hollywood bath between them while Bedroom 2, located on the other side of the staircase from Bedroom 3, enjoys its own bath.

In line with affordability, the house on page 154 offers more for the money with its bonus room allowing future expansion. Located upstairs and down the hall from the other secondary bedrooms, this room—with its potential full bath—would make a perfect guest room or additional family bedroom.

The home on page 138 brings family living to the forefront. On the outside, this one-story plan takes on a pleasing volume look with attention-getting features such as pointed rooflines and keystone detailing. On the inside, it's pure pleasure. The family room and adjacent kitchen act as family centers. Beyond the formal areas, double doors open to the master suite where delightful design creates gratifying living. Note how the secondary sleeping wing and the covered patio create a wonderful back yard for the kids.

Design AA9716

Square Footage: 2,097
Width 54'
Depth 72'-4"

● A bank of ventilating skylights flood the large family room with natural light and fresh air in this three-bedroom ranch. Many other special features—uncommon in a home this size—make an appearance. For example, the breakfast area, family room and master bath open to a spacious deck with a spa area. In the family room you'll find a cathedral ceiling and a fireplace. The plan provides both formal living and dining rooms. The U-shaped kitchen epitomizes the best in efficiency. The large master bedroom has a private deck and pampers with a whirlpool tub, a separate shower and a double-bowl vanity. Two secondary bedrooms each find ample closet space and share a full hall bath.

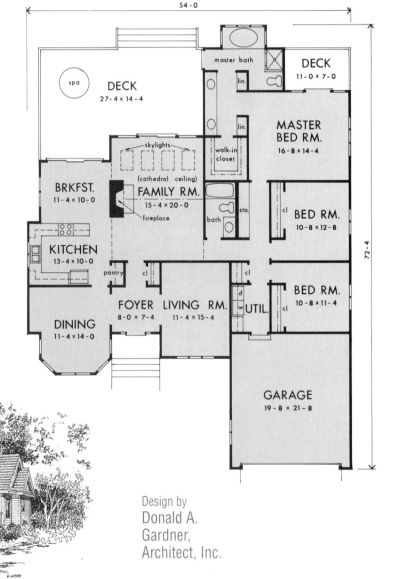

54 - 0

spa

DECK
27-4 × 14-4

master bath

DECK
11-0 × 7-0

skylights

MASTER
BED RM.
16-8 × 14-4

BRKFST.
11-4 × 10-0

(cathedral ceiling)

walk-in
closet

lin.

lin.

FAMILY RM.
15-4 × 20-0

fireplace

sto.

bath

BED RM.
10-8 × 12-8

KITCHEN
13-4 × 10-0

pantry

cl

cl

cl

FOYER
8-0 × 7-4

LIVING RM.
11-4 × 15-4

UTIL.

d
w

cl

BED RM.
10-8 × 11-4

DINING
11-4 × 14-0

GARAGE
19-8 × 21-8

72-4

Design by
Donald A.
Gardner,
Architect, Inc.

FRONT

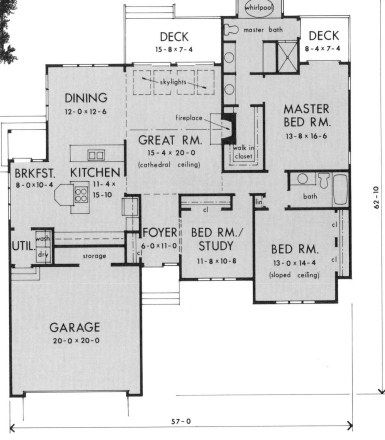

REAR

Design by
Donald A.
Gardner,
Architect, Inc.

Design AA9612

Square Footage: 1,874
Width 57'
Depth 62'-10"

● An arched window adds beauty to this modest traditional ranch. The generous entrance foyer opens to the great room and optional study. The great room provides a cathedral ceiling with exposed wood beams and skylights allowing natural ventilation. The large kitchen has an attached breakfast area and an island. The master suite has a large walk-in closet and master bath with double-bowl vanity, shower and whirlpool tub.

whirlpool

master bath

DECK
15-8 x 7-4

DECK
8-4 x 7-4

skylights

DINING
12-0 x 12-6

fireplace

MASTER
BED RM.
13-8 x 16-6

GREAT RM.
15-4 x 20-0
(cathedral ceiling)

walk in closet

BRKFST.
8-0 x10-4

KITCHEN
11-4 x
15-10

bath

FOYER
6-0 x11-0

BED RM./
STUDY
11-8 x 10-8

lin.

cl

UTIL.

wash

dry

storage

cl

BED RM.
13-0 x 14-4
(sloped ceiling)

cl

cl

GARAGE
20-0 x 20-0

62-10

57-0

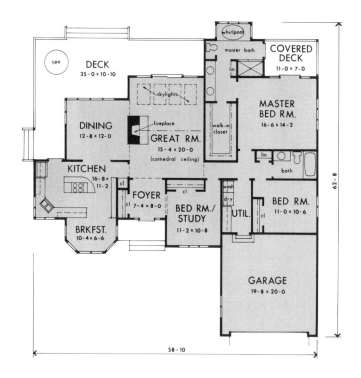

DECK
35-0 x 10-10

spa

DINING
12-8 x 12-0

skylights

fireplace

GREAT RM.
15-4 x 20-0
(cathedral ceiling)

whirlpool

master bath

lin

COVERED
DECK
11-0 x 7-0

MASTER
BED RM.
16-6 x 14-2

walk-in
closet

KITCHEN
16-8 x
11-2

FOYER
7-4 x 8-0

cl

cl

lin

bath

BRKFST.
10-4 x 6-6

BED RM./
STUDY
11-2 x 10-8

wash

dry

UTIL.

cl

BED RM.
11-0 x 10-6

GARAGE
19-8 x 20-0

58 - 10

62 - 8

Design AA9611

Square Footage: 1,817
Width 58'-10"
Depth 62'-8"

● This inviting ranch offers many special features uncommon to the typical house this size. A large entrance foyer leads to the spacious great room with cathedral ceiling, fireplace, and operable skylights that allow for natural ventilation. A bedroom just off the foyer doubles nicely as a study. The large master suite contains a walk-in closet and a pampering master bath with double-bowl vanity, shower and whirlpool tub. For outdoor living, look to the open deck with spa at the great room and kitchen, as well as the covered deck at the master suite.

Design by
Donald A.
Gardner,
Architect, Inc.

Design AA9661

First Floor: 1,416 square feet
Second Floor: 445 square feet
Total: 1,861 square feet
Width 58'-3"
Depth 68'-9"

● An arched entrance and windows provide a touch of class to the exterior of this plan. The foyer leads to all areas of the house minimizing corridor space. The dining room displays round columns at the entrance while the great room boasts a cathedral ceiling, fireplace and arched window over exterior doors to the deck. In the master suite is a walk-in closet and lavish bath. On the second level are two bedrooms and a full bath. Bonus space over the garage can be developed later. The plan is available with a crawl-space foundation.

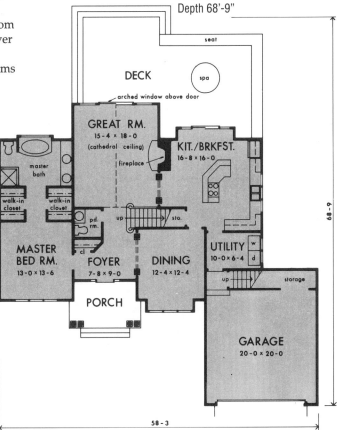

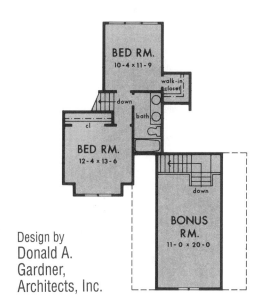

Design by
Donald A.
Gardner,
Architects, Inc.

Design AA2878

Square Footage: 1,521
Width 51'-4"
Depth 52'-4"

L **D**

● This charming one-story design offers plenty of livability in a compact size. Thoughtful zoning puts all the bedroom sleeping areas to one side of the house, apart from household activity in the living and service areas. The home includes a spacious gathering room with a sloped ceiling, in addition to a formal dining room and a separate breakfast room. There's also a handy pass-through between the breakfast room and the large, efficient kitchen. The laundry is strategically located adjacent to the garage and the breakfast/kitchen areas for handy access. The master bedroom enjoys its own suite with a private bath and a walk-in closet. A third bedroom can double as a sizable study just off the central foyer. This design offers the elegance of traditional styling with the comforts of modern lifestyle.

California Engineered Plans and California Stock Plans are available for this home. Call 1-800-521-6797 for more information.

51'-4"

TERRACE

TERRACE

MASTER BEDROOM
12⁰x14⁸

BEDROOM
11⁰x11⁰

GATHERING RM.
15⁰x16⁰

DINING RM.
9⁰x13⁴

SLOPED CEILING

LIN.

CL.

DRESSING RM

WALK-IN CLOSET

BATH

BRKFST RM.
9⁶x8⁰

KITCHEN
11⁰x9⁸

RANGE

DW.

PASS THRU

BATH

TUB

REF'G.

BROOM CL.

PANTRY

STUDY/ BEDROOM
11⁰x11⁰

FOYER

LAUND.

W.

D.

CL.

COVERED PORCH

CURB

52'-4"

GARAGE
21⁴x21⁴

Design by
Home Planners, Inc.

Photo by Andrew D. Lautman

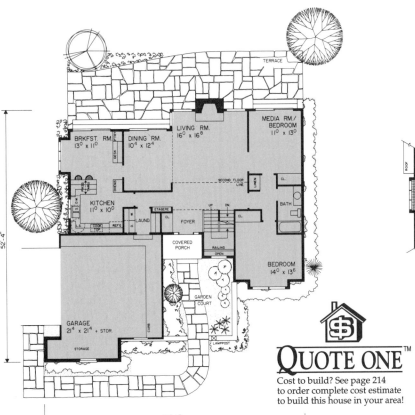

Design by
Home Planners,
Inc.

Design AA2927

First Floor: 1,425 square feet
Second Floor: 704 square feet
Total: 2,129 square feet
Width 55'-4"
Depth 52'-4"

D

● This charming Early American design with its stone-and-board exterior is just as warm on the inside. Features include a complete second-floor master bedroom suite with an upper living room, a studio, an upper foyer and a master bathroom. The upper living room and the master bathroom contain sloped ceilings. The first floor features an efficient kitchen with a pass-through to the breakfast room. There's also a formal dining room just steps away in the rear of the house. An adjacent rear living room enjoys its own fireplace. Other highlights include a rear media room or optional third bedroom. This could be a great place for VCR's, computers, stereos and even TV's. A downstairs bedroom enjoys an excellent front view. Notice the garden court, the covered porch and the large garage with extra storage. This is one well-packaged house, indeed, with plenty to offer the entire family.

California Engineered Plans and California Stock Plans are available for this home. Call 1-800-521-6797 for more information.

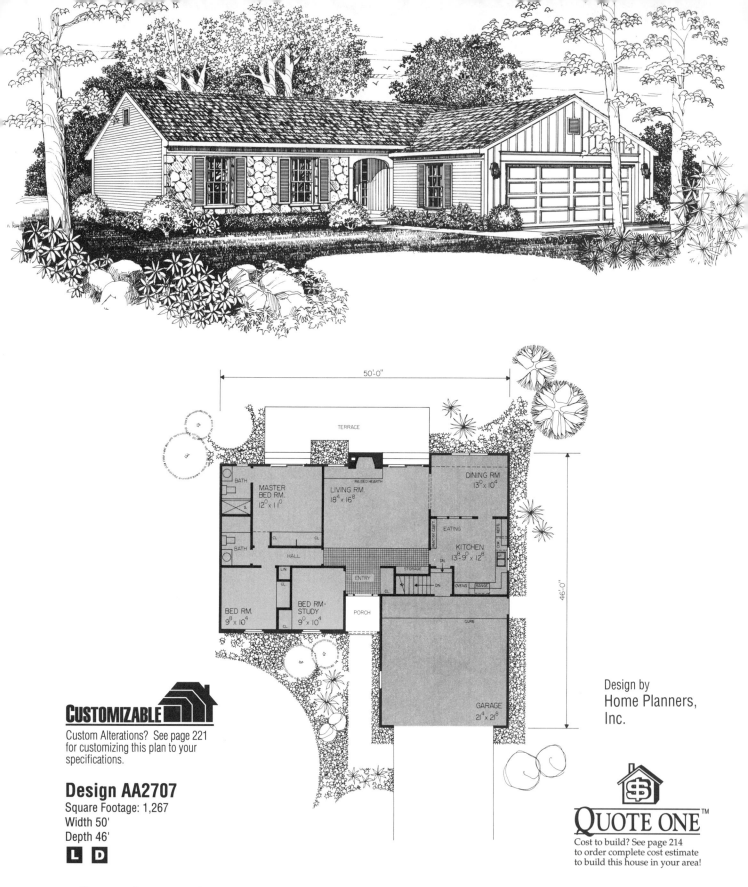

50'-0"

TERRACE

RAISED HEARTH

BATH

MASTER
BED RM.
12⁰ x 11⁰

LIVING RM.
18⁴ x 16⁸

DINING RM.
13⁰ x 10⁴

CL   CL

BATH

EATING

KITCHEN
13⁴-9⁰ x 12⁸

HALL

LIN

CL

STORAGE

ENTRY

OVENS   RANGE

46'-0"

BED RM.
9⁸ x 10⁴

BED RM-
STUDY
9⁸ x 10⁴

CL

PORCH

CURB

GARAGE
21⁴ x 21⁸

Design by
Home Planners,
Inc.

CUSTOMIZABLE

Custom Alterations? See page 221
for customizing this plan to your
specifications.

Design AA2707

Square Footage: 1,267
Width 50'
Depth 46'

L **D**

QUOTE ONE™

Cost to build? See page 214
to order complete cost estimate
to build this house in your area!

● Here is a charming Early American adaptation that will serve as a picturesque and practical retirement home. Also, it will serve admirably those with a small family in search of an efficient, economically built home. The living area, highlighted by the raised-hearth fireplace, is spacious. The kitchen features eating space and easy access to the garage and the basement. The dining room is adjacent to the kitchen and enjoys views of the rear yard. Then, there is the basement for recreation and hobby pursuits. The bedroom wing offers three bedrooms and two full baths. Don't miss the sliding doors to the terrace from the living room and the master bedroom. Storage units are plentiful and include a pantry cabinet in the eating area of the kitchen.

Design AA3372

First Floor: 1,259 square feet
Second Floor: 942 square feet
Total: 2,201 square feet
Width 52''
Depth 38'-4"

L **D**

● Charm is the key word for this delightful plan's exterior, but don't miss the great floor plan inside. Formal living and dining rooms flank the entry foyer to the front; a family room and breakfast room with beamed ceilings are to the rear. The kitchen and service areas function well together and are near the garage and service entrance for convenience. Upstairs are the sleeping accommodations: two family bedrooms and a master suite of nice proportion.

Design by
Home Planners,
Inc.

Cost to build? See page 214
to order complete cost estimate
to build this house in your area!

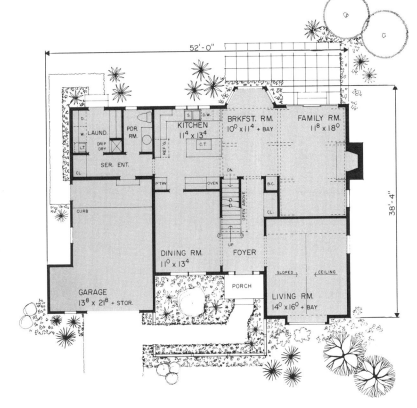

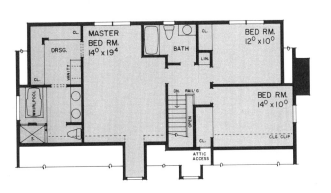

Design AA9502

Square Footage: 1,865
Width 50'
Depth 59'

● Don't let the small size of this home fool you. It adequately serves both formal and informal situations. A living room and dining room are found to the right of the plan and are open to one another. Elegant ceilings may be found in both rooms. The well-planned kitchen is nearby and also serves a nook eating area and the casual family room. A central fireplace lends warmth to this room. Double doors open to the master suite where amenities abound. An extensive, private bath consists of a spa tub, dual vanities, a compartmented commode and an ample walk-in closet. One secondary bedroom has a full bath nearby. Note that the den may double as a bedroom when needed.

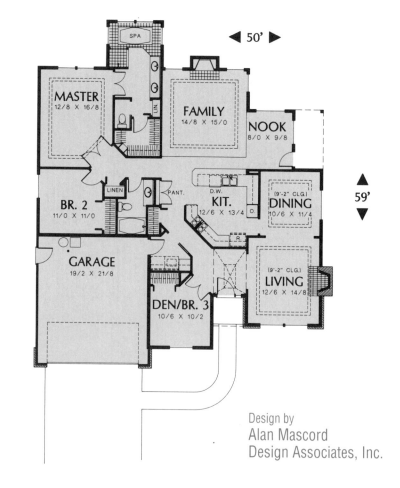

Design by
Alan Mascord
Design Associates, Inc.

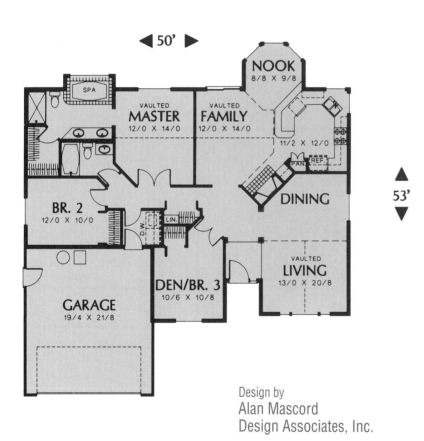

◀ **50'** ▶

SPA

VAULTED
MASTER
12/0 X 14/0

VAULTED
FAMILY
12/0 X 14/0

NOOK
8/8 X 9/8

11/2 X 12/0

PAN. REF.

DINING

BR. 2
12/0 X 10/0

LIN.

D.W.

DEN/BR. 3
10/6 X 10/8

VAULTED
LIVING
13/0 X 20/8

GARAGE
19/4 X 21/8

▲
53'
▼

Design by
Alan Mascord
Design Associates, Inc.

Design AA9403

Square Footage: 1,565
Width 50'
Depth 53'

● If you're looking for a traditional-styled ranch, this one with front-facing gables and a combination of cedar shingles and vertical cedar siding may be just right for you. The vaulted living room faces the street and is set off with a gorgeous Palladian window. The family room (note angled fireplace here) and master bedroom also have vaulted ceilings. Look for a spa tub, large shower and walk-in closet in the master bedroom. Through French doors in the entry is a den that could be used as a third bedroom.

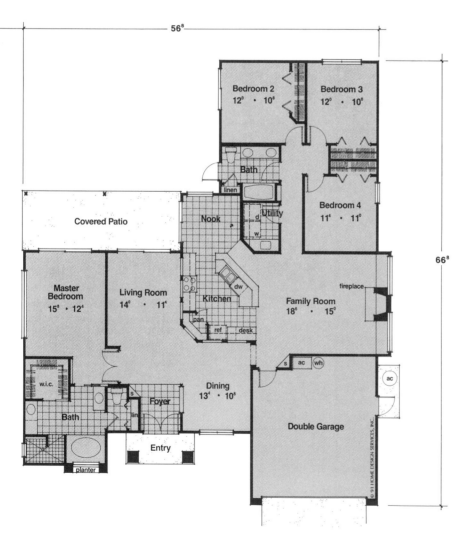

Covered Patio

Bedroom 2
12⁰ • 10⁸

Bedroom 3
12⁰ • 10⁸

Bath

linen

Nook

Utility

Bedroom 4
11⁴ • 11⁰

Master
Bedroom
15⁸ • 12⁴

Living Room
14⁰ • 11⁴

Kitchen

dw

Family Room
18⁶ • 15⁰

fireplace

w.i.c.

pan

ref   desk

s   ac   wh

ac

Bath

Dining
13⁴ • 10⁸

Foyer

lin

Double Garage

planter

Entry

56⁸

66⁸

© 91 HOME DESIGN SERVICES, INC.

Design AA8638

Square Footage: 2,144
Width 56'-8"
Depth 66'-8"

● This is the ultimate family house! This unique arrangement of rooms creates spaces which are functional and individual. The entry opens to the formal living and dining room areas with a magnificent view of the outdoor living space and yard. Double doors lead to the master suite located in its very own private wing of the home for perfect privacy and quiet. The His and Hers sinks, soaking tub and step-down shower add luxury. The private toilet room and huge walk-in closet add practicality. Beyond the formal and master wing is the family space with the kitchen at its hub. The bedroom wing has great amenities for the kids—outdoor access in the shared bath and a nearby laundry room.

Design by
Home Design
Services, Inc.

Bedroom 2
11⁴ • 10⁰

Covered Patio

Breakfast

Master Bedroom
15⁰ • 13⁰

dw desk

ref.

Kitchen

pan.

W.I.C.

Bath

Lin

Family Room
17⁴ • 15⁰

opt. fireplace

Lin

Bath

w

Utility

d

Bedroom 3
11⁴ • 10⁴

Foyer

Living Room
11⁰ • 10⁸

Dining
11⁰ • 10⁰

Entry

ac

wh

opt.

Double Garage

WIDTH 59'
DEPTH 55'-4"

Design by
Home Design
Services, Inc.

Design AA8644
Square Footage: 1,831
Width 59'
Depth 55'-4"

● A two-level entry, varying rooflines and multi-pane windows add to the spectacular street appeal of this three-bedroom home. To the right of the foyer is the dining room surrounded by elegant columns. Adjacent is the angular kitchen, which opens to the bayed breakfast nook. The elegant living room sits across the foyer from the dining room. The family room includes plans for an optional fireplace. The master bedroom is tucked in the back of the home and features a walk-in closet and a full bath with a dual vanity, spa tub and oversized shower. Two additional bedrooms—each with a large closet—share a full bath. Don't miss the covered patio that adds to outdoor livability.

Design AA8618

First Floor: 1,352 square feet
Second Floor: 1,000 square feet
Total: 2,352 square feet
Width 55'
Depth 52'

Design by
Home Design
Services, Inc.

● A covered patio shades the entry to the foyer of this home—it is lit by an arched window. Double doors to the right open to a guest room with arched picture window. The great room, open to the level above, has a wet bar; a large rear patio also offers a wet bar. The tiled kitchen provides a serving bar for the breakfast room. French doors in the master bed-room open onto a deck. The spacious bath here includes a walk-in closet, twin vanities and spa tub. Two additional bed-rooms and a bath complete the second level. The front bed-room includes a study and opens onto a deck. The plan can be built with a flat-tiled or barrel roof.

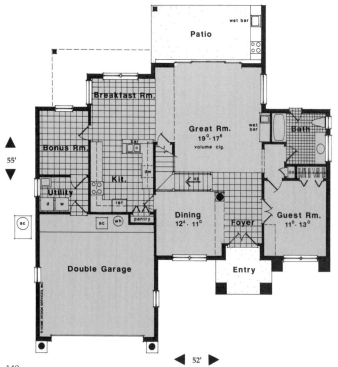

Design AA8661

Square Footage: 1,817
Width 50'
Depth 63'

● First impressions take off in
this one-story, volume-look home.
A traditional split entry finds the
living room on the left and the dining room on the right. The latter
shares a large, open space with the
family room, made more impressive with its volume ceiling. The
tiled kitchen and breakfast room
bespeak charm and efficiency.
On one side of the plan, the master
bedroom boasts a private sitting
space and a lavish bath with shut-
ter doors at the soaking tub and a
room-sized walk-in closet. At the
other side of the house, two family
bedrooms each afford ample closet
space and room to grow. A "kid's"
door leads to the covered patio that
rests at the rear of the plan.

Design by
Home Design
Services, Inc.

Floor Plan Labels

- 50' (width dimension top)
- 63' (depth dimension right)

Bedroom 3 volume ceiling 11⁰ · 10¹⁰
Bath
lin
Covered Patio volume ceiling
Sitting
Master Bedroom volume ceiling 23⁰ · 12⁴
Breakfast
volume ceiling
Family Room volume ceiling 19⁰ · 13⁰
Bedroom 2 volume ceiling 11⁶ · 11⁰
fireplace
Kitchen
dw
ref
Bath
Living Room volume ceiling 11⁴ · 10⁸
Foyer
Dining volume ceiling 12⁴ · 10⁰
w
d
Utility
ac
w.i.c.
wh
Entry
Double Garage

141

Design AA3563

First Floor: 1,023 square feet
Second Floor: 866 square feet
Total: 1,889 square feet
Width 52'-4"
Depth 34'-8"

L **D**

● Practical to build, this wonderful transitional plan combines the best of contemporary and traditional styling. Its stucco exterior is enhanced by arched windows and a recessed arched entry plus a lovely balcony off the second-floor master bedroom. A walled entry court extends the living room to the outside. The double front doors open to a foyer with a hall closet and a powder room. The service entrance is just to the right and accesses the two-car garage. The large living room adjoins directly to the dining room. The family room is set off behind the garage and features a sloped ceiling and a fireplace. Sleeping quarters consist of two secondary bedrooms with a shared bath and a generous master suite with a well-appointed bath.

Design by
Home Planners, Inc.

QUOTE ONE™

Cost to build? See page 214 to order complete cost estimate to build this house in your area!

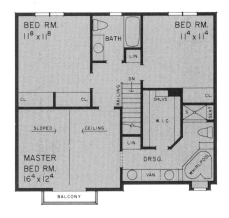

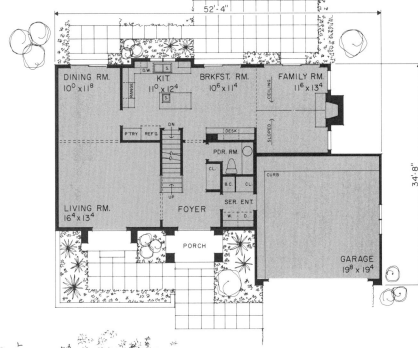

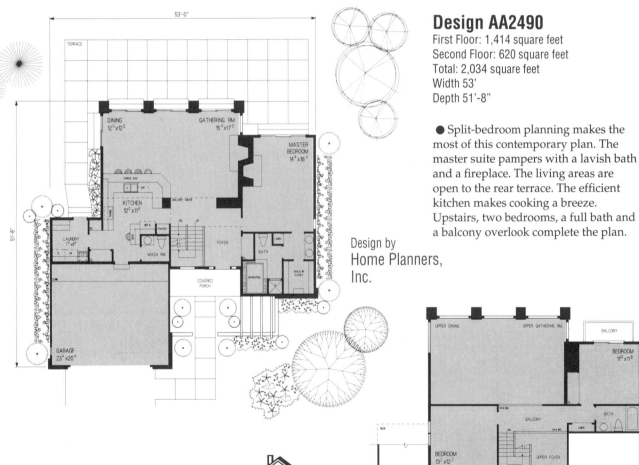

Design AA2490

First Floor: 1,414 square feet
Second Floor: 620 square feet
Total: 2,034 square feet
Width 53'
Depth 51'-8"

● Split-bedroom planning makes the most of this contemporary plan. The master suite pampers with a lavish bath and a fireplace. The living areas are open to the rear terrace. The efficient kitchen makes cooking a breeze. Upstairs, two bedrooms, a full bath and a balcony overlook complete the plan.

Design by
Home Planners, Inc.

CUSTOMIZABLE

Custom Alterations? See page 221 for customizing this plan to your specifications.

QUOTE ONE™

Cost to build? See page 214 to order complete cost estimate to build this house in your area!

143

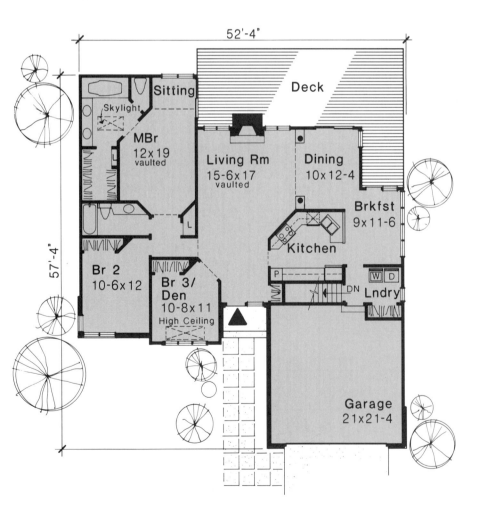

Design AA8890

Square Footage: 1,630
Width 52'-4"
Depth 57'-4"

● This home design effectively
separates living and sleeping
zones for added comfort. A
vaulted living room offers a
fireplace flanked by bright windows. Columns define the dining room which accesses a rear
wraparound deck. The well-
designed kitchen easily serves
the airy breakfast room. A nearby laundry room makes chores
a breeze. In the sleeping wing,
the master bedroom suite
impresses with its vaulted ceiling, sitting room and skylit
bathroom with dual vanities,
compartmented toilet and walk-
in closet. Bedroom 3 could also
be a den, perfect for home
computing.

Design by
LifeStyle
HomeDesigns

Design AA8889
Square Footage: 1,283
Width 51'-5"
Depth 40'-9"

● This fine ranch home offers distinction with its Palladian windows, shingle siding and stone enhancements. The vaulted great room focuses on a fireplace. The dining room shares views with this room. A pass-through from the kitchen assures ease in serving meals. A vaulted breakfast room enjoys access to a rear deck for added enjoyment. Three bedrooms include a master bedroom with a private bath. As a starter home or a retirement home, this design has it all!

Design by
LifeStyle
HomeDesigns

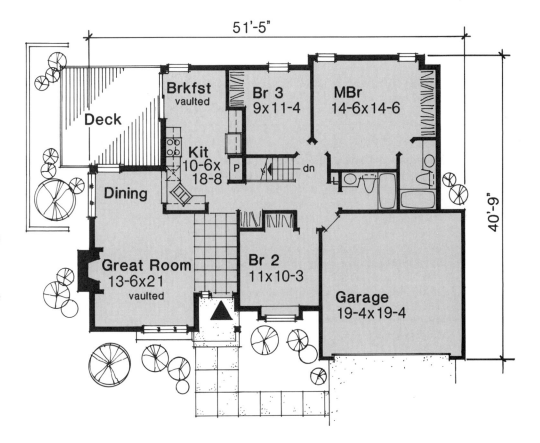

Design AA9320

First Floor: 1,042 square feet
Second Floor: 953 square feet
Total: 1,995 square feet
Width 48'
Depth 40'

● Clean rooflines and a delightful covered front porch accentuate this two-story home's elevation. Livability is enriched through careful segregation of the formal and informal living spaces. A measure of versatility characterizes the formal dining room which is open to the volume living room. The bayed breakfast area is open to a well-planned kitchen with a snack bar and two lazy Susans. A spacious family room provides a view out the back, plus a cozy raised-hearth fireplace. On the second level, three secondary bedrooms with bright windows share a centrally located bath. In the master suite is a formal boxed ceiling and a luxurious dressing area. Envision yourself in the angled whirlpool.

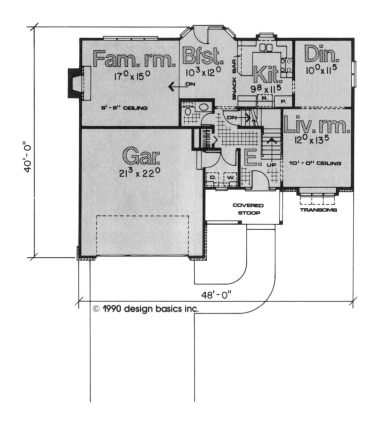

© 1990 design basics inc.

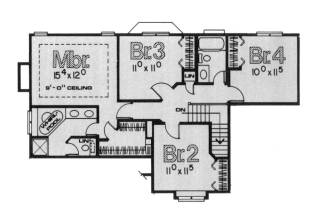

Design by
Design
Basics,
Inc.

Design AA9309

First Floor: 1,506 square feet

Second Floor: 633 square feet

Total: 2,139 square feet

Width 50'

Depth 58'

● Graceful lines and arched windows create a delightful country flair for this 1½-story home. From the volume entry, there's a clear view of the stunning great room enhanced by the handsome fireplace and windows with a view. The adjacent dining room is perfect for entertaining. A dinette, open to the island kitchen, allows sunlight to brighten and warm this family-sized eating area. The covered patio is accessed from the dinette. In the gourmet kitchen, convenience is evident through features such as a snack bar, planning desk and walk-in pantry. The main-floor master suite sports a beautiful arched window, double doors and sloped ceiling. A two-person whirlpool, His and Hers vanities and a decorator plant ledge complement the master dressing area. Three secondary bedrooms upstairs share a hall bath.

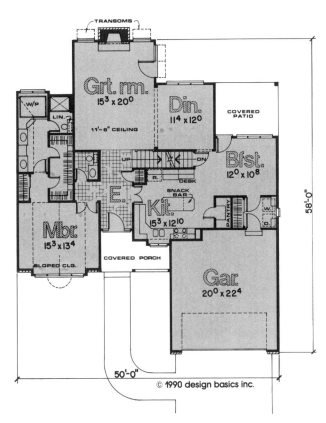

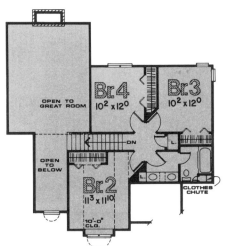

Design by
Design Basics, Inc.

Design AA9818

First Floor: 1,640 square feet
Second Floor: 1,030 square feet
Total: 2,670 square feet
Width 53'
Depth 59'

● This home, with its classic Georgian detailing, features brick jack arches that frame the arched front door and windows. Dormers above and a motor-court entry garage add to the charm and elegance of this home. Inside, the foyer leads direct-ly to a large great room with a fireplace and French doors that lead outside. Just off the foyer, the dining room is separated by an open colonnade and receives brilliant light from the arched window. The kitchen and breakfast room offer every convenience, including a handy cooking island and on-line work areas. Adjacent to the breakfast room is the keeping room which includes a corner fireplace and French doors that lead to the large rear porch. Comfort and privacy describe the master suite, complete with elegant tray ceilings, a large and accommodating bath and a spacious walk-in closet. Upstairs, two additional bedrooms share convenient access to a bath while, down the hall, a fourth bedroom has its own private bath.

WIDTH 53'
DEPTH 59'

Design by
Design Traditions

Copyright 1992 Stephen S. Fuller, Inc.

Design AA9875

First Floor: 1,475 square feet
Second Floor: 545 square feet
Total: 2,020 square feet
Width 53'
Depth 50'-6"

● This quaint country manor combines stucco and stone to create unrivaled warmth and charm. The two-story foyer is highlighted by the beautiful open-railed staircase and view of the living and dining rooms. The kitchen, equipped with ample space and work island, makes preparations a breeze. The breakfast area opens to a keeping room with corner fireplace and French doors, bringing the out of doors comfortably inside. Privately located on the opposite side of the home is the luxurious master suite with sitting area and master bath complete with dual vanities, garden tub, enclosed shower and large walk-in closet. Upstairs, the gallery overlooks the living and dining rooms below. Down the hallway two bedrooms and a bonus room share access to a centrally located hall bath.

MASTER BEDROOM

LIVING ROOM
12'-0" X 13'-6"

DINING ROOM
11'-0" X 12'-0"

KEEPING ROOM
13'-0" X 14'-0"

MASTER BATH

DN.   UP

FOYER

BREAKFAST
11'-0" X 8'-8"

POWDER

W.I.C.

KITCHEN
12'-0" X 11'-0"

LAUNDRY

STOOP

WIDTH 53'
DEPTH 50'-6"

TWO CAR GARAGE
20'-4" X 20'-8"

BATH

BEDROOM
NO. 2
10'-8" X 11'-8"

OPEN TO BELOW

DN.   GALLERY

OPEN TO BELOW

BEDROOM NO. 3
12'-0" X 12'-6"

Design by
Design Traditions

UNFIN.
BONUS RM.
11'-0" X 21'-0"

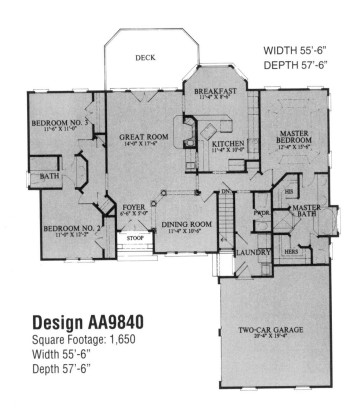

DECK

BREAKFAST
11'-4" X 8'-6"

BEDROOM NO. 3
11'-6" X 11'-0"

GREAT ROOM
14'-0" X 17'-6"

KITCHEN
11'-4" X 10'-0"

MASTER
BEDROOM
12'-4" X 15'-6"

BATH

DN

HIS

FOYER
6'-6" X 5'-0"

DINING ROOM
11'-4" X 10'-6"

PWDR.

MASTER
BATH

BEDROOM NO. 2
11'-0" X 12'-2"

STOOP

LAUNDRY

HERS

TWO-CAR GARAGE
20'-4" X 19'-4"

WIDTH 55'-6"
DEPTH 57'-6"

Design AA9840

Square Footage: 1,650
Width 55'-6"
Depth 57'-6"

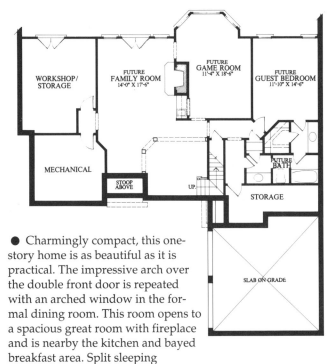

WORKSHOP/
STORAGE

FUTURE
FAMILY ROOM
14'-0" X 17'-6"

FUTURE
GAME ROOM
11'-4" X 18'-6"

FUTURE
GUEST BEDROOM
11'-10" X 14'-6"

MECHANICAL

FUTURE
BATH

STOOP
ABOVE

UP

STORAGE

SLAB ON GRADE

● Charmingly compact, this one-story home is as beautiful as it is practical. The impressive arch over the double front door is repeated with an arched window in the formal dining room. This room opens to a spacious great room with fireplace and is nearby the kitchen and bayed breakfast area. Split sleeping arrangements put the master suite with His and Hers walk-in closets at the right of the plan and two family bedrooms at the left. Additional space in the basement can later be developed as the family grows.

Design by
Design Traditions

Copyright 1992 Stephen S. Fuller, Inc.

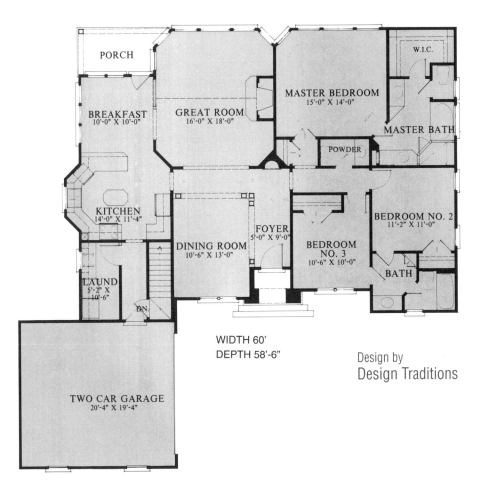

PORCH

BREAKFAST
10'-0" X 10'-0"

GREAT ROOM
16'-0" X 18'-0"

MASTER BEDROOM
15'-0" X 14'-0"

W.I.C.

MASTER BATH

POWDER

KITCHEN
14'-0" X 11'-4"

FOYER
5'-0" X 9'-0"

BEDROOM NO. 2
11'-2" X 11'-0"

DINING ROOM
10'-6" X 13'-0"

BEDROOM
NO. 3
10'-6" X 10'-0"

BATH

LAUND
5'-2" X
10'-6"

DN.

TWO CAR GARAGE
20'-4" X 19'-4"

WIDTH 60'
DEPTH 58'-6"

Design by
Design Traditions

Design AA9872

Square Footage: 1,815
Width 60'
Depth 58'-6"

● The approach to this European home has an inviting quality about it. The stucco exterior with arched detail on the windows furthers the feel of style and grace while the front door adds a majestic touch to an already stately presence. Inside, the foyer opens into the great room with a vaulted ceiling and a dining room defined by an asymmetrical column arrangement. Kitchen tasks are made easy with this home's step-saving kitchen and breakfast bar. Nestled away at the opposite end of the home, the master suite combines perfect solitude with elegant luxury. Features include a double door entry, tray ceiling, niche detail and private rear deck. Additional bedrooms and bath are provided for children and guests.

151

Design AA9717

First Floor: 1,377 square feet
Second Floor: 714 square feet
Total: 2,091 square feet
Width 55'-8"
Depth 62'-4"

● An inviting covered porch and roundtop windows offer an irresistible appeal to this four-bedroom plan. The two-level foyer allows a more spacious feeling uncommon in plans of similar size. The generous great room with a fireplace and the breakfast bay both provide access to a rear deck. The master bedroom, located on the first level, has a large walk-in closet and a bath consisting of a double-bowl vanity, a shower and a garden tub with a skylight overhead. The second level has three bedrooms and a full bath with a double-bowl vanity. As an added feature, the bonus room over the garage does not take away from any of the attic storage space.

Design by
Donald A.
Gardner,
Architect, Inc.

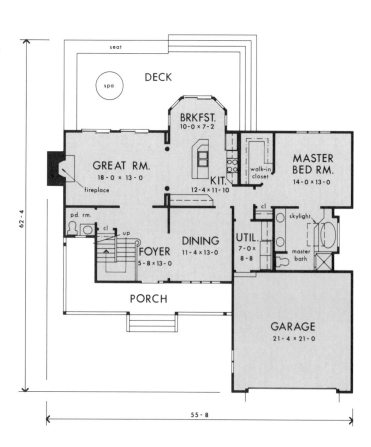

152

Design by
Donald A.
Gardner,
Architect, Inc.

Design AA9662

First Floor: 1,025 square feet
Second Floor: 911 square feet
Total: 1,936 square feet
Width 53'-8"
Depth 67'-8"

● The exterior of this three-bedroom home is enhanced by its many gables, arched windows and wraparound porch. A large great room with impressive fireplace leads to both the dining room and screened porch with access to the deck. An open kitchen offers a country-kitchen atmosphere. The second-level master suite has two walk-in closets and an impressive bath. There is also bonus space over the garage. The plan is available with a crawl-space foundation.

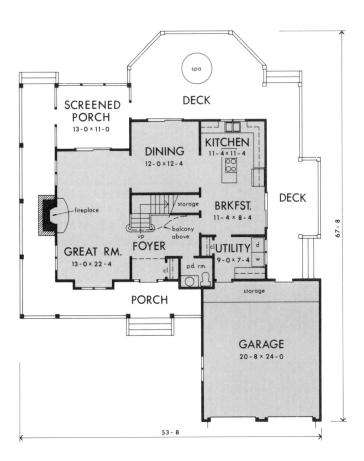

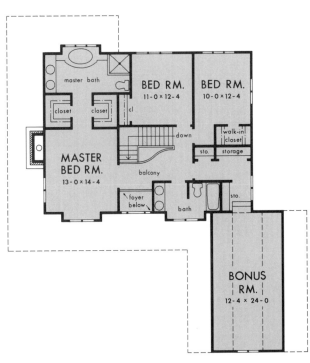

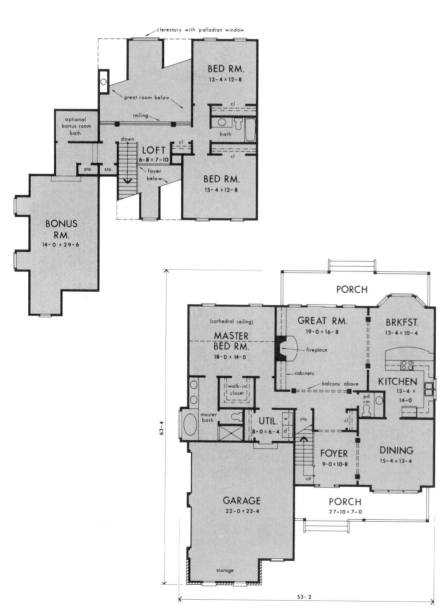

clerestory with palladian window

BED RM.
13-4 × 12-8

great room below

railing

optional
bonus room
bath

down

LOFT
6-8 × 7-10

foyer
below

cl

bath

cl

sto. sto.

cl

BED RM.
15-4 × 12-8

BONUS
RM.
14-0 × 29-6

PORCH

(cathedral ceiling)

MASTER
BED RM.
18-0 × 14-0

GREAT RM.
19-0 × 16-8

BRKFST.
13-4 × 10-4

fireplace

cabinets

balcony above

KITCHEN
13-4 ×
14-0

walk-in
closet

master
bath

UTIL.
8-0 × 6-4

w
d

sto.

pd.
rm.

cl

63-4

FOYER
9-0 × 10-8

DINING
15-4 × 13-4

up

GARAGE
22-0 × 23-4

PORCH
27-10 × 7-0

storage

53-2

Design AA9701

First Floor: 1,720 square feet
Second Floor: 652 square feet
Total: 2,372 square feet
Bonus Room: 553 square feet
Width 53'-2"
Depth 63'-4"

● This elegant country home, with both front and rear porches, offers a pleasing appearance with its variety of materials and refined detailing. The open floor plan is reinforced by the vaulted great room and entrance foyer with clerestory windows in dormers above. Both spaces are open to a balcony/loft area above. The master suite with cathedral ceiling and large walk-in closet is located on the first floor for privacy and accessibility. Nine-foot ceilings grace much of the first floor. The second floor, with its eight-foot ceilings, has two large bedrooms, a full bath and a bonus room over the garage with space available for another bath. The plan is available with a crawl-space foundation.

Design by
Donald A.
Gardner,
Architect, Inc.

Design AA9705

First Floor: 1,675 square feet
Second Floor: 448 square feet
Total: 2,123 square feet
Width 53'-8"
Depth 69'-8"

● This attractive, three-bedroom house offers a touch of country with its covered front porch. The entrance foyer, flanked by a dining room and a bedroom/study, leads to a spacious great room. Here, a clerestory and a fireplace add both charm and warmth. The dining room and breakfast room have cathedral ceilings with arched windows flooding the house with natural light. The deck off the great room will delight with its spa and seat. The master bedroom boasts a cathedral ceiling and a bath with a whirlpool, shower and double-bowl vanity. The second floor allows for two additional bedrooms along with a bonus room. The plan is available with a crawl-space foundation.

Design by
Donald A. Gardner, Architect, Inc.

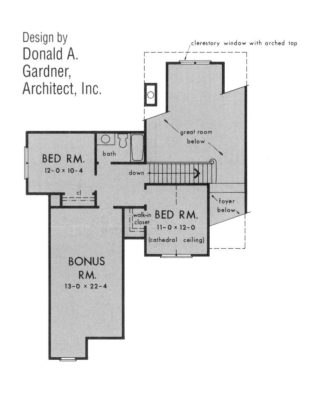

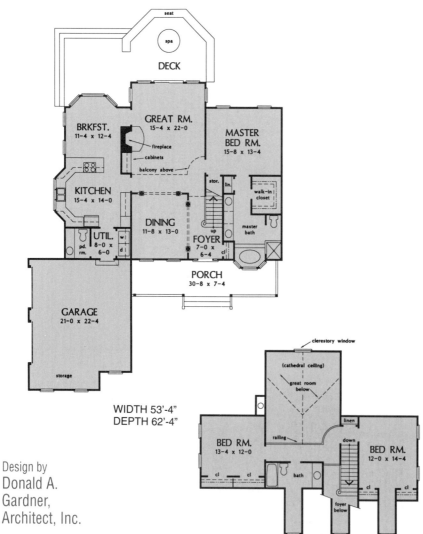

seat

spa

DECK

GREAT RM.
15-4 x 22-0

BRKFST.
11-4 x 12-4

MASTER
BED RM.
15-8 x 13-4

fireplace

cabinets

balcony above

KITCHEN
15-4 x 14-0

stor.

lin.

walk-in
closet

DINING
11-8 x 13-0

master
bath

UTIL.
8-0 x
6-0

pd.
rm.

d

up

FOYER
7-0 x
6-4

cl

PORCH
30-8 x 7-4

GARAGE
21-0 x 22-4

storage

WIDTH 53'-4"
DEPTH 62'-4"

Design by
Donald A.
Gardner,
Architect, Inc.

clerestory window

(cathedral ceiling)

great room
below

linen

BED RM.
13-4 x 12-0

railing

down

BED RM.
12-0 x 14-4

cl

cl

bath

cl

cl

foyer
below

Design AA9710

First Floor: 1,540 square feet
Second Floor: 654 square feet
Total: 2,194 square feet
Width 53'-4"
Depth 62'-4"

● This charmer opens up
with a foyer leading into a
columned dining room—per-
fect for entertaining. Just
beyond, with a view out the
rear of the house, is the great
room. A cozy fireplace separates the great room from a
delightful bayed breakfast
nook, also with a view out
the rear of the house. A
U-shaped kitchen provides
ample counter space for food
preparation or countertop
appliances. The master bedroom occupies the right side
of the house. Highlights
include a stupendous master
bath with a large walk-in
closet, dual-vanities and a
whirlpool tub set in a window bay. Both of the upstairs
bedrooms have twin closets;
both share a full bath. The
plan is available with a
crawl-space foundation.

156

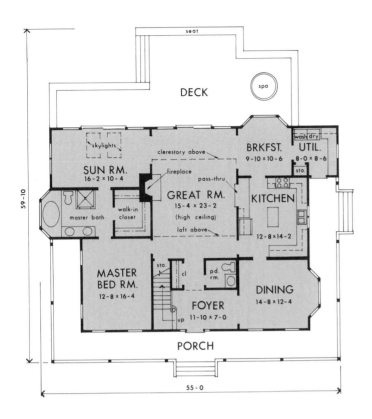

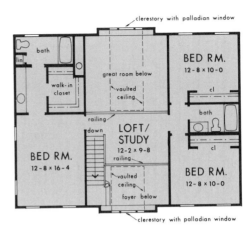

Design AA9616

First Floor: 1,734 square feet
Second Floor: 958 square feet
Total: 2,692 square feet
Width 55'
Depth 59'-10"

● A wraparound covered porch at the front and sides of this home and the open deck with spa and seating provide plenty of outside living area. A central great room features a vaulted ceiling, fireplace and clerestory windows above. The loft/study on the second floor overlooks this gathering area. Besides a formal dining room, kitchen, breakfast room and sun room on the first floor, there is also a generous master suite with garden tub. Three second-floor bedrooms complete sleeping accommodations. The plan includes a crawl-space foundation.

Design by
Donald A.
Gardner,
Architect, Inc.

REAR

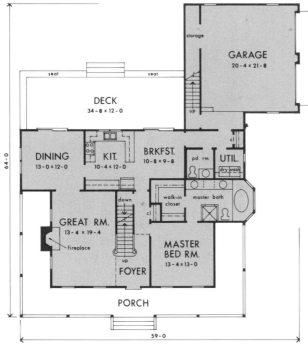

seat | seat

DECK
34 - 8 x 12 - 0

storage

GARAGE
20 - 4 x 21 - 8

up

64 - 0

DINING
13 - 0 x 12 - 0

KIT.
10 - 4 x 12 - 0

BRKFST.
10 - 8 x 9 - 8

pd. rm.

UTIL.

dry wash

cl

down

walk-in closet

master bath

GREAT RM.
13 - 4 x 19 - 4

fireplace

up

cl

MASTER BED RM.
13 - 4 x 13 - 0

FOYER

PORCH

59 - 0

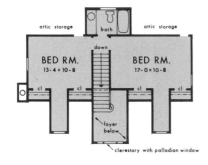

attic storage

attic storage

bath

down

BED RM.
13 - 4 x 10 - 8

BED RM.
17 - 0 x 10 - 8

cl | cl | cl | cl

foyer below

clerestory with palladian window

down

BONUS RM.
23 - 8 x 14 - 4

Design AA9645

First Floor: 1,356 square feet
Second Floor: 542 square feet
Total: 1,898 square feet
Width 59'
Depth 64'

● The welcoming charm of this country farmhouse is expressed by its many windows and its covered, wraparound porch. A two-story entrance foyer is enhanced by a Palladian window in a clerestory dormer above to allow natural lighting. A first-floor master suite allows privacy and accessibility. The master bath includes a whirlpool tub, shower and double-bowl vanity along with a walk-in closet. The first floor features a nine-foot ceiling throughout with the exception of the kitchen area which features an eight-foot ceiling. The second floor provides two additional bedrooms, a full bath and plenty of storage space. An unfinished basement and bonus room provide room to grow. Order Design AA9645 for a crawl-space foundation; order Design AA9645-A for a basement foundation.

Design by
Donald A.
Gardner,
Architect, Inc.

DECK

seat

seat

spa

skylights

SUN RM.
16-2 x 8-10

GREAT RM.
15-4 x 21-0
(cathedral ceiling)

fireplace

master bath

walk-in closet

balcony above

pass-thru

BRKFST.
9-10 x 9-10

wash dry

UTILITY
8-0 x 7-10

KITCHEN
12-8 x 13-0

53-10

MASTER BED RM.
12-8 x16-4

sto.

cl

pd. rm.

FOYER
11-10 x 7-2
(sloped ceiling)
up

DINING
14-8 x 12-8

PORCH

55-0

Design by
Donald A.
Gardner,
Architect, Inc.

Design AA9623

First Floor: 1,651 square feet
Second Floor: 567 square feet
Total: 2,218 square feet
Width 55'
Depth 53'-10"

● A wonderful wraparound covered porch at the front and sides of this house and the open deck with spa at the back provide plenty of outside living area. Inside, the spacious great room has a fireplace, a cathedral ceiling and a clerestory with an arched window. The kitchen is centrally located for maximum flexibility in layout and has a food preparation island for convenience. Besides the master bedroom and its access to the sun room, there are two second-level bedrooms that share a full bath. For a crawl-space foundation, order Design AA9623; for a basement foundation, order Design AA9623-A.

clerestory with arched window

(cathedral ceiling)

great room below

storage

storage

railing

BED RM.
12-8 x 12-0

BED RM.
12-8 x 12-0

balcony

down

cl

cl

bath

cl

cl

foyer below

clerestory with palladian window

B. NATHAN

Design by
Home Planners,
Inc.

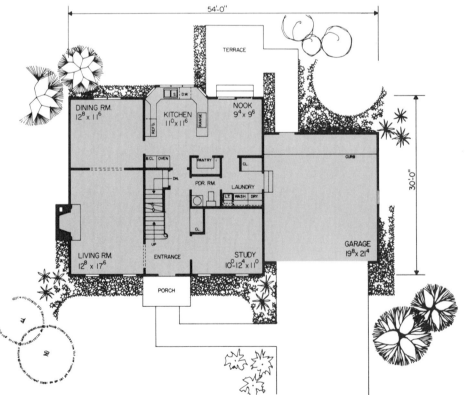

Design AA2731

First Floor: 1,039 square feet
Second Floor: 973 square feet
Total: 2,012 square feet
Width 54'
Depth 30'

L **D**

● Affordable style is the hallmark of this Colonial design. The U-shaped kitchen with large pantry and adjacent breakfast nook is a big center of attention. Next to it is a formal dining room. Living room with fireplace, first-floor study, and efficient service area round out a hard-working downstairs plan. The second floor features a sizable master suite, complete with twin vanities and roomy walk-in closet.

Design AA1957

First Floor: 1,042 square feet
Second Floor: 780 square feet
Total: 1,822 square feet
Width 50'
Depth 34'-10"

L **D**

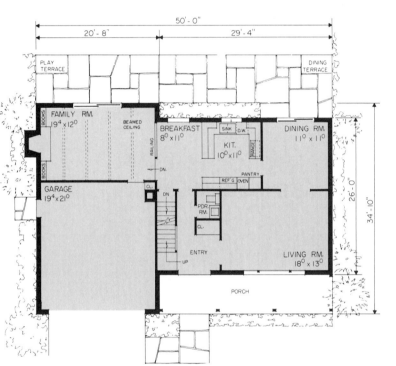

Design by
**Home Planners,
Inc.**

● When you order your blueprints for this design you will receive details for the construction of each of the three charming exteriors pictured above. Whichever the exterior you finally decide to build, the floor plan will be essentially the same except the location of the windows. This will be a fine home for the growing family. It will serve well for many years. There are four bedrooms and two full baths (one with a stall shower) upstairs.

Design AA2668 First Floor: 1,206 square feet
Second Floor: 1,254 square feet; Total: 2,460 square feet
Width 52'
Depth 42'

L

● This elegant exterior houses a very livable plan. Every bit of space has been put to good use. The front country kitchen is a good place to begin. It is efficiently planned with its island cook top, built-ins and pass-thru to the dining room. The large great room will be the center of all family activities. Quiet times can be enjoyed in the front library. Study the second floor sleeping areas.

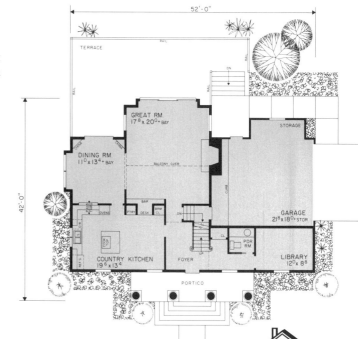

Design by
Home Planners,
Inc.

Cost to build? See page 214
to order complete cost estimate
to build this house in your area!

Design by
Home Planners,
Inc.

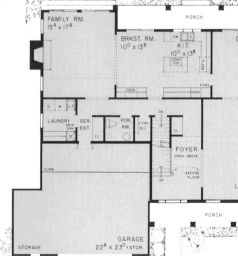

Design AA3570

First Floor: 1,578 square feet
Second Floor: 1,546 square feet
Total: 3,124 square feet
Bonus Room: 380 square feet
Width 56'
Depth 52'

L D

● The unique design of this
Colonial will satisfy the most
refined tastes. Well-designed
traffic patterns define family
and formal areas. But that
doesn't mean all the amenities
are left for company. For
example, the family room and
its fireplace create a warm
atmosphere for playing a
board game with the kids or
just relaxing. The kitchen features an island cooktop and a
view onto the back porch. The
roomy first-floor laundry
includes space for drip drying.
If it's not laundry day then
take in the good weather
from the second-floor balcony
or slip into the master bath's
whirlpool. With an additional
three bedrooms and two bath-
rooms as well as a large bonus
room above the garage, your
family will have plenty of
room to grow.

Design AA9500

First Floor: 1,568 square feet
Second Floor: 1,227 square feet
Total: 2,795 square feet
Width 50'
Depth 61'

● A pleasing mix of traditional and contemporary elements, this gracious home has all the living space your family could ever ask. On the first floor are formal living and dining rooms, complemented by a private den in its own gazebo-like space. The family room is found to the rear of the plan, contains a fireplace and connects to the eating nook and adjacent island kitchen. The three-car garage holds family vehicles easily. Upstairs, three bedrooms and two full baths meet sleeping-space requirements. The master suite has a private deck, whirlpool spa and gigantic walk-in closet.

◀ 50' ▶

▲
61'
▼

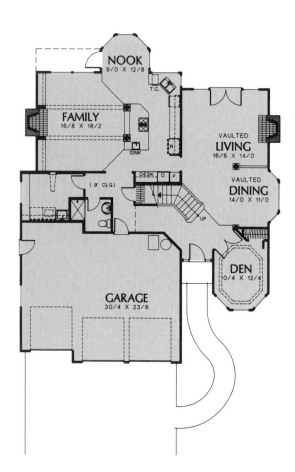

NOOK
9/0 X 12/8

FAMILY
16/8 X 18/2

SINK

VAULTED
LIVING
16/6 X 14/0

VAULTED
DINING
14/0 X 11/0

DESK O. P.

(9' CLG.)

UP

DEN
10/4 X 12/4

GARAGE
30/4 X 23/8

DECK

SPA

FIREPLACE

MASTER
16/8 X 17/4

DN.

FOYER
BELOW

BR. 2
14/6 X 11/0

LINEN

BR. 3
12/6 X 11/8

SHELVES

Design by
Alan Mascord
Design Associates, Inc.

Narrow Houses For Sloping Sites

For a narrow lot, a sloping site translates into welcome added livability. The extra finished space of a walk-out or day-light basement may support a family room, family bedrooms or such desirable features as a recreation room or workshop. With this increase in square footage—kept within narrow-lot dimensions—the home builder's cost per square foot decreases quite dramatically.

Many of the designs in this section display rear living rooms and wraparound decks—both features of waterfront living. A good example of this is the outstanding design on page 194. This home sports soaring contemporary looks—natural wood siding contributes to this grand appearance. The entry level entertains an expansive great room with a central fireplace and a walk-out to a deck. Three bedrooms on the upper level include two with a rear deck. For more casual living, and delightful direct access to the sands, a lower-level family room provides ample space for kid's play. And note that all of this comes in a package only 32' x 36'!

Truly unique in both narrow lot and sloping-site terms, the home on page 183 also enjoys thoughtful contemporary styling. To cater to a range of narrow lots, the two-car garage may occupy any space desired. Further the flexibility of the design by orienting the entry to the street or to the side. Inside, three bedrooms, including a master suite with a pampering private bath, comprise the walk-out basement. The main level facilitates open living and, when the occasion arises, grand entertaining. For both warmth and effect, a two-way fireplace connects the great room and dining room. A wraparound deck will delight family and guests alike with its fine presentation of outdoor living.

For something a little more traditional, the design on page 178 may be the one for you. Ideal for a suburban setting, this quad-level maximizes available space for the best in livability. The garage offers passage to three of the levels: the basement—an ideal location for a workshop; the family-room level which includes a laundry room; and the formal living area comprised of the living and dining rooms. A terrace extends from the family room while another opens off the dining room. Upstairs, four bedrooms include a master suite with a balcony.

Perhaps the quintessential narrow-lot, sloping-site design, the home on page 168 presents the home builder with a most inspiring plan—inside and out. With dimensions that span 40' x 46', and two floors of living space, nearly 2,000 square feet come into play. All of this is enhanced by the fine features of a family plan: formal living and dining rooms; a kitchen with a nook; a vaulted and sunken family room. Three bedrooms assure room to grow. To make this design even more desirable—with no sacrifice of available space—you'll find plenty of room for a back yard.

Design AA9509

Main Level: 1,022 square feet
Upper Level: 813 square feet
Total: 1,835 square feet
Width 36'
Depth 33'

● This house not only accommodates a narrow lot, but it also fits a sloping site. Notice how the two-car garage is tucked away under the first level of the house. The angled corner entry gives way to a two-story living room with a tiled hearth. The dining room shares an interesting angled space with this area and enjoys easy service from the efficient kitchen. A large pantry and an angled corner sink add character to this area. The family room offers double doors to a refreshing balcony. A powder room and a laundry room complete the main level. Upstairs, three bedrooms include a vaulted master suite with a private bath. Bedrooms 2 and 3 each take advantage of direct access to a full bath.

Design by
Alan Mascord
Design Associates, Inc.

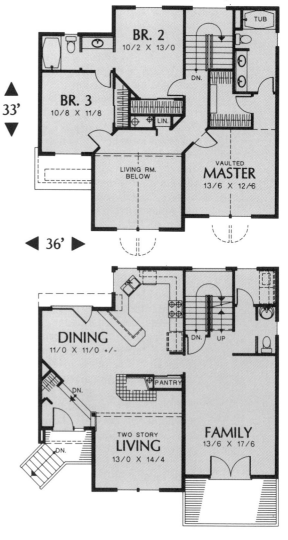

Design AA9510

Main Level: 800 square feet
Upper Level: 462 square feet
Lower Level: 732 square feet
Total: 1,994 square feet
Width 40'
Depth 42'-6"

● With undeniable style, this home would easily serve steep, daylight-basement lots. The lower level houses two bedrooms and the family room where sliding glass doors provide outdoor access. A utility area is tucked away near the full bath here. On the main level, the foyer opens to a two-story kitchen which affords room enough for a dinette set. A formal living room/dining room combination speaks for the rest of this level. Notice that the dining room is vaulted and enjoys a balcony over-looking the backyard. With true flair, the master bedroom impresses with its private upper-level location. A deck opens off the back of the room. The bath spoils with its dual lavatories and bumped-out spa tub.

Design by
Alan Mascord
Design Associates, Inc.

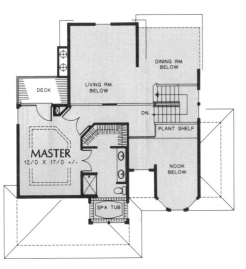

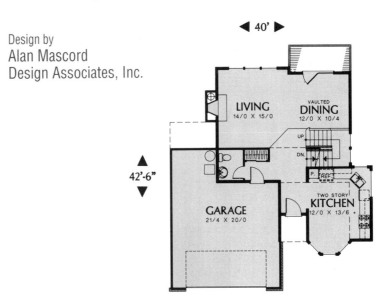

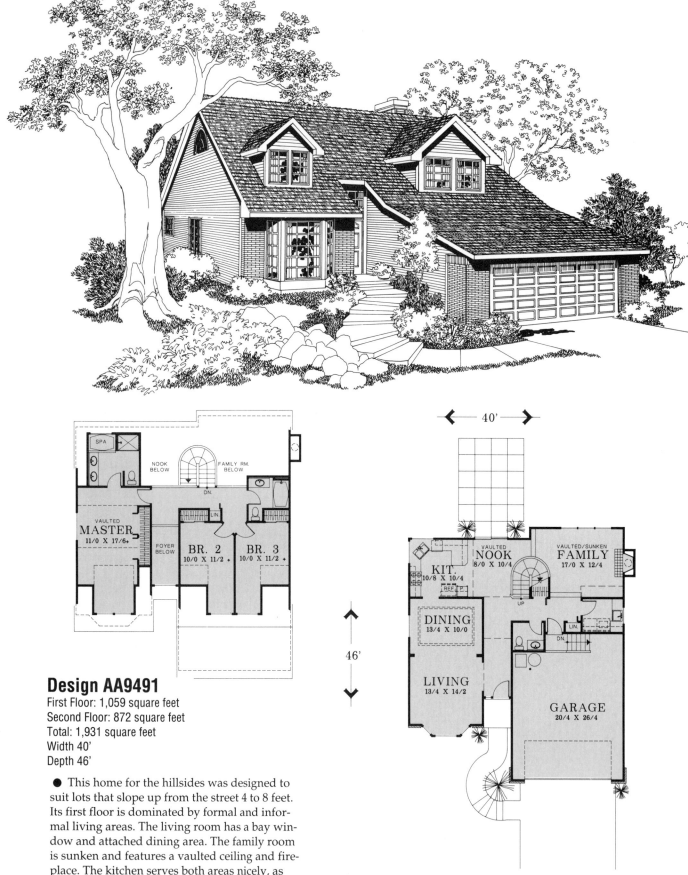

Design AA9491

First Floor: 1,059 square feet
Second Floor: 872 square feet
Total: 1,931 square feet
Width 40'
Depth 46'

● This home for the hillsides was designed to suit lots that slope up from the street 4 to 8 feet. Its first floor is dominated by formal and informal living areas. The living room has a bay window and attached dining area. The family room is sunken and features a vaulted ceiling and fireplace. The kitchen serves both areas nicely, as well as the casual nook eating area. Upstairs are three bedrooms. The master bedroom has a vaulted ceiling and luxurious bath. Two family bedrooms share a full bath. The upper floor balcony overlooks the nook and family room below.

Design by
Alan Mascord
Design Associates, Inc.

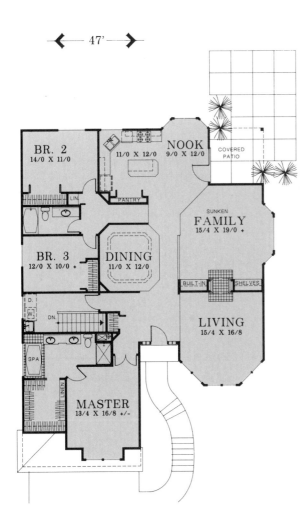

← 47' →

BR. 2
14/0 X 11/0

NOOK
9/0 X 12/0

11/0 X 12/0

COVERED
PATIO

PANTRY

LIN.

SUNKEN
FAMILY
15/4 X 19/0 +

BR. 3
12/0 X 10/0 +

DINING
11/0 X 12/0

BUILT-IN   SHELVES

D.

W.

DN.

SPA

LIVING
15/4 X 16/8

LINEN

MASTER
13/4 X 16/8 +/-

63'

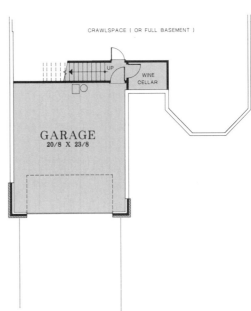

CRAWLSPACE (OR FULL BASEMENT)

UP

WINE
CELLAR

GARAGE
20/8 X 23/8

Design AA9492

Square Footage: 2,198
Width 47'
Depth 63'

● This home is perfect for a sloping lot with the garage at the lower level and the remainder of the house above. Special features of the home include a see-through fireplace between the living and family rooms, a bay-windowed nook, a large walk-in closet and spa in the master bedroom and a wine cellar just off the garage. The family room is sunken and also has a bay window. A covered patio is found just off the nook.

Design by
Alan Mascord
Design Associates, Inc.

PATIO   PATIO

REC ROOM
13'-4" x 18'-4"

FAMILY ROOM
23'-0" x 14'-8"

SHOP
32'-0" x 10'-4"

UNEX

UNEX   CRAWL SPACE   ACCESS

BEDROOM #2
14'-10" x 15'-0"

LIVING ROOM BELOW

BALCONY   DN

WALK-IN CLOSET

LINEN

FOYER BELOW

FURN

BEDROOM #3
18'-8" x 14'-0"

LINEN   STORAGE

Design AA4406

Main Level: 1,497 square feet
Upper Level: 848 square feet
Lower Level: 1,497 square feet
Total: 3,842 square feet
Width 38'
Depth 60'-9"

Design by
Home Planners,
Inc.

38'-0"

60'-9"

WINDOWS AT TOP OF WALL

BOOKS
FIREPLACE
BOOKS

MASTER BEDROOM
13'-10" x 18'-8"

LIVING ROOM
20'-8" X 15'-0"

SLOPED CEILING

WALK-IN CLOSET

LAUNDRY
WASH DRY

WET BAR

UP

FOYER

MECH

2 STORY FOYER

ENTRY

COATS

GARAGE
20'-0" X 20'-0"

DINING ROOM
12'-0" X 14'-0"

TRAY CEILING

CHINA   PANTRY

REF

KITCHEN
12'-0" X 10'-8"

VAULTED CEILING

DW

● Tame a narrow lot with this unique side-entry design. The front kitchen and dining room feature high ceilings while the sloped-ceiling living room has a fireplace and built-in bookshelves. The master suite on the first floor is separated from two bedrooms on the second floor, each with its own full bath. A lower-level basement holds a family room and a recreation room.

Design AA4391

Main Level: 1,315 square feet
Upper Level: 1,312 square feet
Lower Level: 1,273 square feet
Total: 3,900 square feet
Width 38'
Depth 33'

● This hillside home opens with formal and informal living areas to the left of the central foyer and dining and cooking areas to the right. A large deck to the back adds outdoor enjoyment. The master bedroom, with full bath, misses nothing in the way of luxury and is joined by two family bedrooms and baths. Bonus space to the front makes a perfect office or computer room. Note recreation room with fireplace.

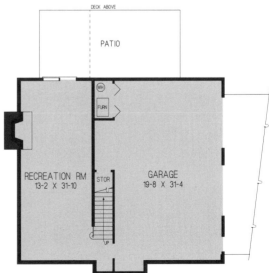

Design by
Home Planners, Inc.

Design AA4405

Main Level: 1,483 square feet
Upper Level: 882 square feet
Lower Level: 1,439 square feet
Total: 3,804 square feet
Width 37'-4"
Depth 54'

WOODEN DECK | GREENHOUSE | WOODEN DECK

PANTRY

KITCHEN
(SLOPED CEILING)

MASTER
BEDROOM
13'-8" x 18'-0"

DINING
ROOM
12'-0" x 14'-4"
(SLOPED CEILING)

REFR.

37'-4"

54'-0"

PANTRY

W D

DN

UP

LINENS

MASTER
BATH #1

WALK-IN
CLOSET

POWDER
ROOM

WET BAR

LIVING ROOM
15'-0" x 19'-8"
(SLOPED CEILING)

GARAGE
20'-0" x 20'-0"

BOOKS

COATS

FOYER

BEDROOM #2
13'-8" x 18'-0"
(TRAY CEILING)

SKYLIGHT

MEDIA BALCONY
(VAULTED CEILING)
10'-0" 12'-4"

DN

CLOSET

CLOSET

LINEN

CLOSET

BEDROOM #3
14'-0" x 16'-8"
(TRAY CEILING)

DECK ABOVE
PATIO

DECK ABOVE
PATIO

RECREATION ROOM
36'-4" x 17'-10"

UP

SHOP
21'-8" x 10'-8"

UNEX

UNFINISHED
BASEMENT

● There's no skimping on amenities here. Notice the special
extras: wet bar, fireplace, and built-in bookshelves in the
living room, greenhouse off the island kitchen, double decks
to the rear, skylights in the master bath and the vaulted ceiling
media balcony. Split-bedroom designing makes the master
suite a private retreat.

Design by
Home Planners,
Inc.

● By placing living areas to the back of this plan, a wide rear and side deck can be enjoyed in privacy away from street noise. The large central dining room has access to the deck and leads to the sunken living room. Sleeping accommodations on the second floor allow for a large master suite and two more bedrooms with full bath.

Design by
Home Planners,
Inc.

Design AA4404

Main Level: 1,336 square feet
Upper Level: 1,210 square feet
Lower Level: 1,332 square feet
Total: 3,878 square feet
Width 30'
Depth 73'

L

CUSTOMIZABLE

Custom Alterations? See page 221 for customizing this plan to your specifications.

Copyright 1992 Stephen S. Fuller, Inc.

Design AA9879

Square Footage: 1,770
Width 48'
Depth 47'

● The country cottage styling of this stately brick home includes brick detailing framing the front entry and windows. Gambles and a multi-level roof help create the soft charm of this design. The foyer provides views into both the large great room with warming hearth and the dining room with vaulted ceiling, making a tremendous first impression. From the great room, one enters the kitchen with spacious work area and adjacent breakfast room including a boxed bay window. The second level offers two bedrooms and a bath in an arrangement well-suited for children. The master bedroom is entered through large double doors and features a tray ceiling and French doors leading to a private deck. The master bath is generous and complete with His and Hers vanities, garden tub and large walk-in closet.

Design by
Design Traditions

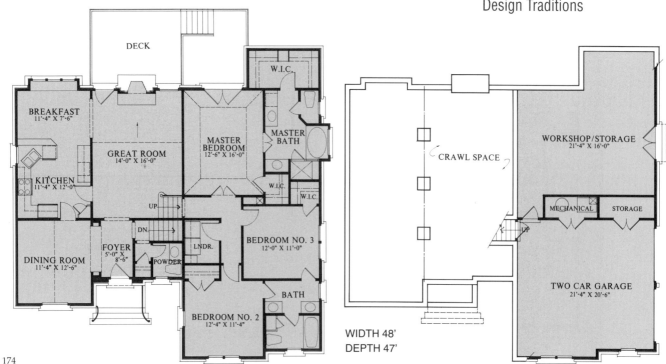

DECK

BREAKFAST
11'-4" X 7'-6"

W.I.C.

GREAT ROOM
14'-0" X 16'-0"

MASTER
BEDROOM
12'-6" X 16'-0"

MASTER
BATH

KITCHEN
11'-4" X 12'-0"

W.I.C.

UP

W.I.C.

DN

BEDROOM NO. 3
12'-0" X 11'-0"

FOYER
5'-0" X
8'-6"

LNDR.

POWDER

DINING ROOM
11'-4" X 12'-6"

BATH

BEDROOM NO. 2
12'-4" X 11'-4"

CRAWL SPACE

WORKSHOP/STORAGE
21'-4" X 16'-0"

MECHANICAL

STORAGE

UP

TWO CAR GARAGE
21'-4" X 20'-6"

WIDTH 48'
DEPTH 47'

Design AA9841

Square Footage: 1,725 (without basement)
Width 47'-6"
Depth 45'-6"

● European style takes beautifully to a sloped lot. This design tames a slight grade by making use of a hillside garage. The main living area is split into two levels accessed from the foyer. The lower entry level holds living and dining space; the upper level houses bedrooms.

Design by
Design Traditions

WIDTH 47'-6"
DEPTH 45'-6"

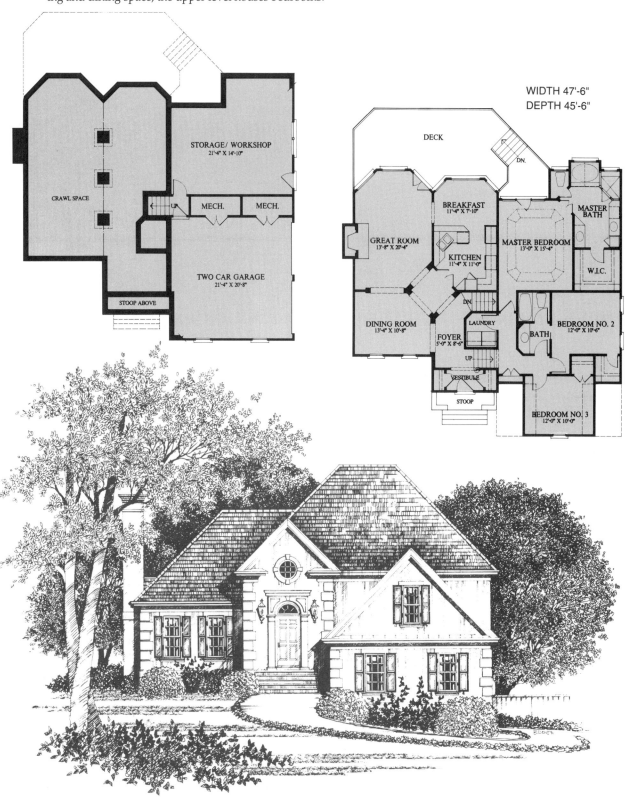

CRAWL SPACE

STORAGE/ WORKSHOP
21'-4" X 14'-10"

MECH.   MECH.

UP

TWO CAR GARAGE
21'-4" X 20'-8"

STOOP ABOVE

DECK

DN.

GREAT ROOM
13'-8" X 20'-4"

BREAKFAST
11'-4" X 7'-10"

KITCHEN
11'-4" X 11'-0"

MASTER BEDROOM
13'-0" X 15'-4"

MASTER BATH

W.I.C.

DN

DINING ROOM
13'-4" X 10'-8"

LAUNDRY

BATH

BEDROOM NO. 2
12'-0" X 10'-6"

FOYER
5'-0" X 8'-6"

UP

VESTIBULE

STOOP

BEDROOM NO. 3
12'-0" X 10'-0"

Design AA9345

Main Level: 1,499 square feet
Lower Level: 57 square feet
Total: 1,556 square feet
Width 50'
Depth 40'

● A high-impact entry defines the exterior of this special multi-level home design. A formal dining room with interesting ceiling detail and a boxed window is open to the entry. In the volume great room, homeowners will enjoy a handsome brick fireplace and large windows to the back. Wrapping counters, a corner sink, Lazy Susan and pantry add convenience to the thoughtful kitchen. The adjoining bayed breakfast area has a sloped ceiling and arched transom window. The three bedrooms in this home provide privacy from the main living areas. Two secondary bedrooms share the hall bath. Last, but not least, the master suite offers a vaulted ceiling, skylit dressing/bath area with double vanity, walk-in closet and whirlpool tub.

Design by
Design
Basics,
Inc.

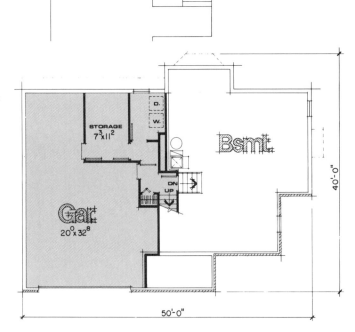

© 1987 design basics inc.

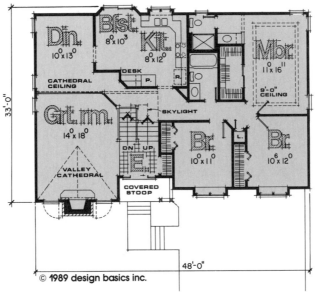

Dn.
10⁰ x 13⁰

Bfst.
8⁰ x 10³

Kit.
8⁰ x 12⁰

DESK

P.

R.

CATHEDRAL CEILING

Mbr.
11⁰ x 16⁰

9'-0" CEILING

Grt. rm.
14⁰ x 18⁰

SKYLIGHT

DN UP

Br.
10⁰ x 11⁰

L.

Br.
10⁶ x 12⁰

VALLEY CATHEDRAL

COVERED STOOP

33'-0"

48'-0"

© 1989 design basics inc.

Design AA9291

Square Footage: 1,458
Width 48'
Depth 33'

● From the volume entry, expansive views of the great room and dining room captivate home owners and guests. The great room with a fireplace centered under the valley cathedral ceiling beckons. An efficient kitchen which serves the bright dinette has a pantry and planning desk. The cathedral ceiling in the dining room adds to the atmosphere of meals and entertaining. Two secondary bedrooms with boxed windows are accessed by the corridor hallway. Comfort abounds in the master suite with 9-foot tiered ceiling plus mirrored bi-pass doors for the walk-in closet and private bath.

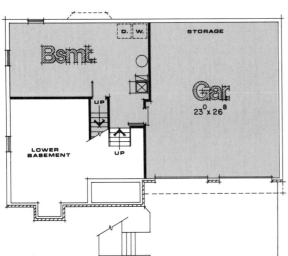

Bsmt.

STORAGE

D. W.

Gar.
23⁰ x 26⁸

UP

UP

LOWER BASEMENT

Design by
Design Basics, Inc.

177

Design AA2608 Main Level: 728 square feet
Upper Level: 874 square feet; Lower Level: 310 square feet
Total: 1,912 square feet
Width 56'-8"
Depth 36'-5"

L **D**

Cost to build? See page 214
to order complete cost estimate
to build this house in your area!

● Here is tri-level livability with a fourth basement level for bulk storage and, perhaps, a shop area. There are four bedrooms, a handy laundry, two eating areas, formal and informal living areas and two fireplaces. Sliding glass doors in the formal dining room and the family room open to a terrace. The U-shaped kitchen has a built-in range/oven and a storage pantry. The breakfast nook overlooks the family room. The sleeping quarters consist of three secondary bedrooms and a master bedroom. The master suite enjoys a private bath with a dressing area and a walk-in closet. There's also a balcony off this bedroom. The two-car garage will accommodate the family vehicles and storage.

Design by
Home Planners,
Inc.

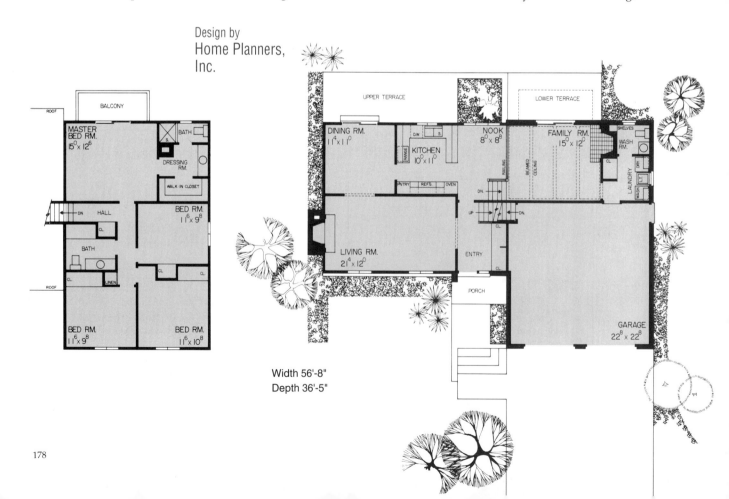

Width 56'-8"
Depth 36'-5"

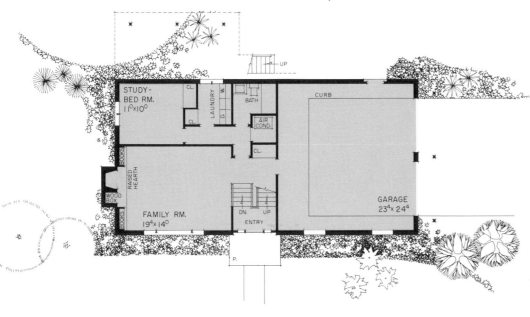

DECK

RAILING

DN.

DINING RM.
11⁰x12⁰

BREAKFAST
7⁰x12⁰

RANGE

KIT.
9⁰x12⁰

REF'G.

D.W.

S.

CL. CL.

DRESS.
RM.

BATH

VANITY

MASTER
BED RM.
14⁰x13⁶

PANTRY
DESK
CHINA

CL.

BATH

VANITY

CL.

LINEN

3' HI. STORAGE

DN. UP

ENTRY

CL.

BED RM.
10⁰x10⁰

CL.

BED RM.
11⁰x13⁶

LIVING RM.
19⁸x15⁰

P.

Width 54'-8"
Depth 28'

Design AA1850

Main Level: 1,456 square feet
Lower Level: 728 square feet
Total: 2,184 square feet
Width 54'-8"
Depth 28'

● A perfect rectangle, this
split-level is comparatively
inexpensive to build and very
appealing to live in. It features
a large upper-level living room
with fireplace, formal dining
room, three bedrooms (with
two full baths nearby), and an
outdoor deck. Another fireplace warms the family room
on the lower level, which also
has a full bath and room for a
study or fourth bedroom.

UP

STUDY-
BED RM.
11⁰x10⁰

CL.

LAUNDRY

W

D

BATH

AIR
COND.

CL.

CURB

BOOKS

RAISED HEARTH

WOOD
BOX

BOOKS

FAMILY RM.
19⁴x14⁰

DN. UP

ENTRY

GARAGE
23⁴x24⁴

P.

Design by
Home Planners,
Inc.

Quote One™

Cost to build? See page 214
to order complete cost estimate
to build this house in your area!

54'-0"

TERRACE

TERRACE

BALCONY

DINING RM.
11⁰+BAY x 13⁶

KITCHEN
9⁸x13⁶

BRKFST RM.
9⁰x13⁶

FAMILY RM.
23⁰x13⁶

MASTER
BED RM.
13⁰x19⁴

WALK-IN
CLOSET

RANGE

DRESSING
RM.

BRM. OVEN
CL.

DESK

PANTRY

BATH

44'-4"

CL.

DN

W.R.

LT. W D

LAUNDRY
7⁰x7⁶

BED RM./
STUDY
11⁰x11⁰

UP

HALL

LIVING RM.
20⁴+BAY x 13⁶

FOYER

BATH

CL.

LINEN

CURB

CL.

CL.

COVERED PORCH

GARAGE
23⁴x21⁸

BED RM.
12⁰x11⁰

STOR

BED RM.
11⁰x16⁸

Design AA2786
Main Level: 871 square feet
Upper Level: 1,132 square feet
Lower Level: 528 square feet
Total: 2,531 square feet
Width 54'
Depth 44'-4"

Design by
Home Planners,
Inc.

● A bay window in each the formal living room and dining room. A great interior and exterior design feature to attract attention to this tri-level home. The exterior also is enhanced by a covered front porch to further the

Colonial charm. The interior livability is outstanding, too. An abundance of built-ins in the kitchen create an efficient work center. Features include an island range, pantry, broom closet, desk and breakfast room with

sliding glass doors to the rear terrace. The lower level houses the informal family room, wash room and laundry. Further access is available to the outdoors by the family room to the terrace and laundry room to the side yard.

TERRACE

TERRACE

BALCONY

FAMILY RM.
15² x 19²

AIR COND.

LAUNDRY
D.
W

CL.

WASH ROOM

BREAKFAST RM.
10⁴ x 12⁶

KITCHEN
10⁴ x 12⁶

RANGE

DINING RM.
11⁰ x 14⁶

REF'S.

DW

LS

S

PANTRY

DESK

OVENS

BRM. CL.

RAISED HEARTH

DN

CL.

FOYER

UP.

CL.

LIVING RM.
23⁰ x 16⁶

CURB

GARAGE
24⁸ x 20⁴

PORCH

MASTER BEDROOM
18⁰ x 14⁰

SHLVS.

WALK-IN CLOSET

ROOF

DRESSING RM.

BEDROOM/ STUDY
12⁰ x 11⁰

LINEN

BATH

DN

CL.

CL.

CL.

LEDGE

BATH

CL.

ROOF

BEDROOM
12⁰ x 14⁴

BEDROOM
13⁰ x 11⁰

Width 58'
Depth 45'-4"

Design by
Home Planners, Inc.

Design AA2787

Main Level: 976 square feet; Upper Level: 1,118 square feet; Lower Level: 524 square feet; Total: 2,618 square feet
Width 58'
Depth 45'-4"

L **D**

● Three level living! Main, upper and lower levels to serve you and your family with great ease. Start from the bottom and work your way up. Family room with raised hearth fireplace, laundry and wash room on the lower level. Formal living and dining rooms, kitchen and breakfast room on the main level. Stop and take note at the efficiency of the kitchen with its many outstanding extras. The upper level houses the three bedrooms, study (or fourth bedroom if you prefer) and two baths. This design has really stacked up its livability to serve its occupants to their best advantage. This design has great interior livability and exterior charm.

DECK

arched window above door

GREAT RM.
15-4 × 20-0

BRKFST.
8-0 × 10-0

w
d

MASTER
BED RM.
13-4 × 13-4

fireplace

(cathedral ceiling)

KIT.
13-4 × 7-4

walk-in
closet

walk-in
closet

master
bath

down

DINING
13-4 × 10-4

cl   FOYER
10-0 × 9-4

BED RM.
13-4 × 13-4

bath

PORCH
24-0 × 6-0

55 – 1

45 - 8

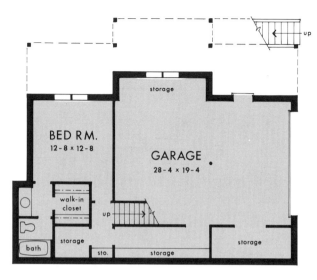

storage

BED RM.
12-8 × 12-8

GARAGE
28-4 × 19-4

up

walk-in
closet

up

storage

bath

storage

sto.   storage

storage

Design AA9684

Square Footage: 1,528
Basement (heated): 394; (unheated): 851
Width 45'-8"
Depth 55'-1"

Design by
**Donald A.
Gardner,
Architects, Inc.**

● Loaded with charm, this compact plan has plenty of
livability within its walls. The main floor contains a great
room, a formal dining room, an island kitchen with an
attached breakfast nook, a grand master suite and one
family bedroom. On the garage level is a wealth of storage in addition to the bedroom with a full bath. A rear
deck adds great outdoor livability. For a crawl-space
foundation, order Design AA9684; for a basement foundation, order Design AA9684-A.

B·NATHAN

Design AA9683

Square Footage: 1,004
Basement (heated): 923 square feet
Total: 1,927 square feet
Width 65'-8"
Depth 82'-8"

● This three-bedroom contemporary is designed for a hillside view. The great room and dining room share a fireplace open on both sides and a large deck accessible to both spaces. The great room has a sloped ceiling with a clerestory for natural light and ventilation. The dining room has a cathedral ceiling. The kitchen offers a pass-through to the dining room. All bedrooms are on the lower level for privacy. The generous master bath accommodates a shower, garden tub and a double-bowl vanity. Two additional bedrooms share a separate full bath.

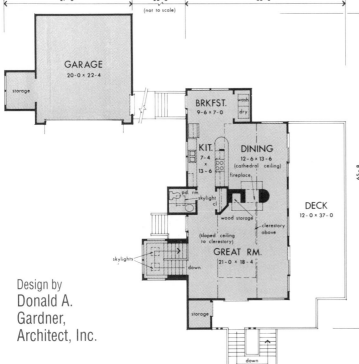

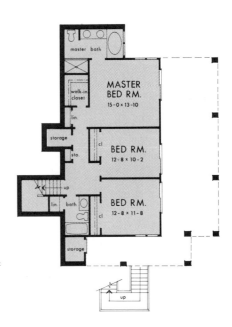

Design by
Donald A.
Gardner,
Architect, Inc.

GARAGE
20-0 x 22-4

storage

BRKFST.
9-6 x 7-0

wash
dry

KIT.
7-4
x
13-6

DINING
12-6 x 13-6
(cathedral ceiling)

fireplace

pd. rm.

cl

skylight

wood storage

DECK
12-0 x 37-0

clerestory
above

(sloped ceiling
to clerestory)

skylights

GREAT RM.
21-0 x 18-4

down

storage

down

master bath

walk-in
closet

lin.

storage

sto.

lin.

bath

MASTER
BED RM.
15-0 x 13-10

BED RM.
12-8 x 10-2

up

BED RM.
12-8 x 11-8

storage

up

27-0

22-0
(not to scale)

33-8

65-8

Design AA2841

Main Level: 1,044 square feet
Upper Level: 851 square feet
Lower Level: 753 square feet
Total: 2,648 square feet
Width 44'   Depth 62'-4"

L

● This spacious tri-level with traditional stone exterior offers excellent comfort and zoning for the modern family. The rear opens to balconies and a deck that creates a covered patio below. A main floor gathering room is continued above with an upper gathering room. The lower level offers an activities room with raised hearth, in addition to an optional bunk room with bath. A modern kitchen on main level features a handy snack bar, in addition to a dining room. A study on main level could become an optional bedroom. The master bedroom is located on the upper level, along with a rectangular bunk room with its own balcony.

TERRACE

ACTIVITIES RM.
15⁰ x 18⁰

BUNK RM. OPTIONAL
11⁴ x 15⁴

BASEMENT

RAISED HEARTH

AIR COND.

BATH

UP

STORAGE CABINETS

L.T. WASH DRY CL

UNEX

WIDTH 44'
DEPTH 62'-4"

UNEX

Design by
Home Planners, Inc.

DECK

GATHERING RM.
15⁰ x 18⁰

BALCONY

STUDY/ BEDROOM
11⁸ x 12⁸

BALCONY ABOVE

DINING RM.
11⁸ x 10⁰

SNACK BAR
RANGE

KITCHEN
11⁸ x 11⁰

CL
SEAT

BATH

FOYER

BRM CL

REF'G. DW

PORCH

CURB

GARAGE
21⁰ x 22⁰ + STORAGE

STORAGE

BALCONY

UPPER GATHERING RM.

BALCONY

BEDROOM
11⁸ x 12⁸

BUNK RM.
11⁸ x 18⁸

RAILING

LOUNGE
15⁰ x 6⁰

LINEN

RAILING   RAILING

BATH

SEAT

UPPER FOYER

DN

CL   CL

Design AA2842

Entrance Level: 156 square feet; Upper Level: 1,038 square feet
Lower Level: 1,022 square feet; Total: 2,216 square feet
Width 42'
Depth 58'-4"

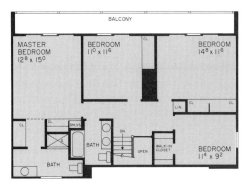

● This narrow, 42 foot width, house can be built on a narrow lot to cut down overall costs. Yet its dramatic appeal surely is worth a million. The projecting front garage creates a pleasing curved drive. One enters this house through the covered porch to the entrance level foyer. At this point the stairs lead down to the living area consisting of formal living room, family room, kitchen and dining area then up the stairs to the four bedroom-two bath sleeping area. The indoor-outdoor living relationship at the rear is outstanding.

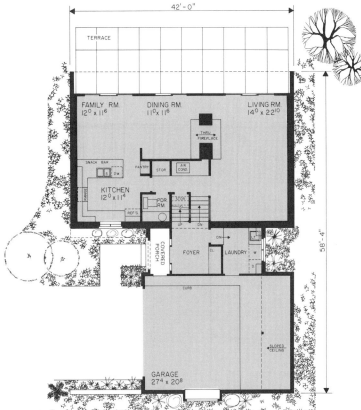

Design by
Home Planners,
Inc.

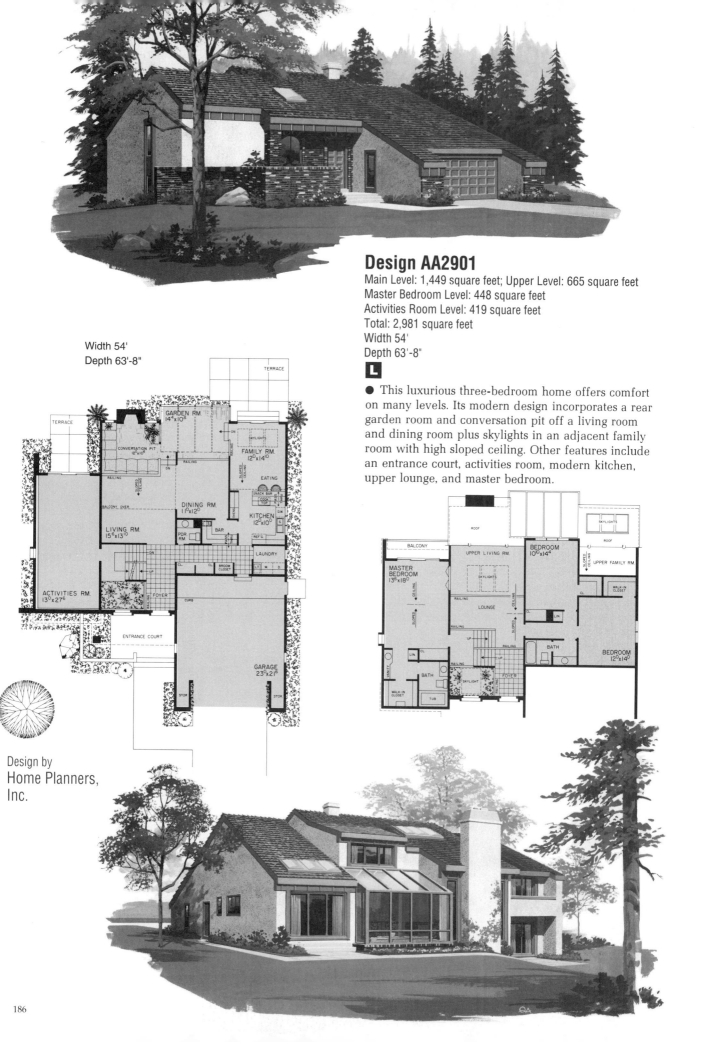

Design AA2901

Main Level: 1,449 square feet; Upper Level: 665 square feet
Master Bedroom Level: 448 square feet
Activities Room Level: 419 square feet
Total: 2,981 square feet
Width 54'
Depth 63'-8"

L

● This luxurious three-bedroom home offers comfort
on many levels. Its modern design incorporates a rear
garden room and conversation pit off a living room
and dining room plus skylights in an adjacent family
room with high sloped ceiling. Other features include
an entrance court, activities room, modern kitchen,
upper lounge, and master bedroom.

Width 54'
Depth 63'-8"

Design by
Home Planners,
Inc.

Design AA2828

First Floor: 817 square feet (Living Area); Foyer & Laundry: 261 square feet
Second Floor: 852 square feet (Living Area); Foyer & Storage: 214 square feet; Total: 2,144 square feet
Width 44'-8"
Depth 52'

● A fine contemporary design in two stories, this home also extends its livability to the basement where bonus space could be converted later to an activities or hobby room. On the first floor, living areas revolve around a central kitchen with snack bar in the dining room. The first-floor bedroom could also serve as a study, family room or library. Note the raised-hearth fireplace in the living room. Upstairs are three bedrooms, or two and a lounge, and a sewing or hobby room. Two long balconies here overlook the terrace below.

Design by
Home Planners,
Inc.

Design AA2511

Main Level: 1,043 square feet
Upper Level: 703 square feet
Lower Level: 794 square feet
Total: 2,540 square feet
Width 40'-4"
Depth 52'

L **D**

QUOTE ONE™

Cost to build? See page 214
to order complete cost estimate
to build this house in your area!

● Study this outstanding multi-level with its dramatic outdoor deck and balconies. This home is ideal if you are looking for a home that is new and exciting. The livability that it offers will efficiently serve your family.

Design by
Home Planners,
Inc.

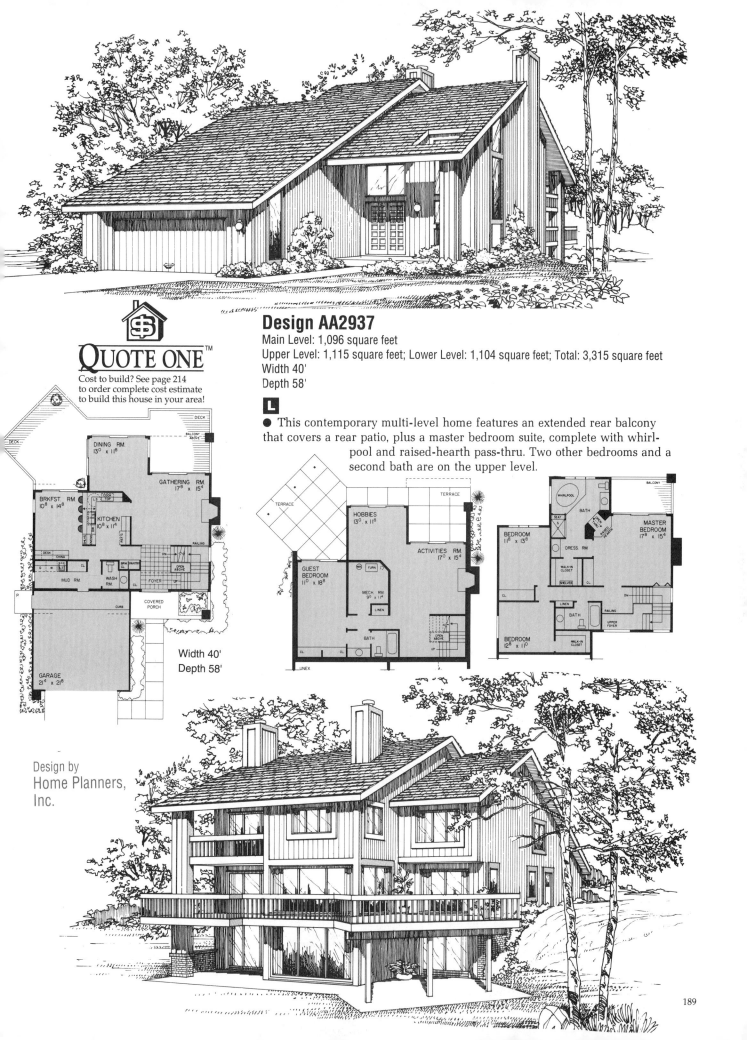

Design AA2937

Main Level: 1,096 square feet
Upper Level: 1,115 square feet; Lower Level: 1,104 square feet; Total: 3,315 square feet
Width 40'
Depth 58'

L

● This contemporary multi-level home features an extended rear balcony that covers a rear patio, plus a master bedroom suite, complete with whirlpool and raised-hearth pass-thru. Two other bedrooms and a second bath are on the upper level.

Width 40'
Depth 58'

Design by
Home Planners,
Inc.

DECK

DINING RM.
13⁰ x 11⁸

BALCONY
ABOVE

DECK

BRKFST. RM.
10⁸ x 14⁸

GATHERING RM.
17⁶ x 15⁴

KITCHEN
10⁸ x 11⁴

DESK
CHINA
CL

MUD RM.

PANTRY

WASH RM.

FOYER

RAILING

OPEN ABOVE

UP

COVERED
PORCH

CURB

GARAGE
21⁴ x 21⁸

TERRACE

HOBBIES
13⁰ x 11⁸

TERRACE

ACTIVITIES RM.
17⁰ x 15⁴

GUEST
BEDROOM
11⁰ x 18⁸

MECH. RM.
9⁰ x 11⁰

LINEN

BATH

OPEN ABOVE

UP

UNEX

WHIRLPOOL

BATH

SEAT

RAISED HEARTH

MASTER
BEDROOM
17⁸ x 15⁴

BEDROOM
11⁸ x 13⁸

BALCONY

DRESS. RM.

WALK-IN
CLOSET

SHELVES

CL

LINEN

BATH

DN

RAILING

UPPER
FOYER

BEDROOM
12⁸ x 11⁰

WALK-IN
CLOSET

189

● You can't help but feel spoiled by this design. Behind the handsome facade lies a spacious, amenity-filled plan. Downstairs from the entry is the large living room with sloped ceiling and fireplace. Nearby is the U-shaped kitchen with a pass-through to the din-ing room — a convenient step-saver. Also on this level, the master suite boasts a fireplace and a sliding glass door onto the deck. The living and din-ing rooms also feature deck access. Upstairs are two bedrooms and shared bath. A balcony sitting area overlooks the living room. The enormous lower-level playroom includes a fireplace, a large bar, and sliding glass doors to the patio. Also notice the storage room with built-in workbench.

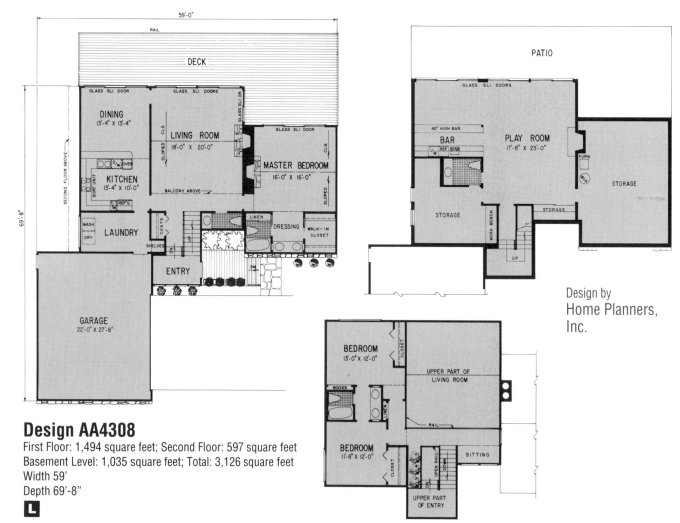

Design by
Home Planners, Inc.

Design AA4308

First Floor: 1,494 square feet; Second Floor: 597 square feet
Basement Level: 1,035 square feet; Total: 3,126 square feet
Width 59'
Depth 69'-8"

L

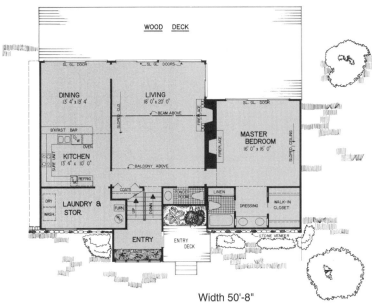

WOOD DECK

DINING
13' 4" x 13' 4"

LIVING
18' 0" x 20' 0"

BEAM ABOVE

MASTER BEDROOM
16' 0" x 16' 0"

SL. GL. DOOR

B'K'FAST BAR

OVEN

KITCHEN
13' 4" x 10' 0"

REFRIG

BALCONY ABOVE

DRY
WASH

LAUNDRY & STOR.

FURN

UP

DOWN

COATS

POWDER ROOM

LINEN

DRESSING

WALK-IN CLOSET

ENTRY

ENTRY DECK

STONE VENEER

Width 50'-8"
Depth 47'-8"

Design AA4115

Main Level: 1,494 square feet
Upper Level: 597 square feet
Total: 2,091 square feet
Width 50'-8"
Depth 47'-8" (including deck)

Design by
Home Planners,
Inc.

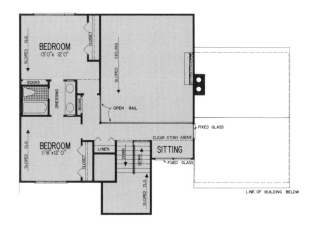

BEDROOM
13'0"x 12'0"

BOOKS

DRESSING

OPEN RAIL

CLEAR STORY ABOVE

FIXED GLASS

BEDROOM
11'8"x12'0"

LINEN

DOWN

SITTING

FIXED GLASS

LINE OF BUILDING BELOW

● Here is a home that's moderately sized without sacrificing livability. Just off the entry is a large, two-story living room. There's also a dining room with a breakfast bar/pass-through to the kitchen. To the rear is an enormous deck for sunning and relaxing. A split-sleeping area features two upper-level bedrooms and a main-level master bedroom. Notice the fireplace and sloped ceilings.

There's a lot to love in this wood-and-stone contemporary. From three wood decks to the second-floor balcony overlook, the planning is just right. The split-bedroom design puts the master bedroom on the first floor. It is luxuriously appointed with a sloped ceiling, fireplace, walk-in closet, and deck access. A U-shaped kitchen serves both breakfast room and dining room. On the basement level is a large playroom, a washroom, and shop area that could be converted to a fourth bedroom with full bath.

Design AA4331

First Floor: 1,580 square feet
Second Floor: 730 square feet
Basement Level: 1,323 square feet
Total: 3,633 square feet
Width 58'
Depth 60'

Design by
Home Planners,
Inc.

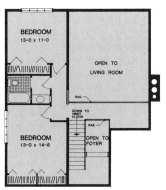

BEDROOM
13-0 x 11-0

OPEN TO
LIVING ROOM

RAIL

DOWN TO
FIRST
FLOOR

RAIL

BEDROOM
13-0 x 14-8

OPEN TO
FOYER

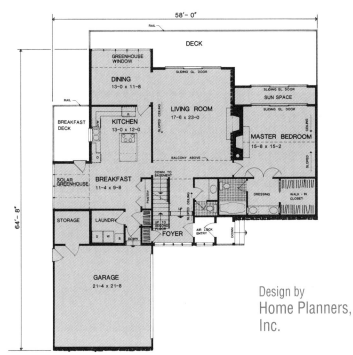

58'-0"

RAIL

DECK

GREENHOUSE
WINDOW

DINING
13-0 x 11-8

SLIDING GL. DOOR

SLIDING GL. DOOR

SUN SPACE

RAIL

BREAKFAST
DECK

KITCHEN
13-0 x 12-0

LIVING ROOM
17-6 x 23-0

SLOPED CEILING

SLIDING GL. DOOR

MASTER BEDROOM
15-8 x 15-2

SLOPED CEILING

BALCONY ABOVE

64'-8"

SOLAR
GREENHOUSE

BREAKFAST
11-4 x 9-8

DOWN TO
BASEMENT

PANTRY

SLOPED CEILING

DRESSING

WALK-IN
CLOSET

STORAGE

LAUNDRY

D   W   S

UP TO
SECOND
FLOOR

DOWN

UP TO
SECOND
FLOOR

FOYER

AIR LOCK
ENTRY

DOWN

GARAGE
21-4 x 21-8

Design by
Home Planners,
Inc.

Design AA4334

First Floor: 1,838 square feet
Second Floor: 640 square feet
Total: 2,478 square feet
Width 58'
Depth 64'-8"

● Grand sloping rooflines and a design
created for southern orientation are the
unique features of this contemporary
home. Outdoor living is enhanced by a
solar greenhouse off the breakfast room,
a sun space off the master bedroom, a
greenhouse window in the dining room,
a casual breakfast deck, and full-width
deck to the rear. The split-bedroom plan
allows for the master suite (with fireplace, and huge walk-in closet) to be situated on the first floor and two family
bedrooms and a full bath to find space
on the second floor. Be sure to notice
the balcony overlook to the sloped-
ceiling living room below.

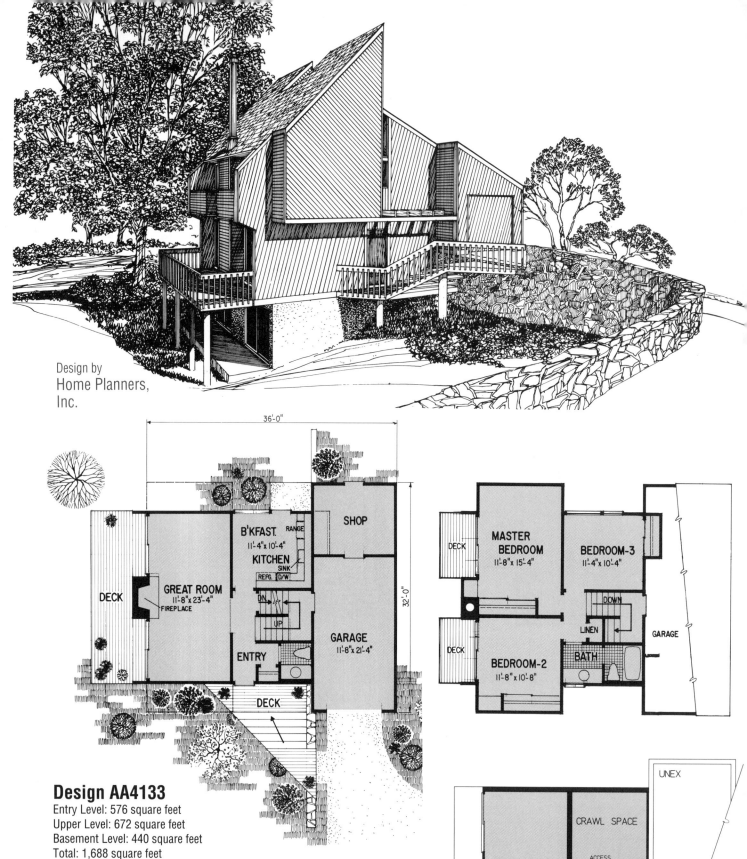

36'-0"

32'-0"

DECK

GREAT ROOM
11'-8" x 23'-4"
FIREPLACE

B'KFAST.
11'-4" x 10'-4"

RANGE

SHOP

KITCHEN
SINK
REFG. D/W

DN

UP

ENTRY

GARAGE
11'-8" x 21'-4"

DECK

DECK

DECK

MASTER BEDROOM
11'-8" x 15'-4"

BEDROOM-3
11'-4" x 10'-4"

DOWN

LINEN

GARAGE

BEDROOM-2
11'-8" x 10'-8"

BATH

UNEX

PATIO

FAMILY RM
11'-8" X 22'-8"

CRAWL SPACE

ACCESS

STOR

UP

STORAGE

FURN

WH

Design AA4133

Entry Level: 576 square feet
Upper Level: 672 square feet
Basement Level: 440 square feet
Total: 1,688 square feet
Width 36'
Depth 32'

L

● Narrow hillside lots are easily tamed with this unique design. At entry level are all the elements of modern livability: large great room with fireplace and deck, powder room off the entry, and an L-shaped kitchen with breakfast room. Of three second-floor bedrooms, two have private decks. The basement can be developed into casual living space. Note the workshop area just next to the garage.

Design by
Home Planners,
Inc.

Narrow Houses For Corner Lots Or Side Entry

Encompassing greater variety in lot arrangement while maintaining a fine selection of home styles, this section on narrow houses for corner lots or side entry acts as an appropriate conclusion to the array of homes offered in this book. With an added design feature—a side-load garage—the houses in this section present not only a greater variety in appearances, but also new opportunities for the building site. A corner-lot site is perfect for showcasing a house, and any of the designs in this section will make a grand statement.

A true suburban delight, the Colonial featured on page 205 will dignify any neighborhood. With its side-load garage located on the right and a wraparound porch accounting for the front and left sides this home has a handsome facade. And the inside lives up to the introduction: formal living takes precedence with separate living and dining rooms while a beamed family room, a sun room and four upstairs bedrooms spoil the family.

Maintaining narrow-lot variety, page 200 presents a plan with two different exterior elevations available. One offers sheer elegance with stucco, columns and arched windows while the other offers a more countrified appearance. Whichever you choose, the amenities and conveniences remain the same. A detached garage allows for flexibility in placement; if you like, move the garage back and extend the deck. The deck and the privacy afforded by the placement of the garage presents an ideal environment for a pool.

Versatility is displayed in the plan featured on page 210. Totally Southwestern, this house utilizes all of the modern amenities while maintaining its exquisite character. The clever masking of the garage helps to maintain an authentic appearance. A front courtyard, a covered porch, beam ceilings and rounded corners further this authenticity.

Perhaps most recognizable as a classic corner-lot house, the home on page 208, measuring only 44' wide, makes use of a rear garage connected by a covered porch. A quaint flower court rests in the area between the main house and the garage. A snack-bar pass-through to the kitchen makes the covered porch a delightful place to enjoy breakfast, lunch or dinner!

Design AA9848 First Floor: 915 square feet
Second Floor: 935 square feet; Total: 1,850 square feet
Width 38'
Depth 43'

Design by
Design Traditions

DECK

BREAKFAST
13'-4" x 10'-0"

DINING
9'-6" x 13'-6"

FAMILY ROOM
13'-6" x 20'-0"

KITCHEN
11'-0" x 10'-0"

POWDER

UP
FOYER

TWO-CAR GARAGE
20'-0" x 22'-6"

Width 38'
Depth 43'

● The appearance of this home suggests classic values. On entry, the foyer opens to a generous family room with a fireplace and views to the large deck beyond. The adjacent dining room is framed by columns. In the kitchen, the design maximizes convenience. The staircase off the foyer leads to the upper level where the master suite and two family bedrooms are found. A bonus room completes the second floor. This home is designed with a basement foundation.

W.I.C.

M.BATH

BEDROOM No.2
11'-8" x 10'-0"

BATH

W.I.C.

MASTER SUITE
13'-0" x 15'-0"

BEDROOM No.3
10'-8" x 10'-0"

LAUN.

DN

BONUS

Design AA9847

First Floor: 1,225 square feet
Second Floor: 565 square feet
Total: 1,790 square feet
Width 42'
Depth 50'

● The exterior of this home is intriguing and inviting. The combination of materials and shapes is reminiscent of an English country home. Beyond the columned entry is a classic raised foyer which leads to a sunken dining room and a great room. The openness of the plan is evident in the kitchen and the breakfast area. The master bedroom boasts a tray ceiling, a fireplace and a bay window. The open gallery staircase overlooks the great room and provides entry to two more bedrooms as well as an unfinished bonus room. This home is designed with a basement foundation.

Design by
Design Traditions

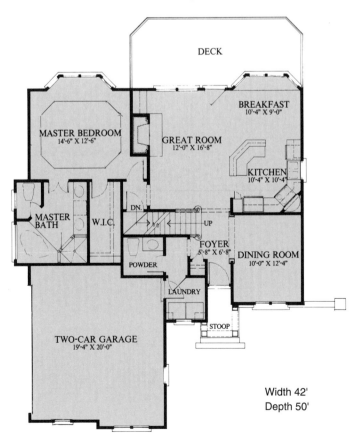

Width 42'
Depth 50'

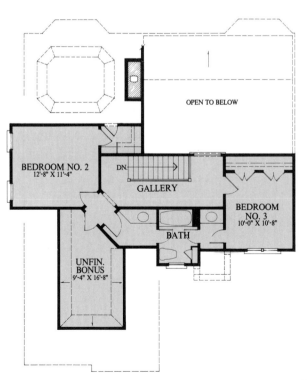

Copyright 1992 Stephen S. Fuller, Inc.

Design AA9876

First Floor: 1,720 square feet
Second Floor: 545 square feet
Total: 2,265 square feet
Width 50'
Depth 53'-6"

● The foyer opens to the living and dining areas, providing a spectacular entrance to this English country cottage. Just beyond the dining room is a gourmet kitchen with work island and food bar opening onto the breakfast room. Accented by a fireplace and built-in bookcase, the family room with a ribbon of windows is an excellent setting for family gatherings. Remotely located off the central hallway, the master suite includes a rectangular ceiling detail and access to the rear deck, while the master bath features His and Hers vanities, garden tub, and spacious walk-in closet. The central staircase leads to the balcony overlook and three bedrooms with spacious closets and baths.

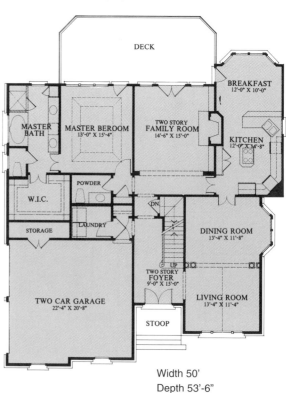

Design by
Design Traditions

Width 50'
Depth 53'-6"

Design AA9849

First Floor: 780 square feet
Second Floor: 915 square feet
Total: 1,695 square feet
Width 41'
Depth 41'

● The lines of this home are very clean, as well as traditional. Inside, contemporary priorities reign. To the left of the foyer is the powder room. Opposite is a formal dining room with passage to the kitchen, which is open to the breakfast area and the great room. This area is particularly well-suited to entertaining both formally and informally, with an open, airy design to the kitchen. The large fireplace is well placed and framed by glass and light. Opening from the great room is a two-car garage and a staircase to the second level. The master suite's double-door entrance, tray ceiling and fireplace are of special interest. The adjoining master bath and the walk-in closet complement this area well. The laundry room is found on this level, convenient to all three bedrooms. This home is designed with a basement foundation.

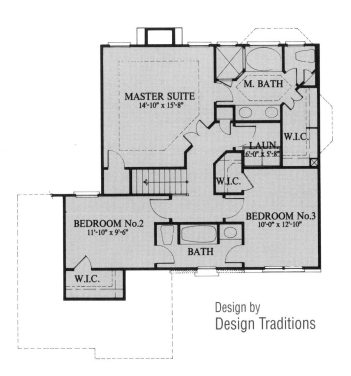

Design by
Design Traditions

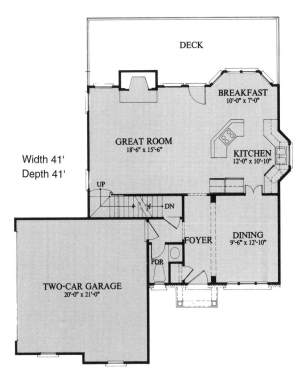

AA9655

AA9655-REAR

Designs by
Donald A.
Gardner,
Architect, Inc.

GARAGE
20-4 × 20-4

DECK
43-0 × 10-0

covered
breezeway

skylights
hot tub
SUN RM.
15-8 × 7-10

fireplace
GREAT RM.
20-0 × 15-6
(cathedral ceiling)

UTILITY
8-10 × 5-4

wash

powder rm.

bath

lin.

BED RM.
11-4 × 13-8

master bath

walk-in closet

FOYER
4-6 × 12-4

DINING
12-0 × 12-0

KITCHEN
14-4 × 12-0

cl

MASTER
BED RM.
13-4 × 17-8

cl

PORCH
19-2 × 5-6

BRKFST.
13-4 × 8-8

BED RM.
14-8 × 11-0

66-4

67-6

Design AA9655/ AA9619

Square Footage: 2,032   Square Footage: 2,021
Width 67'-6"   Width 67'-6"
Depth 66'-4"   Depth 67'-4"

● Multi-pane windows, shutters and a
delightful covered porch grace the facade
of this one-story home. Inside, the floor
plan is no less appealing. Note that the
great room has a fireplace, a cathedral
ceiling and sliding glass doors with an
arched window above to allow for natural illumination of the room. A sun room
with a hot tub leads to an adjacent deck.
This space can also be reached from the
master bath. The spacious master bedroom has a walk-in closet and a bath
with a double-bowl vanity, a separate
shower and a garden tub. Two family
bedrooms are located at the other end of
the house for privacy. The garage is connected to the house by a breezeway.
Another design, AA9619, offers the same
floor plan with a different exterior elevation and an optional basement plan.
Order AA9619 for a crawl-space foundation; order AA9619-A for a
basement foundation.

AA9619

GARAGE
20-4 × 20-4

DECK
36-8 × 10-0

covered
breezeway

SUN RM.
15-8 × 7-10
hot tub

GREAT RM.
20-0 × 15-6
(cathedral ceiling)

fireplace

UTILITY
9-0 × 5-4

wash
dry

powder rm.

bath

cl

BED RM.
11-4 × 13-8

master bath

walk-in closet

rail

FOYER
4-6 × 12-4

DINING
12-0 × 12-0

KITCHEN
14-4 × 12-0

cl

MASTER
BED RM.
13-4 × 16-8

cl

PORCH
19-2 × 5-0

BRKFST.
13-4 × 7-8

BED RM.
14-8 × 11-0

67-4

67-6

AA9619-REAR

Design AA9718

Square Footage: 1,998
Width 69'
Depth 75'-4"

● The country cottage gets all dressed up with multi-pane windows, dormers, shed windows and a covered porch. Inside, skylights, a paddle fan and a wet bar make the sun room something to talk about. You'll also find a deck off this room; it leads to the covered breezeway connecting the garage to the house. In the great room, exposed beams, built-in shelves and a dramatic fireplace set off this wonderfully warm room. The country kitchen with its island cooktop features a pass-through counter to the great room. The generous master suite is privately located and luxuriously appointed with a whirlpool tub, a separate shower and dual lavatories. Two family bedrooms find peace and quiet at the other end of the house and share a full hall bath with a compartmented vanity.

Design by
Donald A.
Gardner,
Architect, Inc.

Floor Plan Labels

GARAGE
20-4 x 20-4

DECK
33-0 x 13-4

seat

covered breezeway

75-4

skylights
wet bar
SUN RM.
14-0 x 9-0

UTIL.
7-0 x 7-4
wash
dry

linen
whirlpool

BRKFST.
9-2 x 10-6

walk-in closet

master bath

book shelves
(cathedral ceiling)
GREAT RM.
18-0 x 16-2
fireplace

KITCHEN
12-8 x 10-0

MASTER BED RM.
15-0 x 15-10

BED RM.
11-4 x 12-0

cl

bath

columns

lin
cl
FOYER
11-8 x 5-6

DINING
12-8 x 12-0

cl

BED RM.
11-4 x 12-0

PORCH
16-0 x 5-2

69-0

Design AA9719

First Floor: 1,168 square feet
Second Floor: 917 square feet
Total: 2,085 square feet
Width 62'-6"
Depth 36'-2"

● This elegant, three-bedroom Colonial has an inventive, well-zoned, solar floor plan. Perfect for entertaining, the sun room with ventilating skylights shares its wet bar with the adjoining great room. A contemporary center-island kitchen services the dining and breakfast areas. Notice how both the breakfast area and the sun room open to a large rear deck. Upstairs, the master bedroom acts as a calm retreat with a luxurious bath featuring a whirlpool tub, a separate shower and a double-bowl vanity. The two family bedrooms enjoy privacy by design—one even features a walk-in closet. A two-car garage extends storage space as well as entrance to the house through a utility area.

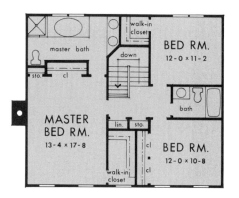

Design by
Donald A.
Gardner,
Architect, Inc.

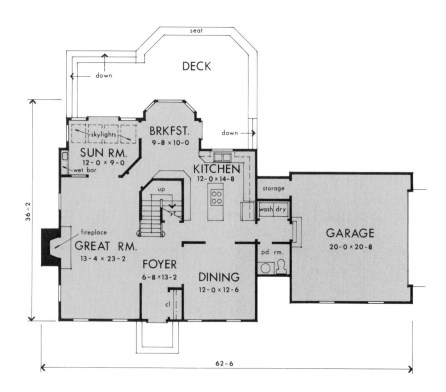

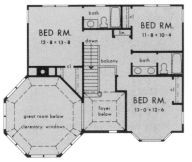

Design by
Donald A.
Gardner,
Architect, Inc.

Design AA9699
First Floor: 1,519 square feet
Second Floor: 792 square feet
Total: 2,311 square feet
Width 62'-10"
Depth 80'-4"

Design AA9698
First Floor: 1,790 square feet
Second Floor: 792 square feet
Total: 2,582 square feet
Width 63'
Depth 80'-4"

● One great exterior; two floor plans. The second floor is the same for both plans—the difference lies only in the first-floor layout. It features a great room and formal dining room on Design AA9699; a formal living room, dining room and family room on Design AA9698. Order Design AA9698 for living room option; order Design AA9699 for great room option.

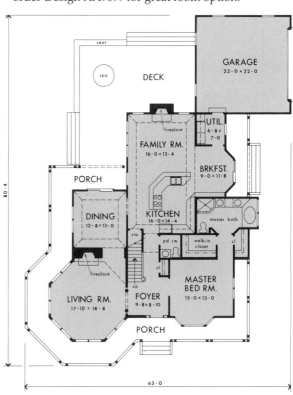

Design AA9303

First Floor: 1,428 square feet
Second Floor: 1,304 square feet
Total: 2,732 square feet
Width 54'
Depth 38'

● Nine-foot main level walls are a nice feature not readily apparent in the design of this popular Colonial home. Comfortable traffic patterns segregate formal and informal living spaces. To the left of the spacious two-story entry is a formal dining room with hutch space. Sunny windows bring light into the living room and throughout the whole home. The built-in bookcases in a generous family room can easily be converted to a wet bar. Highlights of the island kitchen/breakfast area are a wraparound counter, planning desk, walk-in pantry and a butler pantry. Upstairs, secondary bedrooms are served by a compartmented hall bath with double lavs. The large master suite sports a vaulted ceiling, His and Hers closets, corner whirlpool and double vanity with makeup counter.

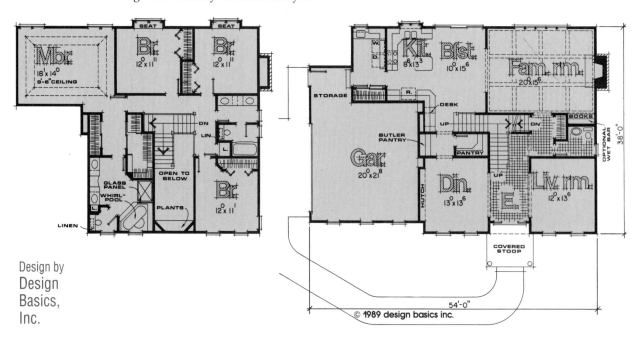

Design by
Design
Basics,
Inc.

© 1989 design basics inc.

Design AA9242

First Floor: 1,322 square feet
Second Floor: 1,272 square feet
Total: 2,594 square feet
Width 56'
Depth 48'

● Here's the luxury you've been looking for—from the wraparound covered front porch to the bright sun room at the rear off the breakfast room. A sunken family room with fireplace serves everyday casual gatherings, while the more formal living and dining rooms are reserved for special entertaining situations. The kitchen has a central island with snack bar and is located most conveniently for serving and cleaning up. Upstairs are four bedrooms, one a lovely master suite with French doors into the master bath and a whirlpool tub in a dramatic bay window. A double vanity in the shared bath easily serves the three family bedrooms.

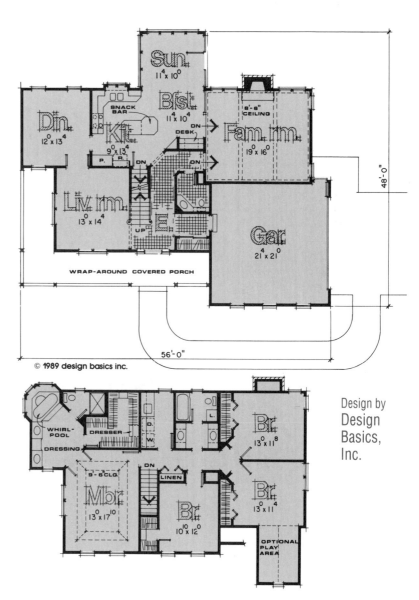

Sun.
11⁴ x 10⁰

Dn.

Bkfst.
11⁴ x 10⁴

SNACK BAR

DESK

Fam. rm.
19⁰ x 16⁰

8'-8" CEILING

Din.
12⁰ x 13⁰

Kit.
9⁰ x 13⁴

P. R.

Dn.

Dn.

Liv. rm.
13⁰ x 14⁰

UP

UP

Gar.
21⁴ x 21⁰

WRAP-AROUND COVERED PORCH

48'-0"

56'-0"

© 1989 design basics inc.

WHIRL-POOL

DRESSING

DRESSER

D. W.

L.

Br.
13⁰ x 11⁸

9'-6" CLG.

Mbr.
13⁰ x 17¹⁰

DN

LINEN

Br.
10⁰ x 12⁰

Br.
13⁰ x 11⁴

OPTIONAL PLAY AREA

Design by
Design Basics, Inc.

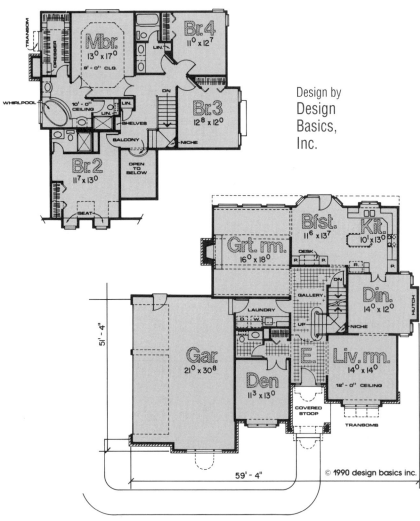

Design by
Design
Basics,
Inc.

Design AA9319

First Floor: 1,523 square feet
Second Floor: 1,282 square feet
Total: 2,805 square feet
Width 59'-4"
Depth 51'-4"

● Breathtaking details inside
and out lend elegance to this
stunning two-story home. A
gallery wall visible from the
entry is a perfect way to display your favorite pictures.
Tall boxed windows accent
the formal living room while
French doors access a private
den. Entertaining is a breeze in
the formal dining room with
hutch space and service doors
into the island kitchen with
three pantries. Large windows
and a fireplace provide comfort and livability in the great
room. Upstairs, an arched balcony overlooks the entry
below. One secondary bed-
room includes a private bath
and window seats while double doors lead into the master
suite with boxed ceiling. An
irresistible oval whirlpool sets
the pampering tone of the
master dressing area which is
enhanced by the large walk-in
closet and a decorator plant
shelf.

Design AA9286

First Floor: 1,583 square feet
Second Floor: 1,331 square feet
Total: 2,914 square feet
Width 58'
Depth 59'-4"

● A dramatic elevation with bright windows hints at the luxurious floor plan of this four-bedroom, two-story home. Upon entry, a beautiful staircase and formal living spaces are in sight. To the right, transom windows and a volume ceiling grace the living room. The dining room was designed to accommodate a hutch. The large family room includes elegant bowed windows and a showy three-sided fireplace. A bright dinette and snack bar are served by the open, island kitchen. Step up a half-flight of stairs to a private den with double doors and a special ceiling treatment. All secondary bedrooms have access to a Hollywood bath or private bath. The tiered ceiling and two closets highlight the master suite.

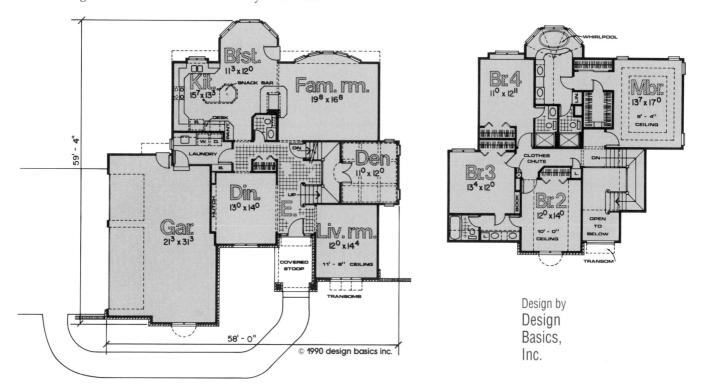

Design by
Design
Basics,
Inc.

Design AA2145

First Floor: 1,182 square feet
Second Floor: 708 square feet
Total: 1,890 square feet
Width 44'
Depth 64'

L

● Historically referred to as a "half house", this authentic adaptation has its roots in the heritage of New England. With completion of the second floor, the growing family doubles their sleeping capacity. Notice that the overall width of the house is only 44 feet. Take note of the covered porch leading to the garage and the flower court.

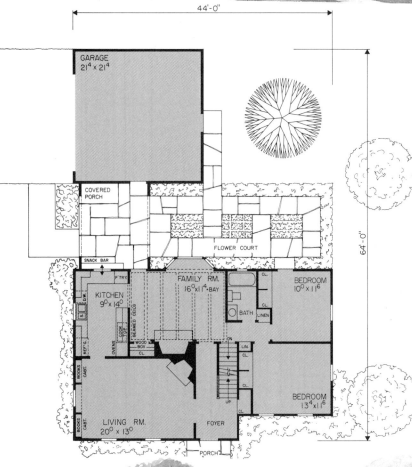

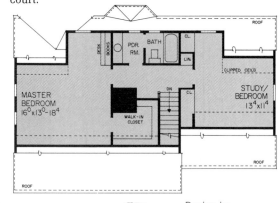

Design by
Home Planners,
Inc.

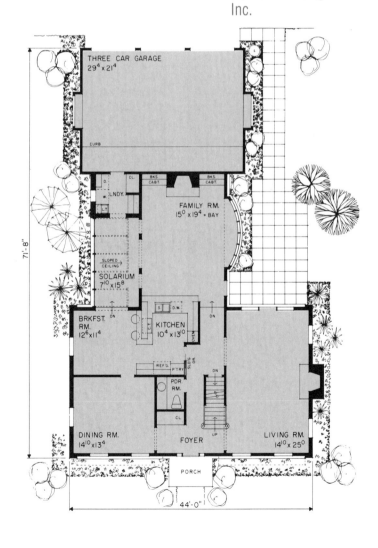

Design AA3552

First Floor: 1,784 square feet
Second Floor: 1,192 square feet
Total: 2,976 square feet
Width 44'
Depth 71'-8"

L D

● Smart exterior features mark this home as a classic: second-story pop-outs with half-round windows above multi-pane windows, charming lintels and a combination of horizontal wood siding and brick. Inside, the foyer is flanked by the formal living and dining rooms. An extra-special feature of this design is its large breakfast room. A solarium opens off this area and will, no doubt, delight all. The family room utilizes built-ins. Upstairs, three bedrooms may become four with the sitting room. The master suite enjoys a walk-in closet, a dressing area with a vanity, a whirlpool tub and a separate shower in the bath. A three-car garage provides all the space necessary for the family vehicles and plenty of additional paraphernalia.

Design by
Home Planners,
Inc.

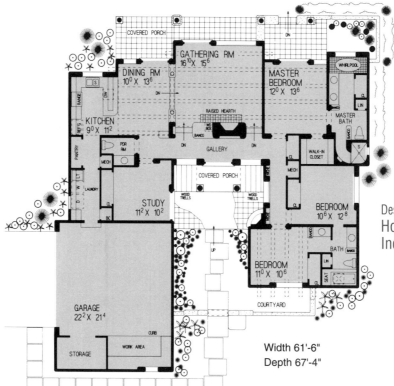

COVERED PORCH

GATHERING RM
16¹⁰ X 15⁶

DINING RM
10⁰ X 13⁶

MASTER
BEDROOM
12⁰ X 13⁶

WHIRLPOOL

KITCHEN
9⁰ X 11²

RAISED HEARTH

MASTER
BATH

PDR
RM

MECH

GALLERY

WALK-IN
CLOSET

PANTRY

LAUNDRY

MECH

STUDY
11² X 10²

WOOD
TRELLS

COVERED PORCH

WOOD
TRELLS

BEDROOM
10⁶ X 12⁸

BATH

UP

BEDROOM
11⁰ X 10⁶

GARAGE
22² X 21⁴

COURTYARD

STORAGE

WORK AREA

CURB

Width 61'-6"
Depth 67'-4"

Design by
**Home Planners,
Inc.**

QUOTE ONE™

Cost to build? See page 214
to order complete cost estimate
to build this house in your area!

CUSTOMIZABLE

Custom Alterations? See page 221
for customizing this plan to your
specifications.

Design AA3431

Square Footage: 1,907
Width 61'-6"
Depth 67'-4"

● Graceful curves welcome you into
the courtyard of this Santa Fe home.
Inside, the gallery directs traffic to the
work zone on the left or the sleeping
zone on the right. Straight ahead lies a
sunken gathering room with a beam
ceiling and a raised-hearth fireplace. A
large pantry offers extra storage space
for kitchen items. The covered rear
porch is accessible from the dining
room, the gathering room and the
secluded master bedroom. The master
bath has a whirlpool tub, a separate
shower, a double vanity and closet
space. Two family bedrooms share a
compartmented bath.

**California Engineered Plans and
California Stock Plans are available
for this home. Call 1-800-521-6797 for
more information.**

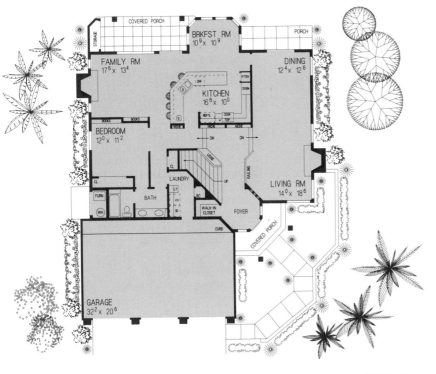

First floor plan labels:
COVERED PORCH · STORAGE · BRKFST RM 10⁹ x 10⁹ · PORCH · FAMILY RM 17⁶ x 13⁴ · DINING 12⁴ x 12⁸ · PTRY · OVEN · KITCHEN 16⁶ x 10⁰ · DW · REF'S · COOK TOP · NICHE · NICHE · BOOKS · BOOKS · BEDROOM 12⁰ x 11² · DN · DN · RAILING · LEDGE · CL · UP · LIVING RM 14⁰ x 18⁶ · CL · LAUNDRY · W · D · BC · WALK-IN CLOSET · FOYER · FURN · BATH · WH · CURB · COVERED PORCH · GARAGE 32² x 20⁶

Width 52'
Depth 64'-4"

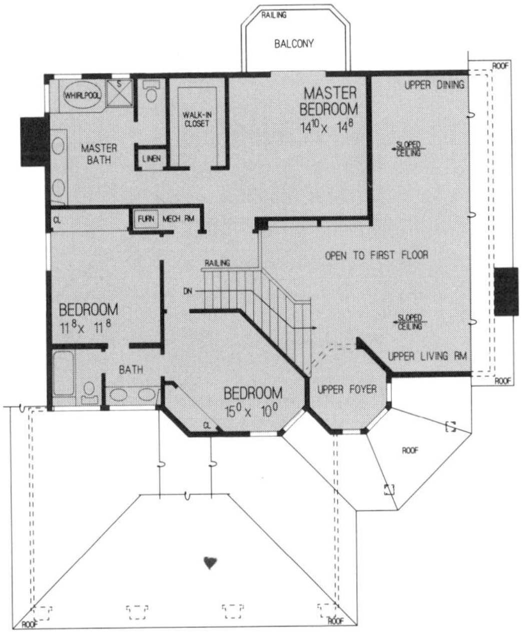

Design AA3425

First Floor: 1,776 square feet
Second Floor: 1,035 square feet
Total: 2,811 square feet
Width 52'
Depth 64'-4"

● Here's a two-story Spanish design with an appealing, angled exterior. Inside is an interesting floor plan containing rooms with a variety of shapes. Formal areas are to the right of the entry tower: a living room with fireplace and large dining room. The kitchen has loads of counter space and is complemented by a bumped-out breakfast room. Note the second fireplace in the family room and the first-floor bedroom. Three second-floor bedrooms radiate around the upper foyer.

QUOTE ONE™

Cost to build? See page 214
to order complete cost estimate
to build this house in your area!

CUSTOMIZABLE

Custom Alterations? See page 221
for customizing this plan to your
specifications.

Second floor plan labels:
RAILING · BALCONY · ROOF · WHIRLPOOL · S · WALK-IN CLOSET · MASTER BEDROOM 14¹⁰ x 14⁸ · UPPER DINING · MASTER BATH · LINEN · SLOPED CEILING · CL · FURN MECH RM · OPEN TO FIRST FLOOR · RAILING · DN · BEDROOM 11⁸ x 11⁸ · SLOPED CEILING · UPPER LIVING RM · BATH · BEDROOM 15⁰ x 10⁰ · UPPER FOYER · ROOF · CL · ROOF · ROOF · ROOF

Design by
Home Planners,
Inc.

When You're Ready To Order . . .

Let Us Show You Our Home Blueprint Package.

Building a home? Planning a home? Our Blueprint Package has nearly everything you need to get the job done right, whether you're working on your own or with help from an architect, designer, builder or subcontractors. Each Blueprint Package is the result of many hours of work by licensed architects or professional designers.

QUALITY

Hundreds of hours of painstaking effort have gone into the development of your blueprint set. Each home has been quality-checked by professionals to insure accuracy and buildability.

VALUE

Because we sell in volume, you can buy professional-quality blueprints at a fraction of their development cost. With our plans, your dream home design costs only a few hundred dollars, not the thousands of dollars that custom architects charge.

SERVICE

Once you've chosen your favorite home plan, you'll receive fast, efficient service whether you choose to mail or fax your order to us or call us toll free at 1-800-521-6797.

SATISFACTION

Our years of service to satisfied home plan buyers provide us the experience and knowledge that guarantee your satisfaction with our product and performance.

ORDER TOLL FREE 1-800-521-6797

After you've looked over our Blueprint Package and Important Extras on the following pages, simply mail the order form on page 221 or call toll free on our Blueprint Hotline: 1-800-521-6797. We're ready and eager to serve you.

Each set of blueprints is an interrelated collection of detail sheets which includes components such as floor plans, interior and exterior elevations, dimensions, cross-sections, diagrams and notations. These sheets show exactly how your house is to be built.

Among the sheets included may be:

Frontal Sheet
This artist's sketch of the exterior of the house gives you an idea of how the house will look when built and landscaped. Large ink-line floor plans show all levels of the house and provide an overview of your new home's livability, as well as a handy reference for deciding on furniture placement.

Foundation Plan
This sheet shows the foundation layout includ-

SAMPLE PACKAGE

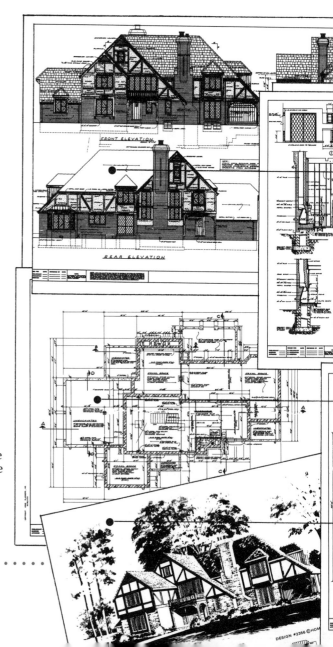

ing support walls, excavated and unexcavated areas, if any, and foundation notes. If slab construction rather than basement, the plan shows footings and details for a monolithic slab. This page, or another in the set, may include a sample plot plan for locating your house on a building site.

Detailed Floor Plans
These plans show the layout of each floor of the house. Rooms and interior spaces are carefully dimensioned and keys are given for cross-section details provided later in the plans. The positions of electrical outlets and switches are shown.

House Cross-Sections
Large-scale views show sections or cut-aways of the foundation, interior walls, exterior walls, floors, stairways and roof details. Additional cross-sections may show important changes in

floor, ceiling or roof heights or the relationship of one level to another. Extremely valuable for construction, these sections show exactly how the various parts of the house fit together.

Interior Elevations
These large-scale drawings show the design and placement of kitchen and bathroom cabinets, laundry areas, fireplaces, bookcases and other built-ins. Little "extras," such as mantelpiece and wainscoting drawings, plus moulding sections, provide details that give your home that custom touch.

Exterior Elevations
These drawings show the front, rear and sides of your house and give necessary notes on exterior materials and finishes. Particular attention is given to cornice detail, brick and stone accents or other finish items that make your home unique.

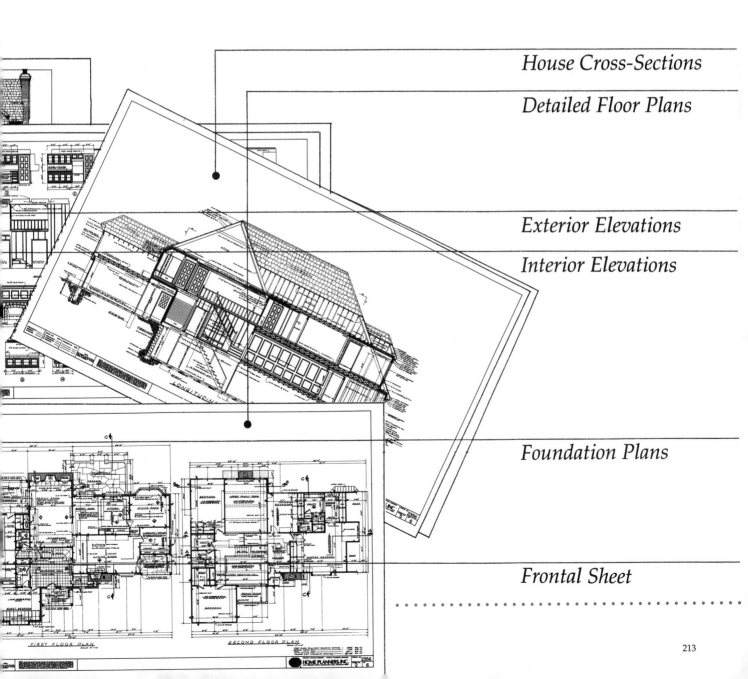

House Cross-Sections

Detailed Floor Plans

Exterior Elevations

Interior Elevations

Foundation Plans

Frontal Sheet

*I*mportant Extras To Do The Job Right!

*Introducing
eight important
planning and
construction aids
developed by our
professionals to
help you succeed
in your home-
building project.*

MATERIALS LIST & DETAILED COST ESTIMATE

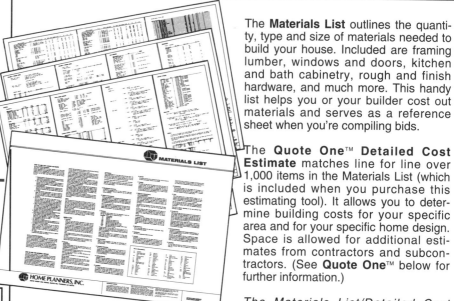

The **Materials List** outlines the quantity, type and size of materials needed to build your house. Included are framing lumber, windows and doors, kitchen and bath cabinetry, rough and finish hardware, and much more. This handy list helps you or your builder cost out materials and serves as a reference sheet when you're compiling bids.

The **Quote One**™ **Detailed Cost Estimate** matches line for line over 1,000 items in the Materials List (which is included when you purchase this estimating tool). It allows you to determine building costs for your specific area and for your specific home design. Space is allowed for additional estimates from contractors and subcontractors. (See **Quote One**™ below for further information.)

The Materials List/Detailed Cost Estimate package can be ordered up to 6 months after a blueprint order. Because of the diversity of local building codes, the Materials List does not include mechanical materials. Detailed Cost Estimates are available for select Home Planners plans only. Consult a customer service representative for currently available designs.

Make informed decisions about your home-building project with a customized materials take-off and a Quote One™ Detailed Cost Estimate. These tools are invaluable in planning and estimating the cost of your new home.

SPECIFICATION OUTLINE

This valuable 16-page document is critical to building your house correctly. Designed to be filled in by you or your builder, this book lists 166 stages or items crucial to the building process. It provides a comprehensive review of the construction process and helps in making choices of materials. When combined with the blueprints, a signed contract, and a schedule, it becomes a legal document and record for the building of your home.

QUOTE ONE™

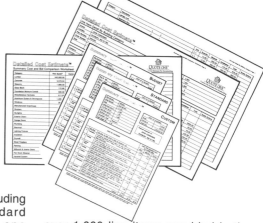

A new service for estimating the cost of building select Home Planners designs, the Quote One™ system is available in two separate stages: The Summary Cost Report and the Detailed Cost Estimate. The Summary Cost Report shows the total cost per square foot for your chosen home in your zip-code area and then breaks that cost down into ten categories showing the costs for building materials, labor and installation. The total cost for the report (including three grades: Budget, Standard and Custom) is just $25 for one home; and additionals are only $15. These reports allow you to evaluate your building budget and compare the costs of building a variety of homes in your area.

The Detailed Cost Estimate furnishes an even more detailed report. The material and installation (labor + equipment) cost is shown for each of over 1,000 line items provided in the Standard grade. Space is allowed for additional estimates from contractors and subcontractors. This invaluable tool is available for a price of $110 ($120 for a Schedule E plan) which includes the price of a materials list which must be purchased with a Blueprint set.

To order these invaluable reports, use the order form on page 221 or call **1-800-521-6797**.

CONSTRUCTION INFORMATION

If you want to know more about techniques—and deal more confidently with subcontractors—we offer these useful sheets. Each set is an excellent tool that will add to your understanding of these technical subjects.

Plan-A-Home®

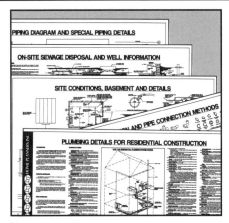

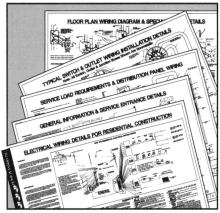

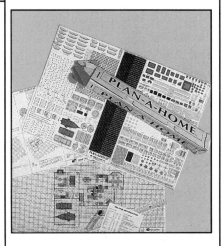

PLUMBING

The Blueprint Package includes locations for all the plumbing fixtures in your new house, including sinks, lavatories, tubs, showers, toilets, laundry trays and water heaters. However, if you want to know more about the complete plumbing system, these 24x36-inch detail sheets will prove very useful. Prepared to meet requirements of the National Plumbing Code, these six fact-filled sheets give general information on pipe schedules, fittings, sump-pump details, water-softener hookups, septic system details and much more. Color-coded sheets include a glossary of terms.

ELECTRICAL

The locations for every electrical switch, plug and outlet are shown in your Blueprint Package. However, these Electrical Details go further to take the mystery out of household electrical systems. Prepared to meet requirements of the National Electrical Code, these comprehensive 24x36-inch drawings come packed with helpful information, including wire sizing, switch-installation schematics, cable-routing details, appliance wattage, door-bell hookups, typical service panel circuitry and much more. Six sheets are bound together and color-coded for easy reference. A glossary of terms is also included.

Plan-A-Home® is an easy-to-use tool that helps you design a new home, arrange furniture in a new or existing home, or plan a remodeling project. Each package contains:

- **More than 700 reusable peel-off planning symbols** on a self-stick vinyl sheet, including walls, windows, doors, all types of furniture, kitchen components, bath fixtures and many more.

- **A reusable, transparent, 1/4-inch scale planning grid** that matches the scale of actual working drawings (1/4-inch equals 1 foot). This grid provides the basis for house layouts of up to 140x92 feet.

- **Tracing paper** and a protective sheet for copying or transferring your completed plan.

- **A felt-tip pen,** with water-soluble ink that wipes away quickly.

Plan-A-Home® lets you lay out areas as large as a 7,500 square foot, six-bedroom, seven-bath house.

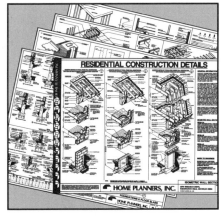

CONSTRUCTION

The Blueprint Package contains everything an experienced builder needs to construct a particular house. However, it doesn't show all the ways that houses can be built, nor does it explain alternate construction methods. To help you understand how your house will be built—and offer additional techniques—this set of drawings depicts the materials and methods used to build foundations, fireplaces, walls, floors and roofs. Where appropriate, the drawings show acceptable alternatives. These six sheets will answer questions for the advanced do-it-yourselfer or home planner.

MECHANICAL

This package contains fundamental principles and useful data that will help you make informed decisions and communicate with subcontractors about heating and cooling systems. The 24x36-inch drawings contain instructions and samples that allow you to make simple load calculations and preliminary sizing and costing analysis. Covered are today's most commonly used systems from heat pumps to solar fuel systems. The package is packed full of illustrations and diagrams to help you visualize components and how they relate to one another.

To Order, Call Toll Free 1-800-521-6797

To add these important extras to your Blueprint Package, simply indicate your choices on the order form on page 221 or call us Toll Free 1-800-521-6797 and we'll tell you more about these exciting products.

D *The Deck Blueprint Package*

Many of the homes in this book can be enhanced with a professionally designed Home Planners' Deck Plan. Those home plans highlighted with a D have a matching or corresponding deck plan available which includes a Deck Plan Frontal Sheet, Deck Framing and Floor Plans, Deck Elevations and a Deck Materials List. A Standard Deck Details Package, also available, provides all the how-to information necessary for building *any* deck. Our Complete Deck Building Package contains 1 set of Custom Deck Plans of your choice, plus 1 set of Standard Deck Building Details all for one low price. Our plans and details are carefully prepared in an easy-to-understand format that will guide you through every stage of your deck-building project. This page contains a sampling of 12 of the 25 different Deck layouts to match your favorite house. See page 218 for prices and ordering information.

SPLIT–LEVEL SUN DECK
Deck Plan D100

BI–LEVEL DECK WITH COVERED DINING
Deck Plan D101

WRAP–AROUND FAMILY DECK
Deck Plan D104

DECK FOR DINING AND VIEWS
Deck Plan D107

TREND–SETTER DECK
Deck Plan D110

TURN–OF–THE–CENTURY DECK
Deck Plan D111

WEEKEND ENTERTAINER DECK
Deck Plan D112

CENTER–VIEW DECK
Deck Plan D114

KITCHEN–EXTENDER DECK
Deck Plan D115

SPLIT–LEVEL ACTIVITY DECK
Deck Plan D117

TRI–LEVEL DECK WITH GRILL
Deck Plan D119

CONTEMPORARY LEISURE DECK
Deck Plan D120

⬛ *The Landscape Blueprint Package*

For the homes marked with an ⬛ in this book, Home Planners has created a front-yard landscape plan that matches or is complementary in design to the house plan. These comprehensive blueprint packages include a Frontal Sheet, Plan View, Regionalized Plant & Materials List, a sheet on Planting and Maintaining Your Landscape, Zone Maps and Plant Size and Description Guide. These plans will help you achieve professional results, adding value and enjoyment to your property for years to come. Each set of blueprints is a full 18" x 24" in size with clear, complete instructions and easy-to-read type. Six of the forty front-yard Landscape Plans to match your favorite house are shown below.

Regional Order Map

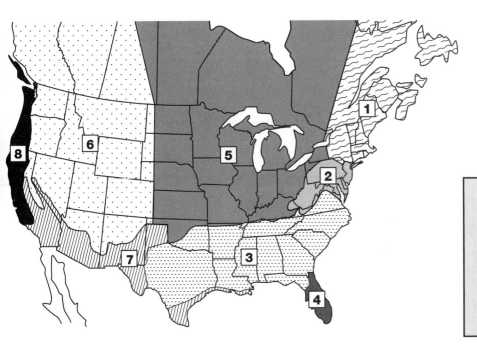

Most of the Landscape Plans shown on these pages are available with a Plant & Materials List adapted by horticultural experts to 8 different regions of the country. Please specify Geographic Region when ordering your plan. See page 218 for prices, ordering information and regional availability.

Region	**1**	Northeast
Region	**2**	Mid-Atlantic
Region	**3**	Deep South
Region	**4**	Florida & Gulf Coast
Region	**5**	Midwest
Region	**6**	Rocky Mountains
Region	**7**	Southern California & Desert Southwest
Region	**8**	Northern California & Pacific Northwest

CAPE COD COTTAGE
Landscape Plan L202

GAMBREL–ROOF COLONIAL
Landscape Plan L203

CENTER–HALL COLONIAL
Landscape Plan L204

CLASSIC NEW ENGLAND COLONIAL
Landscape Plan L205

COUNTRY–STYLE FARMHOUSE
Landscape Plan L207

TRADITIONAL SPLIT–LEVEL
Landscape Plan L228

Price Schedule & Plans Index

These pages contain all the information you need to price your blueprints. In general, the larger and more complicated the house, the more it costs to design and thus the higher the price we must charge for the blueprints. Remember, however, that these prices are far less than you would normally pay for the services of a licensed architect or professional designer.

Custom home designs and related architectural services often cost thousands of dollars, ranging from 5% to 15% of the cost of construction. By ordering our blueprints you are potentially saving enough money to afford a larger house, or to add those "extra" amenities such as a patio, deck, swimming pool or even an upgraded kitchen or luxurious master suite.

House Blueprint Price Schedule
(Prices guaranteed through December 31, 1996)

	1-set Study Package	4-set Building Package	8-set Building Package	1-set Reproducible Sepias
Schedule A	$280	$325	$385	$485
Schedule B	$320	$365	$425	$545
Schedule C	$360	$405	$465	$605
Schedule D	$400	$445	$505	$665
Schedule E	$520	$565	$625	$725

Additional Identical Blueprints in same order..............$50 per set
Reverse Blueprints (mirror image)................................$50 per set
Specification Outlines ....$10 each
Materials Lists (available only from those designers listed below):
- ▲ Home Planners Designs $50
- ✳ Larry Garnett Designs $50
- † Design Basics Designs $75
- ✳ Alan Mascord Designs...$50
- ◆ Donald Gardner Designs $50

Materials Lists for "E" price plans are an additional $10.
Materials Lists are not available for California Engineering Service.

Deck Plans Price Schedule

CUSTOM DECK PLANS

Price Group	Q	R	S
1 Set Custom Plans	$25	$30	$35

Additional identical sets ....$10 each
Reverse sets (mirror image)......................................$10 each

STANDARD DECK DETAILS
1 Set Generic Construction Details..........................$14.95 each

COMPLETE DECK BUILDING PACKAGE

Price Group	Q	R	S
1 Set Custom Plans, plus 1 Set Standard Deck Details	$35	$40	$45

Landscape Plans Price Schedule

Price Group	X	Y	Z
1 set	$35	$45	$55
3 sets	$50	$60	$70
6 sets	$65	$75	$85

Additional Identical Sets ....$10 each
Reverse Sets (mirror image)......................................$10 each

Index

To use the Index below, refer to the design number listed in numerical order (a helpful page reference is also given). Note the price index letter and refer to the House Blueprint Price Schedule above for the cost of one, four or eight sets of blueprints or the cost of a reproducible sepia. Additional prices are shown for identical and reverse blueprint sets, as well as a very useful Materials List for some of the plans. Also note in the Index below those plans that have matching or complementary Deck Plans or Landscape Plans. Refer to the schedules

above for prices of these plans. Some of our plans can be customized through Home Planners' Home Customizer ® Service. These plans are indicated below with this symbol: 🏠. See page 221 for information. Some plans are also part of our Quote One™ estimating service and are indicated by this symbol: 🏠. See page 214 for more information.

To Order: Fill in and send the order form on page 221—or call toll free 1-800-521-6797 or 520-297-8200.

DESIGN	PRICE	PAGE	CALIFORNIA PLANS	CUSTOMIZABLE	QUOTE ONE™	DECK	DECK PRICE	LANDSCAPE	LANDSCAPE PRICE	REGIONS
▲AA1361	A	113				D117	S	L225	X	1-3,5,6,8
▲AA1850	B	179			🏠					
▲AA1956	A	112		🏠	🏠	D117	S			
▲AA1957	A	161			🏠	D100	Q	L228	Y	1-8
▲AA2145	A	208			🏠			L209	Y	1-6,8
▲AA2488	A	117	✓	🏠	🏠	D102	Q			
▲AA2490	A	143		🏠	🏠					
▲AA2493	C	40								
▲AA2511	B	188			🏠	D108	R	L229	Y	1-8
▲AA2608	A	178				D112	R	L228	Y	1-8
▲AA2622	A	110		🏠	🏠	D103	R	L200	X	1-3,5,6,8
▲AA2657	B	114			🏠			L200	X	1-3,5,6,8
▲AA2661	A	38	✓	🏠	🏠	D113	R	L202	X	1-3,5,6,8
▲AA2668	B	162						L214	Z	1-3,5,6,8
▲AA2707	A	134		🏠	🏠	D117	S	L226	X	1-8
▲AA2711	B	116	✓	🏠	🏠	D105	R	L229	Y	1-8
▲AA2731	B	160				D114	R	L205	Y	1-3,5,6,8
▲AA2786	B	180								
▲AA2787	B	181				D105	R	L228	Y	1-8
▲AA2828	B	187								
▲AA2841	B	184						L208	Z	1,2,5,6,8
▲AA2842	B	185								
▲AA2878	B	132	✓	🏠	🏠	D112	R	L200	X	1-3,5,6,8
▲AA2901	C	186						L229	Y	1-8
▲AA2927	B	133	✓	🏠	🏠	D100	Q			
▲AA2937	C	189			🏠			L229	Y	1-8
▲AA2974	A	42	✓		🏠			L223	Z	1-3,5,6,8
▲AA3316	A	43			🏠			L202	X	1-3,5,6,8
▲AA3372	C	135			🏠	D102	Q	L200	X	1-3,5,6,8
▲AA3379	B	41			🏠	D102	Q	L200	X	1-3,5,6,8
▲AA3425	C	211		🏠	🏠					
▲AA3431	B	210	✓	🏠	🏠					
▲AA3453	A	63						L238	Y	3,4,7,8
▲AA3456	C	30						L238	Y	3,4,7,8
▲AA3457	B	100						L217	Y	1-8
▲AA3459	C	101						L220	Y	1-3,5,6,8
▲AA3460	A	62	✓	🏠	🏠			L200	X	1-3,5,6,8
▲AA3463	C	31						L238	Y	3,4,7,8
▲AA3464	C	102			🏠	D110	R	L233	Y	3,4,7
▲AA3476	A	18		🏠	🏠			L205	Y	1-3,5,6,8
▲AA3477	C	19		🏠	🏠			L205	Y	1-3,5,6,8
▲AA3481	B	20		🏠	🏠			L200	X	1-3,5,6,8
▲AA3484	B	21		🏠	🏠	D105	R	L200	X	1-3,5,6,8
▲AA3485	C	22		🏠	🏠			L238	Y	3,4,7,8

Before You Order . . .

Before filling out the coupon at right or calling us on our Toll-Free Blueprint Hotline, you may want to learn more about our services and products. Here's some information you will find helpful.

Quick Turnaround
We process and ship every blueprint order from our office within 48 hours. Because of this quick turnaround, we won't send a formal notice acknowledging receipt of your order.

Our Exchange Policy
Since blueprints are printed in response to your order, we cannot honor requests for refunds. However, we will exchange your entire first order for an equal number of blueprints at a price of $50 for the first set and $10 for each additional set; $70 total exchange fee for 4 sets: $100 total exchange fee for 8 sets. . . *plus* the difference in cost if exchanging for a design in a higher price bracket or *less* the difference in cost if exchanging for a design in a lower price bracket. One exchange is allowed within a year of purchase date. **(Sepias are not exchangeable. No exchanges can be made for the California Engineered Plans since they are tailored to your specific building site.)** All sets from the first order must be returned before the exchange can take place. Please add $10 for postage and handling via ground service; $20 via 2nd Day Air; $30 via Next Day Air.

About Reverse Blueprints
If you want to build in reverse of the plan as shown, we will include an extra set of reverse blueprints (mirror image) for an additional fee of $50. Lettering and dimensions will appear backward. Right-reading reverses of Home Customizer® plans are available. Call 1-800-521-6797, ext. 800 for more details.

Modifying or Customizing Our Plans
With such a great selection of homes, you are bound to find the one that suits you. However, if you need to make alterations to a design that is customizable, you need only order our Customizer® kit or call our Customization representative at 1-800-521-6797, ext. 800 to get you started. We strongly suggest you order sepias if you decide to revise non-Customizable plans significantly.

Architectural and Engineering Seals
Some cities and states are now requiring that a licensed architect or engineer review and "seal" your blueprints prior to building due to local or regional concerns over energy consumption, safety codes, seismic ratings or other factors. For this reason, it may be necessary to talk to a local professional to have your plans reviewed. In some cases, Home Planners can seal your plans through our Customization Service. Call 1-800-521-6797, ext. 800 for more details.

Compliance with Local Codes and Regulations
At the time of creation, our plans are drawn to specifications published by the Building Officials and Code Administrators (BOCA) International, Inc.; the Southern Building Code Congress (SBCCI) International, Inc.; the International Conference of Building Officials; or the Council of American Building Officials (CABO). Our plans are designed to meet or exceed national building standards. Some states, counties and municipalities have their own codes, zoning requirements and building regulations. Before building, contact your local building authorities to make sure you comply with local ordinances and codes, including obtaining any necessary permits or inspections as building progresses. In some cases, minor modifications to your plans by your builder, architect or designer may be required to meet local conditions and requirements. Home Planners may be able to make these changes to Home Customizer® plans providing you supply all pertinent information from your local building authorities.

Foundation and Exterior Wall Changes
Most of our plans are drawn with either a full or partial basement foundation. Depending on your specific climate or regional building practices, you may wish to change this basement to a slab or crawl-space. Most professional contractors and builders can easily adapt your plans to alternate foundation types. Likewise, most can easily change 2x4 wall construction to 2x6, or vice versa. For Home Customizer® plans, Home Planners can easily make the changes for you.

How Many Blueprints Do You Need?
A single set of blueprints is sufficient to study a home in greater detail. However, if you are planning to obtain cost estimates from a contractor or subcontractors—or if you are planning to build immediately—you will need more sets. Because additional sets are cheaper when ordered in quantity with the original order, make sure you order enough blueprints to satisfy all requirements. The following checklist will help you determine how many you need:

_____Owner

_____Builder (generally requires at least three sets; one as a legal document, one to use during inspections, and at least one to give to subcontractors)

_____Local Building Department (often requires two sets)

_____Mortgage Lender (usually one set for a conventional loan; three sets for FHA or VA loans)

_____TOTAL NUMBER OF SETS

Have You Seen Our Newest Designs?

Home Planners is one of the country's most active home design firms, creating nearly 100 new plans each year. At least 50 of our latest creations are featured in each edition of our New Design Portfolio. You may have received a copy with your latest purchase by mail. If not, or if you purchased this book from a local retailer, just return the coupon below for your FREE copy. Make sure you consider the very latest of what Home Planners has to offer.

Yes! Please send my FREE copy of your latest New Design Portfolio.

Name _____

Address _____

City_____State_____Zip _____

HOME PLANNERS, INC.
3275 WEST INA ROAD, SUITE 110
TUCSON, ARIZONA 85741

Order Form Key

TB32NDP

The Home Customizer®

Many of the plans in this book are customizable through our Home Customizer® service. Look for this symbol 🏠 on the pages of home designs. It indicates that the plan on that page is part of The Home Customizer® service.

Some changes to customizable plans that can be made include:

- exterior elevation changes
- kitchen and bath modifications
- roof, wall and foundation changes
- room additions
- and much more!

If the plan you have chosen to build is one of our customizable homes, you can easily order the Home Customizer® kit to start on the path to making your alterations. The kit, priced at only $29.95, may be ordered at the same time you order your blueprint package by calling our toll-free number or using the order blank at right. Or you can wait until you receive your blueprints, spend some time studying them and then order the kit by phone, FAX or mail. If you then decide to proceed with the customizing service, the $29.95 price of the kit will be refunded to you after your customization order is received. The Home Customizer® kit includes:

- instruction book with examples
- architectural scale
- clear acetate work film
- erasable red marker
- removable correction tape
- ¼" scale furniture cutouts
- 1 set of Customizable Drawings with floor plans and elevations

The service is easy, fast and *affordable*. Because we know and work with our plans and have them available on state-of-the-art computer systems, we can make the changes efficiently at prices much lower than those charged by other architectural or drafting services. In addition, you'll be getting custom changes directly from Home Planners—the company whose dedication to excellence and long-standing professional experience are well recognized in the industry.

Call now to learn more about how simple it can be to have the *custom home* you've always wanted.

📞 **Toll Free**
1-800-521-6797, Ext. 800

California Customers!!

For our customers in California, we now offer California Engineered Plans (CEP) and California Stock Plans (CSP) to help in meeting the strict California building codes. Check Plan Index for homes that are available through this new service or call 1-800-521-6797 for more information about the availability of the service and prices.

BLUEPRINTS ARE NOT RETURNABLE

ORDER FORM

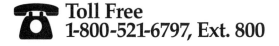

**HOME PLANNERS, INC., 3275 WEST INA ROAD
SUITE 110, TUCSON, ARIZONA 85741**

THE BASIC BLUEPRINT PACKAGE
Rush me the following (please refer to the Plans Index and Price Schedule in this section):

_____ Set(s) of blueprints for plan number(s) _____.	$_____
_____ Set(s) of sepias for plan number(s) _____.	$_____
_____ Additional identical blueprints in same order @ $50 per set.	$_____
_____ Reverse blueprints @ $50 per set.	$_____
_____ Home Customizer® Kit(s) for Plan(s) _____ @ $29.95 per kit.	$_____

IMPORTANT EXTRAS: Rush me the following:
_____ Materials List: $50 Home Planners Designs (not available for CEP service); $50 Larry Garnett Designs; $75 Design Basics Designs; $50 Alan Mascord Designs; $50 Donald Gardner Designs. Add $10 for a Schedule E plan Material List. $_____

_____ **Quote One**™ Summary Cost Report @ $25 for 1, $15 for each additional, for plans _____. $_____
Building location: City _____ Zip Code _____

_____ **Quote One**™ Detailed Cost Estimate @ $110 Schedule A-D; $120 Schedule E for plan _____ $_____
(Must be purchased with Blueprints set; Materials List included)
Building location: City _____ Zip Code _____

_____ Specification Outlines @ $10 each. $_____
_____ Detail Sets @ $14.95 each; any two for $22.95; any three for $29.95; all four for $39.95 (save $19.85). $_____
(These helpful details provide general construction advice and are not specific to any single plan.)
❏ Plumbing ❏ Electrical ❏ Construction ❏ Mechanical

_____ Plan-A-Home® @ $29.95 each. $_____

DECK BLUEPRINTS
_____ Set(s) of Deck Plan _____. $_____
_____ Additional identical blueprints in same order @ $10 per set. $_____
_____ Reverse blueprints @ $10 per set. $_____
_____ Set of Standard Deck Details @ $14.95 per set. $_____
_____ Set of Complete Building Package (Best Buy!) Includes Custom Deck Plan _____ plus Standard Deck Details.
(See Index and Price Schedule) $_____

LANDSCAPE BLUEPRINTS
_____ Set(s) of Landscape Plan _____. $_____
_____ Additional identical blueprints in same order @ $10 per set. $_____
_____ Reverse blueprints @ $10 per set. $_____
Please indicate the appropriate region of the country for
Plant & Material List. (See Map on page 217): Region _____

POSTAGE AND HANDLING	1-3 sets	4+ sets
DELIVERY (Requires street address - No P.O. Boxes)		
•Regular Service (Allow 4-6 days delivery)	❏ $8.00	❏ $10.00
•2nd Day Air (Allow 2-3 days delivery)	❏ $12.00	❏ $20.00
•Next Day Air (Allow 1 day delivery)	❏ $22.00	❏ $30.00
CERTIFIED MAIL (Requires signature)		
If no street address available. (Allow 4-6 days delivery)	❏ $10.00	❏ $14.00
OVERSEAS DELIVERY	fax, phone or mail for quote.	

NOTE: ALL DELIVERY TIMES ARE FROM DATE BLUEPRINT PACKAGE IS SHIPPED.

POSTAGE (From box above) $_____
SUBTOTAL $_____
SALES TAX (Arizona residents add 5% sales tax; Michigan residents add 6% sales tax.) $_____
TOTAL (Sub-total and tax) $_____

YOUR ADDRESS (please print)

Name _____

Street _____

City _____ State _____ Zip _____

Daytime telephone number (_____) _____

FOR CREDIT CARD ORDERS ONLY: Please fill in the information below:

Credit card number _____

Exp. Date: Month/Year _____ Check one: ❏ Visa ❏ MasterCard ❏ Discover Card

Signature _____
Please check appropriate box: ❏ Licensed Builder-Contractor ❏ Homeowner

📞 **ORDER TOLL FREE!**
1-800-521-6797 or 520-297-8200

Order Form Key

TB32BP

Helpful Books & Software

Home Planners wants your building experience to be as pleasant and trouble-free as possible. That's why we've expanded our library of Do-It-Yourself titles to help you along. In addition to our beautiful plans books, we've added books to guide you through specific projects as well as the construction process. In fact, these are titles that will be as useful after your dream home is built as they are right now.

COUNTRY

1 200 country designs from classic to contemporary by 7 winning designers. 224 pages $8.95

BUDGET-SMART

2 200 efficient plans from 7 top designers, that you can really afford to build! 224 pages $8.95

FAMILY HOMES

3 200 stylish designs for today's growing families from 7 hot designers. 224 pages $8.95

NARROW-LOT

4 200 unique homes less than 60' wide from 7 designers. Up to 3,000 square feet. 224 pages $8.95

REGIONAL BEST

5 200 beautiful homes from across America by 8 regional designers. 224 pages $8.95 NEW!

EXPANDABLES

6 200 flexible plans that expand with your needs from 9 top designers. 224 pages $8.95 NEW!

BEST SELLERS

7 NEW! Our 50th Anniversary book with 200 of our very best designs in full color! 224 page $12.95

NEW ENGLAND

8 260 of the best in Colonial home design. Special interior design sections, too. 384 pages $14.95

AFFORDABLE

9 430 cost-saving plans specially selected for modest to medium building budgets. 320 pages $9.95

LUXURY

10 154 fine luxury plans—loaded with luscious amenities! 192 pages $14.95

ONE-STORY

11 470 designs for all lifestyles. 860 to 5,400 square feet. 384 pages $9.95

TWO-STORY

12 478 designs for one-and-a-half and two stories. 1,200 to 7,200 square feet. 416 pages $9.95

VACATION

13 345 designs for recreation, retirement and leisure. 312 pages $7.95 NEW!

MULTI-LEVEL

14 312 designs for split-levels, bi-levels, multi-levels and walkouts. 320 pages $6.95

OUTDOOR

15 42 unique outdoor projects. Gazebos, strombellas, bridges, sheds, playsets and more! 96 pages $7.95 NEW!

DECKS

16 25 outstanding single-, double- and multi-level decks you can build. 112 pages $7.95

ENCYCLOPEDIA

17 500 exceptional plans for all styles and budgets—the best book of its kind! 352 pages $9.95

MODERN & CLASSIC

18 341 impressive homes featuring the latest in contemporary design. 304 pages $9.95

TRADITIONAL

19 403 designs of classic beauty and elegance. 304 pages $9.95

VICTORIAN

20 160 striking Victorian and Farmhouse designs from three leading designers. 192 pages $12.95

SOUTHERN

21 207 homes rich in Southern styling and comfort. 240 pages $8.95 NEW!

WESTERN

22 215 designs that capture the spirit and diversity of the Western lifestyle. 208 pages $9.95

EMPTY-NESTER
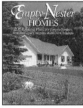
23 200 exciting plans for empty-nesters, retirees and childless couples. 224 pages $8.95

STARTER

24 200 easy-to-build plans for starter and low-budget houses. 224 pages $8.95

Landscape Designs

FRONT & BACK

25 The first book of do-it-yourself landscapes. 40 front, 15 backyards. 208 pages $12.95

BACKYARDS

26 40 designs focused solely on creating your own specially themed backyard oasis. 160 pages $12.95

EASY CARE

27 NEW! 41 special landscapes designed for beauty and low maintenance. 160 pages $12.95

Design Software

BOOK & CD ROM

28 NEW! Both the Home Planners Gold book and matching Windows™ CD ROM with 3D floorplans. $24.95

HOME ARCHITECT

29 The only complete home design kit for Windows™. Draw floor plans and landscape designs easily. Includes CD of 500 floor plans. $59.95

Interior Design

HOME DECORATING

30 Special effects and creative ideas for all surfaces. Includes simple step-by-step diagrams. 96 pages $8.95

BATHROOMS

31 An innovative guide to organizing, remodeling and decorating your bathroom. 96 pages $8.95

KITCHENS
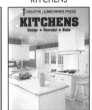
32 An imaginative guide to designing the perfect kitchen. Chock full of bright ideas to make your job easier. 176 pages $12.95

Planning Books & Quick Guides

| TRIM & MOLDING | PAINTING | ROOFING | WALLS & MORE | FLOORS | PATIOS & WALKS | WINDOWS & DOORS | PLUMBING |

  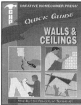   

30 Step-by-step instructions for installing baseboards, window and door casings and more. 80 pages $6.95

31 Tips from the pros on everything from preparation to clean-up. 80 pages $6.95

32 Information on the latest tools, materials and techniques for roof installation or repair. 80 pages $6.95

33 A clear and concise guide to repairing or remodeling walls and ceilings. 80 pages $6.95

34 All the information you need for repairing, replacing or installing floors in any home. 80 pages $6.95

35 Clear step-by-step instructions take you from the basic design stages to the finished project. 80 pages $6.95

36 Installation techniques and tips that make your project easier and more professional looking. 80 pages $6.95

37 Tackle any plumbing installation or repair as quickly and efficiently as a professional. 160 pages $9.95

| ADDING SPACE | HOME REPAIR | TILE | WALLPAPERING | BASIC WIRING | HOUSE CONTRACTING | VISUAL HANDBOOK | CONTRACTING GUIDE |

38 Convert attics, basements and bonus rooms to useful living space. 160 pages $9.95

39 An owner's manual for your home. Sound advice on home maintenance and improvements. 256 pages $9.95

40 Every kind of tile for every kind of application. Includes tips on use installation and repair. 176 pages $12.95

41 Use the book the pros use. Covers tools and techniques for every type of wallcovering. 136 pages $12.95

42 A straight forward guide to one of the most misunderstood systems in the home. 160 pages $12.95

43 Everything you need to know to act as your own general contractor...and save up to 25% off building costs. 134 pages $12.95

44 A plain-talk guide to the construction process; financing to final walk-through, this book covers it all. 498 pages $19.95

45 Loaded with information to make you more confident in dealing with contractors and subcontractors. 287 pages $18.95

| FRAMING |

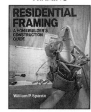

46 For those who want to take a more-hands on approach to their dream. 319 pages $19.95

Additional Books Order Form

To order your books, just check the box of the book numbered below and complete the coupon. We will process your order and ship it from our office within 48 hours. Send coupon and check (in U.S. funds).

YES! Please send me the books I've indicated:

☐	1:FH $8.95	☐	24:ST $8.95
☐	2:BS $8.95	☐	25:MPCD $39.95
☐	3:FF $8.95	☐	26:ARCH $59.95
☐	4:NL $8.95	☐	27:CDP $8.95
☐	5:AA $8.95	☐	28:CDB $8.95
☐	6:EX $8.95	☐	29:CKI $12.95
☐	7:YG $7.95	☐	30:CGT $6.95
☐	8:DP $7.95	☐	31:CGP $6.95
☐	9:AH $9.95	☐	32:CGR $6.95
☐	10:LD2 . . . . . $14.95	☐	33:CGC $6.95
☐	11:V1 . . . . $9.95	☐	34:CGF $6.95
☐	12:V2 . . . . $9.95	☐	35:CGW $6.95
☐	13:VH $7.95	☐	36:CGD $6.95
☐	14:V3 . . . . $6.95	☐	37:CMP $9.95
☐	15:BYL $12.95	☐	38:CAS $9.95
☐	16:HL $12.95	☐	39:CHR $9.95
☐	17:EN $9.95	☐	40:CWT $12.95
☐	18:EC $9.95	☐	41:CW $12.95
☐	19:ET $9.95	☐	42:CBW $12.95
☐	20:VDH $12.95	☐	43:SBC $12.95
☐	21:SH $8.95	☐	44:RVH $19.95
☐	22:WH $9.95	☐	45:BCC $18.95
☐	23:EP $8.95	☐	46:SRF $19.95

Additional Books Sub-Total	$_____
ADD Postage and Handling	$ __3.00__
Ariz. residents add 5% Sales Tax; Mich. residents add 6% Sales Tax	$_____
YOUR TOTAL (Sub-Total, Postage/Handling, Tax)	$_____

YOUR ADDRESS (Please print)

Name _____

Street _____

City _____ State _____ Zip _____

Phone (_____) _____—_____

YOUR PAYMENT

Check one: ☐ Check ☐ Visa ☐ MasterCard ☐ Discover Card
Required credit card information:

Credit Card Number_____

Expiration Date (Month/Year)_____/ _____

Signature Required _____

Home Planners, Inc.
3275 W Ina Road, Suite 110, Dept. BK, Tucson, AZ 85741

TB32BK

Canadian Customers
Order Toll-Free 1-800-561-4169

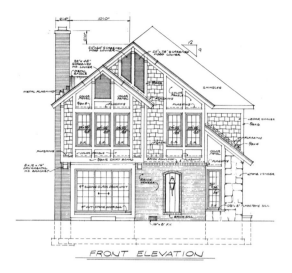

FRONT ELEVATION

OVER 3 MILLION BLUEPRINTS SOLD

"We instructed our builder to follow the plans including all of the many details which make this house so elegant... Our home is a fine example of the results one can achieve by purchasing and following the plans which you offer... Everyone who has seen it has assured us that it belongs in 'a picture book.' I truly mean it when I say that my home 'is a DREAM HOUSE.'"

S.P.
Anderson, SC

"We have had a steady stream of visitors, many of whom tell us this is the most beautiful home they've seen. Everyone is amazed at the layout and remarks on how unique it is. Our real estate attorney, who is a Chicago dweller and who deals with highly valued properties, told me this is the only suburban home he has seen that he would want to live in."

W. & P.S.
Flossmoor, IL

"Your blueprints saved us a great deal of money. I acted as the general contractor and we did a lot of the work ourselves. We probably built it for half the cost! We are thinking about more plans for another home. I purchased a competitor's book but my husband wants only your plans!"

K.M.
Grovetown, GA

"We are very happy with the product of our efforts. The neighbors and passersby appreciate what we have created. We have had many people stop by to discuss our house and kindly praise it as being the nicest house in our area of new construction. We have even had one person stop and make us an unsolicited offer to buy the house for much more than we have invested in it."

K. & L.S.
Bolingbrook, IL

"The traffic going past our house is unbelievable. On several occasions, we have heard that it is the 'prettiest house in Batvia.' Also, when meeting someone new and mentioning what street we live on, quite often we're told, 'Oh, you're the one in the yellow house with the wrap-around porch! I love it!'"

A.W.
Batvia, NY

"I have been involved in the building trades my entire life... Since building our home we have built two other homes for other families. Their plans from local professional architects were not nearly as good as yours. For that reason we are ordering additional plan books from you."

T.F.
Kingston, WA

"The blueprints we received from you were of excellent quality and provided us with exactly what we needed to get our successful home-building project underway. We appreciate your invaluable role in our home-building effort."

T.A.
Concord, TN